THE COMPLETE IDIOT'S GUIDE® TO

Making Money with craigslist

by Skip Press

ALPHA

A member of Penguin Group (USA) Inc.

ALPHA BOOKS

Published by the Penguin Group

Penguin Group (USA) Inc., 375 Hudson Street, New York, New York 10014, USA

Penguin Group (Canada), 90 Eglinton Avenue East, Suite 700, Toronto, Ontario M4P 2Y3, Canada (a division of Pearson Penguin Canada Inc.)

Penguin Books Ltd., 80 Strand, London WC2R 0RL, England

Penguin Ireland, 25 St. Stephen's Green, Dublin 2, Ireland (a division of Penguin Books Ltd.)

Penguin Group (Australia), 250 Camberwell Road, Camberwell, Victoria 3124, Australia (a division of Pearson Australia Group Pty. Ltd.)

Penguin Books India Pvt. Ltd., 11 Community Centre, Panchsheel Park, New Delhi—110 017, India

Penguin Group (NZ), 67 Apollo Drive, Rosedale, North Shore, Auckland 1311, New Zealand (a division of Pearson New Zealand Ltd.)

Penguin Books (South Africa) (Pty.) Ltd., 24 Sturdee Avenue, Rosebank, Johannesburg 2196, South Africa

Penguin Books Ltd., Registered Offices: 80 Strand, London WC2R 0RL, England

Copyright © 2009 by Skip Press

International Standard Book Number: 978-1-59257-949-5
Library of Congress Catalog Card Number: 2009928402

11 10 09   8 7 6 5 4 3 2 1

Interpretation of the printing code: The rightmost number of the first series of numbers is the year of the book's printing; the rightmost number of the second series of numbers is the number of the book's printing. For example, a printing code of 09-1 shows that the first printing occurred in 2009.

Printed in the United States of America

Note: This publication contains the opinions and ideas of its authors. It is intended to provide helpful and informative material on the subject matter covered. It is sold with the understanding that the authors and publisher are not engaged in rendering professional services in the book. If the reader requires personal assistance or advice, a competent professional should be consulted.

The authors and publisher specifically disclaim any responsibility for any liability, loss, or risk, personal or otherwise, which is incurred as a consequence, directly or indirectly, of the use and application of any of the contents of this book.

Most Alpha books are available at special quantity discounts for bulk purchases for sales promotions, premiums, fund-raising, or educational use. Special books, or book excerpts, can also be created to fit specific needs.

For details, write: Special Markets, Alpha Books, 375 Hudson Street, New York, NY 10014.

Publisher: *Marie Butler-Knight*
Senior Managing Editor: *Billy Fields*
Acquisitions Editor: *Tom Stevens*
Development Editor: *Nancy D. Lewis*
Senior Production Editor: *Janette Lynn*
Copy Editor: *Cate Schwenk*

Cartoonist: *Steve Barr*
Cover Designer: *Kurt Owens*
Book Designer: *Trina Wurst*
Indexer: *Heather McNeill*
Layout: *Chad Dressler*
Proofreader: *John Etchison*

I'd like to thank the best friends I've had in recent years, the Friends of Abe, who understand what business and entrepreneurism is all about, and as usual my son and daughter, Haley and Holly, for their love and support.

Contents at a Glance

Contents

Introduction

If the Internet went down for 24 hours, it might bankrupt the majority of businesses across the Western world. Surfing the web is not just a favorite pastime anymore, it's how most people conduct their professional and social lives. The use of craigslist perfectly epitomizes this phenomenon. You probably know someone in your own life that got a job via craigslist, met someone for dating and maybe even married, furnished an apartment from listings on the site, bought a car, or hired personnel when starting a business.

As an Internet phenomenon, craigslist inherited the culture and values of the "community coders"—those who strive for aesthetics, simplicity, and usefulness; and by adopting this idealistic, inclusive philosophy, this book teaches you how to prosper and profit while serving the craigslist community as a buyer and seller, as an employer and employee, and as a generator and consumer of most useful content and commerce.

What began as a list to help others has become a worldwide mainstay in people's lives. It's used by major businesses to find employees. Aspects of craigslist get changed due to legal attention it gets from certain areas of the site. Newspapers complain that the free listings and low-cost ads on craigslist destroy their profits from classified advertising. It's hard to find anyone who doesn't know what craigslist is about.

It's equally difficult, though, to find someone who has explored all the areas and categories of the site. How many of the links on the left side of the home page have you explored? Do you know about the Craigslist Foundation and all the training and seminars available for free, both online and at yearly workshops? Did you ever discover that both Craig Newmark, the founder, and Jim Buckmaster, the long-time CEO of the site, both have blogs that keep craigslist users abreast of all developments?

This book came about simply because there was no resource that fully dealt with the myriad of possibilities offered by the site. In this book, you'll even learn about the hidden places on craigslist.

This is not merely a tour of the site, however. A great many websites have sprung up that tie into and make more efficient the ads on craigslist. You'll find discussions of software, and even an application for use on Facebook, that ties into craigslist. If you ever wanted to search an entire region of craigslist sites all at once, we'll tell you how to do it.

Although the site was originally designed for people making local transactions in San Francisco, and still recommends those interactions take place in person, paying cash, the fact is that people come together from all over the world on craigslist sites. Given that, you need to know how to keep yourself safe while building a business.

From dealing with the government and using its free resources to keeping track of the proper legalities, there are many things you need to know when you begin profiting using the advice in this book. Whether you're just looking for a job, or wanting to hire a staff for your business, you might pick up some tips.

Let us know how it works out for you. Like craigslist, we'll try to stay on top of changes, and will depend on feedback and participation. Hopefully, that will come from you.

How to Use This Book

The Complete Idiot's Guide to Making Money on craigslist is divided into five parts:

Part 1, "How craigslist Works," covers all the basics of the site, from the default location you have when you arrive on the site to all the others around the world. You learn everything about all the columns on the home page, how to set up a craigslist account, and the most efficient ways of using the site, including using outside sites and software.

Part 2, "Getting Down to Business," offers advice on the basics of listings, from the people who work for craigslist to what your responsibilities and recourses are if things don't go well. We offer advice on getting paid while doing Internet business, and where to find and how to use sites that are similar to craigslist.

Part 3, "Jobs, Jobs, Jobs," explains the difference in jobs and gigs, tips on how to use both categories to get hired and stay employed, and everything you should know about how major companies use the site and what they're seeking. You find tips on maximizing a resume, a whole chapter for writers and editors, and advice on staffing your own company from listings on craigslist.

Part 4, "Buying and Selling and Profiting," delves into the age-old practice of bartering (its own category on craigslist), then moves through a hundred other possibilities with collectibles, valuables, and bigger-ticket items like vehicles and real estate. There are opportunities available worldwide via craigslist sites. You find tips on all of them, as well as how to use eBay in conjunction with craigslist for maximizing your profits in your chosen area of interest.

Part 5, "Covering All the Bases," offers advice on keeping everything safe and legal. Should you operate with a dba (doing business as)? Would a corporation be better? Just about everything you need to know about doing business both domestically and internationally is available via government resources and we tell you where to find it. And last but not least, we offer a tour of the discussion forums and how they can help you when you can't find answers elsewhere.

Extras

This book features, sprinkled throughout each chapter, snippets of information in boxed sidebars. These sidebars provide you with basics on the website, additional ideas that make your craigslist journey more interesting and profitable, clues on more effective web surfing in conjunction with craigslist, and things that are a waste of time or troublesome.

List Notes
How things on craigslist work, both basic and those things more complex.

 Skip's Tips

Insider clues to using the areas of craigslist that might not be obvious, and other things off-site.

 List Losers

Warnings and cautions about things that might come up while using the craigslist site.

Online Heat
Information that increases efficiency and results when doing business on the web and craigslist.

Acknowledgments

As anyone who is a parent working at home to provide a living for children knows, it's quite a balance keeping them happy while keeping a business running. The better the kids, the easier it is. I feel blessed that my son, Haley Alexander Press, and my daughter, Holly Olivia Press, are bright, responsible, and loving, thus making my own journey so much more worthwhile. I've told them I love them in many book dedications, but in this one I mean it more than ever.

Obviously, this book would not exist without the craigslist site, and in my opinion that site would not have prospered for so long without the foresight and community mindedness of its founder, Craig Newmark, its CEO Jim Buckmaster, and the dedicated staff of craigslist. So I'd like to thank them all for giving to the world and maintaining such a helpful resource.

Last but not least, I'd like to thank Tom Stevens as an editor for always being kind, thoughtful, and insightful, as well as understanding of everything a writer goes through in coming up with something new, because this one was unexplored territory.

Skip Press
Burbank, California

Special Thanks to the Technical Reviewer

The Complete Idiot's Guide to Making Money on craigslist was reviewed by an expert who double-checked the accuracy of what you'll learn here, to help us ensure that this book gives you everything you need to know about doing business on craigslist. Special thanks are extended to Elliot McGucken.

Trademarks

All terms mentioned in this book that are known to be or are suspected of being trademarks or service marks have been appropriately capitalized. Alpha Books and Penguin Group (USA) Inc. cannot attest to the accuracy of this information. Use of a term in this book should not be regarded as affecting the validity of any trademark or service mark.

Part 1

How craigslist Works

It's a simple web page, or so it seems, yet this site that began as a way to help out friends in San Francisco has sometimes become the subject of controversy while enabling users worldwide to live better lives. Surf along as you learn how to use craigslist in your own area and around the world for fun and profit. Find out about placing effective ads, benefits to be gained from the Craigslist Foundation, and why craigslist and everything else on the site is spelled lowercase!

The Reach of craigslist: A World of Possibilities

In This Chapter

- ◆ Home Page or Main Page?
- ◆ The Column on the Left
- ◆ The Income-Generating Areas
- ◆ Location, Location, Location
- ◆ Utilizing International Cities

craigslist is about connection. That's how it started in San Francisco, where the company is still physically located. Rather than seeking to make a lot of money, Craig Newmark started the site to provide a superior, helpful service, and the spirit lives on! If you want to know about the history of the site and the intentions of its founder, click on "about us" at the bottom of the column on the left side of the home page at www.craigslist.org.

The purpose of this book is not to waste your time telling you about things you can easily find out on the site. We want to give you a much fuller understanding and perhaps more clever route to successfully using this wonderful website, and to help you connect to money-making opportunities.

While we've attempted to provide as much useful information as possible to as many readers as we can, you will find there are chapters specific to certain groups of people, like writers and editors in Chapter 14. craigslist is, like fine writing and great paintings, beautiful in its simplicity, yet wonderful in its layers. It is like worlds within worlds. So let's get started exploring.

Your Home Page

Hmmm, you might ask if you've read the Table of Contents, *what's the difference between a home page and the main page?* Well, it's *your* home page. craigslist knows who you are by the number signature of the computer you use to access it. In case you didn't know, every computer has its own Internet Protocol (IP) address. That knowledge comes in handy later in the book, as we discuss the importance of not "spamming" your ads on craigslist. Meanwhile, here's what your home page is about.

Skip's Tips

At www.whatismyip.com you can find out the IP address of your computer. You'll find a virtual web education there, so take some time browsing on the page. All the tech devices like modems, printers, and routers connected to your computer use this address, and the computers at craigslist make note of it as well. It allows them to identify you when you place an ad, among other things.

How Your Default Location Is Set

There's no elaborate method of setting your home page on craigslist. If you type www.craigslist.org, you'll get a very different page than the one you probably will see after that. Why? Because you will likely, as I did, select a city that you live in or near, and search craigslist that way. In my case, it's http://losangeles.craigslist.org. Once you've picked a city, from that point forward, the craigslist computers will kick you back to the city you've chosen to search from. Try it and see. Click on another city and then go to your browser's title bar and type in www. craigslist.org. You'll get kicked back to the page of the city you were just on. If you want to see the broader site, click on the word craigslist in the upper left. At http://www.craigslist.org/about/sites, you'll see a much simpler page. There's a left-hand column under the word craigslist with links about the site, then to the right in sequence: U.S. cities; states in the United States; provinces in Canada, Canadian cities; countries under **au/nz** (Australia, Micronesia, and New Zealand); countries in Asia and the Americas; countries in Europe, Egypt, and South Africa under **africa;** and a list of international cities in the far-right column.

Locations Within Locations

On my craigslist location page, at the top I see:

> los angeles w wst sfv lac sgv lgb ant

If you click on the **w**, that will take you to the Wikipedia listing for my city. Pretty neat, if you're visiting the page of a city you know little about. **wst** is the Westside/Southbay, **sfv** is the San Fernando Valley, **lac** is central Los Angeles, **sgv** is the San Gabriel Valley, **lgb** is Long Beach / 562 (the telephone area code there), and **ant** stands for the Antelope Valley. Even though you'll go to separate pages by clicking on any of those acronyms, you'll still find that the small **w** to the right of the name will take you to the Wikipedia listing for Los Angeles.

There are similar area breakdowns on the craigslist pages of other American cities. For example, you can search in all the boroughs of New York City. You won't find such a breakdown in international cities except Amsterdam, whose page reads **amsterdam/ranstad.** That's because the city "comprises the northern part of the Randstad, the 6th-largest metropolitan area in Europe," according to Wikipedia. You will find area breakdowns in countries, though. For an example, click on france and have a look.

The Main Page and What's on It

So now you've established the city from where you'll search or place a listing. In my case it's "los angeles" (using the spelling as it looks on craigslist). What do I find there? At the top left:

post to classifieds

my account

help, faq, abuse, legal

Most of those are self-explanatory, and Frequently Asked Questions is faq. We'll explore those in more detail later. Right now let's look at the rest of the page.

Next down the left side is the craigslist search bar. Note that you can (and should) set it by category, the ones listed in the three columns in middle of the page.

Further down is the event calendar, which upon exploration is a catchall hodgepodge of listings that resembles a street fair or massive garage sale, sorted by area. If you're hosting a fundraiser, you'll want to have a listing here, but more on that later.

> **Online Heat**
>
> Have no fear about not being able to read craigslist listings in other countries or international cities. If you surf to the Zurich link, at the top right you're offered a choice of four languages: **de | fr | it | en** (German, French, Italian, English). Das ist kühl. ("That's cool" in German.)

Next you'll find a list of links that you really should spend time reading, if you want to profit from using craigslist and not have any problems in creating or responding to listings. You'll see the following list (explanations provided by me):

avoid scams & fraud—Not just for reporting to craigslist, this page covers generally helpful things like the Federal Trade Commission (FTC) toll free hotline: 1-877-FTC-HELP (1-877-382-4357), and the FTC online complaint form (http://www.ftc.gov). I suggest reading the whole page.

personal safety tips—A short list of very good ideas about making real life transactions, and links off craigslist that will help you with personal safety overall.

craigslist blog—An ongoing discussion lead by craigslist CEO Jim Buckmaster, with continually interesting articles and archives in several categories, filed by month.

craigslist factsheet—A page to read if you really want to make money with the site. You'll discover things like the fact that eBay owns 25 percent of the site.

best-of-craigslist—Listings nominated by craigslist readers that are usually hilarious. Things like "WANTED: ROADKILL" or "FREE VERMIN" can keep you laughing for hours.

job boards compared—Take a look, you might be surprised. As of this writing, craigslist as a job board was rated #1, although they were quoting a year 2000 article.

craigslist movie & dvd—Yes, someone made a movie, "24 Hours on craigslist" (not available as of this writing).

boot camp 2009—The Craigslist Foundation (capitalized unlike craigslist) each year puts on an intensive "one day gathering where people learn how to bring their ideas for stronger communities into reality."

craigslist foundation—This link takes you to http://craigslistfoundation.org, which is about "building a platform for civic engagement." You might want to look into the nonprofit boot camp they offer.

Next down on the left side is system status which is in a larger font than the rest of the page for a reason. You can find out about things like scheduled maintenance. That could be important, because if you want to place ads late at night after your regular job or personal time, you might find the site not available. Many regular craigslist users have no idea this goes on.

Lastly on the left, you'll find a grouping of items:

terms of use	privacy
about us	help

While these are self-explanatory, my guess is you would be hard-pressed to find a single friend or acquaintance who has ever read the **terms of use** in full or explored any of these items other than **help**. That's too bad, because there is a plethora of helpful information that you might not suspect. For example, if you click on the **about us** link you'll find a full page of links including one for **our thanks** leading to www.craigslist.org/about/thanks, a page which lists all the software and hosting companies used by the craigslist site, among other things. If you know anything about the software listed there, you know that page is like a website software workshop.

On the **help** page you'll find not just a listing of answered questions but links to pages that will tell you just about everything you need to know about the site. It's the equivalent of craigslist college.

List Notes

Before CEO of craigslist Jim Buckmaster became Chief Executive Officer in 2000, he "contributed craigslist's homepage design, multi-city architecture, discussion forums, search engine, community moderation system, self-posting process, personals categories (including missed connections), and best-of-craigslist." That's from his blog—you should read it.

The Money-Making Middle Area

The income-generating activity takes place in the middle area of the home page. It has nine categories:

community	housing	jobs
personals	for sale	gigs
discussion forums	services	resumes

On large city community pages, listings are broken down into geographical areas as mentioned earlier. The categories within the community section are:

activities   lost+found   pets
artists musicians   events
childcare   local news   volunteers
general politics classes
groups rideshare

How could you possibly make any money with those? By being creative. For example, in cities where paid clinical medical trials take place, you'll find many listings under the **volunteers** category. In Los Angeles (a Mecca for aspiring musicians) you'll find contests with sizeable prizes. If you're putting on an event, you can locate entertainers and party planners who advertise in the events category.

In short, when you take the time to learn everything about craigslist (reading this book is a good start), you'll find shortcuts that might otherwise take you months or years to discover through use of the site.

We don't cover the personals area of craigslist in this book because we're not interested in any sexually connected means of profit. In recent years there have been legal actions against craigslist because of posters who have used the site for prostitution. Take a look at the March 2009 craigslist blog posting by CEO Jim Buckmaster and you'll see that postings in **erotic services** were drastically reduced over a year's time as the site added phone and credit card authorization when people placed such ads. People might abuse the site, but they got a handle on it.

The discussion forums cover everything from 1099 to writers (two things that are important to me). If you ever find yourself needing information about craigslist not covered in this book, you'll probably find a forum where you can ask (even though I'll be crushed I didn't give you the answer). This area can be a free marketing research tool for a smart entrepreneur. Forums like autos, bikes, crafts, food, gifts, housing, jobs, money, motocy (motorcycle), shop, travel, and wine can provide you with highly knowledgeable people in many areas. And if you're tired of your workday and simply want kindred souls to commiserate with, you can probably find them here.

List Losers

You'll find a lot of sexual discussion forums on craigslist, which might be something that interests you, but if you have in mind doing anything that could be constituted as solicitation, you might want to think twice. This type of thing has been heavily attacked by legal authorities and the site watches closely.

If you need a ride, want to take a class to improve your skills, or want to learn about things like job fairs, you'll find postings on the forums.

In Chapter 3 we'll discuss in further detail some suggestions for making money in the listings in the middle column of craigslist. The purpose of this chapter is to orientate you to what everything on the main page means, so let's continue with the rest of the items in the middle, descriptions provided by me:

>**housing**—In any economy, the craigslist cost of listing property you're renting, leasing, or selling is hard to beat. This is one of the most active areas of the site.

>**for sale**—Part-time entrepreneurs concentrate on this area, which offers 30 areas of potential profit.

>**services**—If you're in business for yourself, this is the area that will probably be most lucrative for you, particularly if you are available nationwide.

>**jobs**—With over 30 different links, this area offers something for everyone, and is where employers looking for full-time employees post most often. While the part-time area usually doesn't offer high-paying possibilities, the ETC can offer very interesting things to explore. The site receives more than 2,000,000 new job listings each month.

>**gigs**—This is the flip side of the services link for independent contractors. Post what you offer on services; find people who need you on gigs.

>**resumes**—Believe it or not, potential employers actually do search here, and by geographic area. If you're comfortable with posting your resume here, you may profit.

My hope with this book is that you never feel like you're being told the obvious. The fact is, as altruistic as the people of craigslist are, they have to deal with the oddities of the public, and things are often not what you might assume from a casual inspection.

People looking to make money on craigslist basically fall into two categories: seekers and providers. Seekers look for jobs, bargains, and housing while providers look for customers, business possibilities, and real estate opportunities. Of course, that's a generality, and people are both seekers and providers at various times. The determining factor is orientation. Chances are, if you're more given to be a provider in your daily life, dreaming up ways to be in business for yourself or move toward that kind of life, you're more likely to have picked up this book. As a freelance writer and editor for over 20 years, I've made a living by being inventive and reinventing myself career-wise whenever necessary.

And craigslist has been a very helpful tool for me, which is why I'm writing about it, for you.

Now let's take a look at the rest of the main page of craigslist and how you might use it for profitability.

Cities, Regions, and Other Places

Although there's no link for Antarctica, a great deal of the rest of the world is covered by craigslist. This is why the site gets more than 12 billion page views per month on over 500 craigslist sites. It's amazing if you think about it, but that's the greatness of the web. The right side column offers:

us cities	us states	countries
canada		
intl cities		

If you're looking to relocate somewhere for family or personal reasons and want to line up a job in advance, it makes sense to use this area of craigslist. The practice is so common employers take advantage of it and post locally as well as in other cities. Although technically, multiple postings of the same ad are not allowed, people abuse it all the time, and that includes employers.

Skip's Tips

Below the us cities column the **more ...** link takes you to over 300 cities and areas. For example, **worcester / central MA** covers a wide area of Massachusetts. Keep that in mind if you're thinking of a specific city, and remember, on the linked page of every large metro area, you'll find links to smaller areas, as previously explained.

You can take the time to laboriously search the job listings by state, city, or area, or you can try a global search using Google or another search engine. Sometimes the latter works. Let's say you're looking for a job as a nurse, a profession which seems to be in higher and higher demand. A Google search for "nurse craigslist" or "nurse site:craigslist. org" will turn up listings from across the country, mostly from employers, but some ads placed by nurses who offer in-home care or other options.

When I Google searched for nurse jobs in Austin, Texas, using the phrase "nurse Austin craigslist" the top hit I got was "austin healthcare jobs classifieds—craigslist" which was a good link, but all sorts of other jobs available in Austin and a myriad of other seemingly unrelated links turned up. A search using Yahoo with the aforementioned phrase turned up roughly the same results.

This means that if you're looking for a job outside your local area and you know where you want to look, you're better off surfing to that city, clicking on a job category, and using the search box on the category page. After all, when you do that, you'll have the following checkboxes to use to narrow your search:

Search options to help narrow your results.

Now, this begs the question, "Can I use one of those keywords to narrow my search with Google?" The answer is "Probably." By using the phrase "nurse austin contract craigslist" in Google, I turned up three times as many listings that were more specific to my original search. Basically, it would depend on employer needs at the time and the listing currently posted, but norms and patterns have emerged as the use of craigslist has evolved.

Anyone who has made use of online job sites for any length of time quickly begins to see that a great number of them are mostly harvesters and repurposers of craigslist postings. This is not true of craigslist competitors like Monster.com, but broadly, craigslist is "everywhere" when it comes to job listings.

We'll go into further detail on job listings and other "middle column" things in Chapter 3. Now let's briefly discuss the basics of the main page if you're a provider, selling things or services outside your local area.

While you can simply post items under the **for sale** area, or offer your expertise under **services,** don't ignore other areas of the main page to build your business. If you're uncertain about differences in U.S. and Canadian law, for example, why not navigate to the Toronto page, check in the **legal** area under **discussion forums,** and see if you can find a lawyer to ask a simple question. Who knows, you might find one who not only likes what you're selling, but has some money to invest and wants to become your Canadian partner.

Let's say you have a product that's seasonal, like the items Americans are used to seeing sold in kiosks during the holiday season. You've done well locally for a couple of years, and you're looking to expand your horizons. An ad for employees or partners placed under **part-time** in the **jobs** area will cost you $25, while an ad placed under **gigs** in one of its nine categories won't cost you anything.

It's up to you to determine how you want to use craigslist to further your income potential. You might have a day job with part-time pursuits, or you may be a full-time entrepreneur. The point is that by being creatively inventive in the use of the site, you will be much more likely to achieve success.

Now let's briefly examine possibilities in international venues (assuming you're living in the United States as you read this book). As the world grows increasingly smaller via the web, the site that began as a simple helpful email list in San Francisco is one of the tools benefiting international commerce in a friendly fashion.

The Possibilities of International Cities

The main page is one thing, but always remember that craigslist is worlds within worlds at just about every level. It can be a bit of a maze sometimes, but you won't get lost in it. You'll find that the **intl cities** and **countries** areas are wide open to people who only speak English. That's because American English is the international language worldwide and, thanks to the Internet which originated in the United States, the one most in use on the web as well.

If you click on an international city, **barcelona** for example, you'll find that on the resultant page the country of Spain is highlighted in yellow and underneath that banner is Barcelona and 10 more Spanish cities. If you click on **berlin** you get a similar result for Germany. With either of those European cities, you'll see on the resultant page a much longer list of European cities below a **europe** banner than you'll find under **int'l cities** on your craigslist home page.

The last column on the right of your craigslist home page is countries, but the links aren't all the same. If you click on **argentina** you're taken to the buenos aires page (the capital), but if you click on **australia** you're taken to a page that gives you a choice between the largest cities, Adelaide, Brisbane, Canberra, Darwin, Hobart, Melbourne, Perth, and Sydney. The page scheme seems to vary, country by country with no absolute pattern. If you click on **UK** on the countries list of your home page, you'll end up on the london page, but under a yellow-highlighted UK banner to the right you'll find a list of cities in the United Kingdom that's a long one, hence a more ... link underneath the link for the city of sheffield.

> ### Online Heat
>
> One way to shortcut craigslist searches is via the site www.crazedlist.org. It's one of my favorite tools as a freelance writer as mentioned in Chapter 14. It enables you to "search craigslist like a madman" both in the United States and worldwide. You can save your search settings and save a lot of search time.

So it's not arranged so that clicking on a country link will take you to the capital city (like london). You'll just have to navigate it country by country. Let's say you're interested in importing pashmina scarves from India for sale in the United States. If you do your research, you'll discover than the city of Jaipur is the textile hub of the country and that's where you'll get the best deals on clothing items. If you click on the link for that city, however, and then under clothes+acc under for sale, you won't find much. Unless you can go there in person, you might be better off finding a website like www.trademart.in or a manufacturer located in Jaipur like www.ratantextiles.com and doing business that way.

In other words, you'll need to be as creative with craigslist sites around the world as you will with those in the United States. Keep in mind, you can use the discussion forums and listings in foreign places to attempt to strike up conversations with potential business partners, but you'll have to use every precaution and possibly more than you would in dealing with someone face to face in your home city. While the international use of craigslist offers wonderful possibilities, nothing at all is guaranteed.

The Least You Need to Know

- ◆ craigslist in its infancy was about connecting people, and that spirit is maintained at a corporate level today, so try to maintain it in your dealings.

- ◆ You'll operate from a default home page on craigslist, so do yourself a favor and learn how the site operates, if you're serious about using it for profitable activities.

- ◆ From how to avoid scams to keeping up with current news about the site and benefiting from things offered by the Craigslist Foundation, you'll save a lot of time and hassle by studying all the items in the left-hand column of the home page.

- ◆ The middle columns of craigslist is where all the money-making opportunities can be found, but only the people who learn to be creative in their use get the most out of the site.

- ◆ An Internet search using a word or phrase followed by the word "craigslist" will often net you the results you want in a much quicker fashion than going through a city page search one by one.

- ◆ Browsing on pages of other countries and international cities has its quirks, but there are over 500 English language craigslist sites available around the world.

Navigating from the Basic Page

In This Chapter

- ◆ Easier navigation
- ◆ Protection and enlightenment
- ◆ Support and the Craigslist Foundation
- ◆ Using what matters

It might seem like a waste of time to read all the explanations on the site. After all, who reads user manuals? Well, the guy who comes to fix your computer because you can't figure it out— remember, the one you paid a lot of money? That guy reads the manuals. So do yourself a favor and find out what craigslist expects of you, the person accustomed to using their site for free, when you actually get down to business. Read the site.

Tips for Easier Navigation

Sorry to disappoint if you thought everything was gratis on craigslist. For business people, things are rarely free. See www.craigslist.org/about/help/posting_fees for details about things you have to pay for:

Job posts in the San Francisco Bay Area

Job posts in Atlanta, Austin, Boston, Chicago, Dallas, Denver, Houston, Los Angeles, New York, Orange County, Philadelphia, Phoenix, Portland, Sacramento, San Diego, Seattle, South Florida, and Washington, D.C.

Brokered apartment rental listings in New York

Erotic services posts on craigslist sites in the United States

As mentioned previously, we're staying out of the erotic business in this book.

You can post ads individually if you want to pay by credit card. If you want to buy a block of ads you can pay with a check. You'll find a link for setting that up at the link just given, leading to this account signup page—https://accounts.craigslist.org/cgi-secure/accountSignup.cgi. As stated on that page:

List Notes

Keep in mind that if you're looking to hire people, you'll have to pay *in each category* where you post your ad. In San Francisco, a job ad costs $75, so if you post in two categories, that's $150. In other U.S. cities, job ads cost only $25, so you'll pay that for each category where you post your ad.

"… you must agree to purchase a minimum block of $675 worth of postings, or show that you have previously bought at least $675 worth of postings. (note: $675 minimum does not apply for NYC housing ads.)"

Hopefully, that gives you a better idea of how actively many businesses use the supposedly "free" craigslist on a regular basis to do business.

Take note that it costs to place job ads in the U.S. cities listed on the page referenced earlier. If you're trying to hire people from other cities in the United States or around the world, you can place those ads for free. Obviously, the cities mentioned are the largest metropolitan areas in America, with the largest concentration of workers and job seekers.

Protection and Enlightenment

How many times have you been notified by email that you're the recipient of several million pounds? All you need to do is provide the sender with who you are, where you live, and other things like your bank account numbers. Or someone sends you an email saying you won the Microsoft lottery and they need the same kind of information. While I don't know what fools ever fall for those emails, spammers keep sending them out, so they must make money. Have you been prompted to respond and ask why, if you already won, they don't know who you are? Of course, that would be the wrong thing to do because then they'd know your email address is valid and you'd just get more scamming emails.

Avoiding Scams and Playing Safe

The folks at craigslist have seen it all as Internet-connected criminals go, so they tell you what to look out for at **avoid scams & fraud.** That link opens to www.craigslist.org/about/scams. Take a look at points of advice on that page (abbreviated for essence):

- Deal locally, meet people in person.
- Never wire funds to strangers.
- Don't trust cashier checks or money orders until you're *sure* they've cleared.
- craigslist is *not* involved in any transaction.
- Don't give out your financial information.
- Avoid middleman service guarantees like shipping.

You might read the full page wondering why anyone wouldn't figure out these are obvious things. Well, given the amount of transactions that take place via craigslist per month, don't you think there's a reason they created the page? They make a very good point that most scams come "from someone far away, often in another country" and advise you to try to make all transactions face-to-face.

Obviously, if you're doing intrastate or international business, in-person meetings don't make sense except in setting up a large deal (like buying a house you travel to inspect) or the beginning of an ongoing business relationship. The page was written for a reason. Most people know someone who was taken in by an Internet scam, maybe even someone who fell for one of the notorious "Nigerian emails," so get your free education before you start doing business and study the craigslist scams page.

Would it ever occur to you that a cashier's check could be fake? It wouldn't to most people, but the page explains it for you. They even post examples of fake emails sent to craigslist users. Remember, eBay owns a 25 percent stake in craigslist and no doubt has some say in the organization. eBay also owns PayPal. If someone can't pay you in that manner, even in a foreign country (PayPal works with most credit and debit cards), there might be something wrong with the transaction they're offering. If you're new to doing business on the web, get your education on craigslist before you dive in headfirst.

Skip's Tips

PayPal might not be available in some countries. While craigslist advises against wiring money to people via Western Union, that doesn't mean you shouldn't *accept* money that way. Someone from Russia might find that wiring money to you at a Western Union station in your local grocery store is the quickest way to do business with you.

Don't forget to peruse the advice at the **personal safety tips** link— www.craigslist.org/about/safety and encourage your older children to do the same. Increasingly, minors use craigslist to find items to buy, and are often naive about making such transactions. The sites linked there, http://getsafeonline.org and http://wiredsafety.org, should be required reading for anyone doing web business. The latter site even offers a WiredKids Summit each year with awards for people who make the Internet safer.

Why the CEO Has a Blog

As pervasive as craigslist is with Internet users, you're likely to find that most people only use it peripherally, when they want to find a used computer, rent an apartment, get a date, or look for a job. More involved users (which would likely be you, if you bought this book) are those who offer services and have entrepreneurial businesses. Larger businesses use the site extensively for job postings, and real estate professionals use it continuously, hence the "block posting" price mentioned earlier. When you're doing regular business via the site, it helps to keep up with current developments.

Here's an example. Let's say you offer legitimate massage services, in the home or office, and there's no hanky-panky involved. You wouldn't be posting under the **erotic** category under **services** on the site, you'd be listed under **therapeutic.** That might not stop a zealous craigslist antiporn crusader from seeing your ad and, due to a single word or phrase like "sensuous," think you're offering prostitution under the guise of massage. In such a case your ad might get "flagged" and removed, costing you business. (If you haven't experienced erroneous flagging and gotten frustrated, you might not understand.)

What the crusader might not know is that San Francisco–based craigslist has worked with 40 state attorney generals to knock out ads that violate laws. If the crusader had read the CEO's blog, he or she would see that "net revenue is accumulating from the fees now required of those posting under 'erotic services,' 100% of which is earmarked for donation to worthy charities" (March 9, 2009 post at http://blog.craigslist.org). In short, craigslist has its own "sin tax" and is making the best of people's foibles.

Jim Buckmaster doesn't post very often, and the posts are never long, so it's worth looking through the blog once a month to keep up with craigslist developments because they might speak to your legitimate moneymaking activities.

"Best of craigslist" Benefits

In doing any kind of business, it helps to have a sense of humor, and you can get a lot of laughs reading through the **best of craiglist** pages.

Since you'll have a regular email list, with some of your customers (we hope) acquired by the use of craigslist, why not send a funny email to remind them of how you met and give them a chuckle?

Here's an example of a "best of" in an ad placed January 23, 2009, at 12:25PM EST, advertising "Antique furniture from former CEO's office—$1.22M." My favorite items on the list were:

> Velvet curtains, very similar to the curtains from Gone With the Wind $28K
>
> Sofa, has been slept in a few times but is very comfortable $15K
>
> Off-white parchment waste can, perfect for shredded documents $1,400

You'll find that ad at www.craigslist.org/about/best/nyc/1004463995.html.

Just think, if you get tired of those curtains, you can make them into a dress, like Scarlett O'Hara did! And who doesn't need a $15,000 slightly used couch?

If someone won't stop irritating you and you're tired of having them as a customer, you could offer them the "opportunity" in the ad "Nitpicker Wanted" posted on the SF Bay area site on January 22, 2009, at 10:57 PST: www.craigslist.org/about/best/sfo/1003255950.html. Hey, they offered $50 an hour!

Obviously, these "ads" are jokes, but if they make you laugh they might do the same for friends, associates, and customers, so it's just another area of the site to use to your advantage.

Online Heat

Linked at **craigslist movie & dvd** on the left is the movie http://24hoursoncraigslist.com. Want to see things like people selling 250 pairs of women's army-surplus pants and everything they own to finance a trip around the world? Watch the movie; you'll get all kinds of ideas. You can even host a screening and make some money; see the site for details.

Supporting craigslist

Let's look a little into the craigslist philosophy. If you're doing business via the site it helps to know what they have in mind on a day-to-day basis. You can read all (well, maybe not *all*) about the main employees at www.craigslist.org/about/teambios. As you'll see, it's mostly a young crowd, and they're all operating out of San Francisco. That could be good or bad, depending on how you view the culture of the City by the Bay, but simply a cursory glance at the information will tell you, *these people know technology*. This means that, if someone (including this book) tells you about means of circumventing a craigslist convention (like not multiposting ads), you'd best pay attention, because you'll get nabbed sooner or later, and not be able to use that particular computer to access craigslist.

Don't say you weren't warned.

At the same time, the **feedbk** link on the discussion forums allows you to provide the people running craigslist with your problems, suggestions, or questions, and keep your experience highly interactive. Even on the web, it's hard to get that kind of service for free, so if you're using craigslist to make money, try to support their policies, procedures, and philosophy. You'll have a better business.

The Craigslist Foundation

As stated in the last chapter, do you *really* want to walk around wearing a craigslist T-shirt? Well, you might, if you had one that said "Ask me about my craiglist business." Funny thing is, you can get a lot of business training for free via craigslist, provided by the site via the **craigslist foundation** link in the left column. You just have to dig a little. But before we get into that, let's examine the purpose of the Foundation.

Who They Are, What They Do

The Craigslist Foundation is meant to use the spirit and culture of craigslist to help strengthen civil society. The Foundation put money into it and they host real world activities like workshops, but you don't have to live in San Francisco or the New York Tri-State Area to ben-efit. You can get more information about the people involved in the Foundation at http://craigslistfoundation.org/about.html. The online contact page and the physical address of the Foundation can be found at http://craigslistfoundation.org/contact.html. One thing about the Foundation is that they look for "exciting partnering opportunities" so if you're civic-minded and have a bright idea, get in touch.

The Nonprofit Boot Camp

From 2006 through 2008, the Craigslist Foundation held instructional boot camps in both San Francisco and the New York Tri-State area. You'll find links to minisites at http://www.craigslistfoundation.org/bootcamp.html. There are downloadable PDFs of what was on the program and each site has many pages and links, but each boot camp was basically about "a day of knowledge, resources, and networking, all focused on how to start and run a vibrant nonprofit." You'll also find a link to sign up for newsletters regarding the following areas:

List Notes
If you use craigslist a lot and make money with it, particularly if you aren't pay-ing for job listings, why not give back something? You can do that by donating to the Craigslist Foundation on its site. As stated onsite, "All contributions to Craigslist Foundation are 100% tax-deductible to fullest extent of the law."

Craigslist Foundation Newsletter
San Francisco
New York
Boston
Chicago
Los Angeles
New Orleans
Philadelphia
Seattle
Texas
Washington, DC
Environment/Sustainability

The signup link is also found on the main Craigslist Foundation page under (you guessed) **newsletter.**

Podcasts and More

One of the better benefits of perusing the Foundation site is that a number of presentations from past boot camps are available as QuickTime downloads right there on the site. Just click on **podcasts.** Some that might help you in putting together a web-based business are:

How to Create a Website and How Much Might It Cost
David Taylor

Dirty Sexy Money ... Online
Marc Ruben

Internet Strategy on the Cheap
Britt Bravo & Eric Leland

A Practical Approach to Fundraising Online
Andrew Mosawi

Be Bold—Creating Careers With Impact
Laura Galinsky (moderator), Lucas Welch, Angela Coleman, Taz Tagore & Anthony Lopez

Planning And Enhancing IT
Mark Topping & Alex Wilkinson

Free and Low Cost Tech Resources
Cristine Cronin

Collaborative & Competitive Strategies
David LaPiana

Financial Management 101
Sojeila Maria Silva

Internet Marketing Stategies: Extending Your Online Reach
Brent Blackaby, Jeff Patrick & Favianna Rodriguez

If you're interested in creating a nonprofit organization, there are even more interesting podcasts to hear, and you'll probably want to be on the mailing list for the next boot camp. Remember, these podcasts are all free. You'll also on occasion be linked to the websites of some speakers who are actively involved in creating and running nonprofits, and thus you have access to even more free information.

Help and Other Stuff

Every basic question you might have is answered on the **help** page. Just click on that word in the left column and your education will begin. There are six categories:

classified postings   job classified postings
frequently asked questions   paid housing post (NYC only)
general help   harassment, legal stuff, spam, email

Remember what we said earlier about there being worlds within worlds on craigslist? That was never truer than on the help page. You'll find things here that you might not suspect existed by a simple look at the home page.

Under **classified postings** you'll find information on:

◆ how much does it cost?

◆ how to submit a post

◆ how to reply to a post

◆ how to edit or delete a post

◆ how to repost

◆ how to include a picture

◆ resend publish/edit/delete email

◆ craigslist user accounts

Those are all self-explanatory (click on them, you'll see) and need not be discussed here, with the exception of **craigslist user accounts.** More than any other link in getting started with using craiglist, you need to read this page at www.craigslist.org/about/help/user_accounts. You don't have to have a user account to post on craigslist, but if you post frequently or post paid ads, having an account makes it all much easier.

List Notes

It's not difficult to contact real people at craigslist, but they usually only make phone contact available for payment. You can pay an account invoice by credit card online, or if that makes you uncomfortable you can call. See http://www.craigslist.org/about/help/paying_invoices. They don't accept gift cards.

When you set up a listing, you're sent an email that you must respond to, to make the listing go live. From that email, you'll have the link you use to manage your ad, be that editing it or deleting it.

If you plan to do serious business, set up a user account, using the email address you want to use for craigslist, at https://accounts.craigslist.org/login/signup. On that page, you'll have to enter your email address and some "captcha" words in a box to verify that you're a human and that a software robot isn't placing the ad. You've seen these plenty of times, but if you don't know that word, see http://en.wikipedia.org/wiki/Captcha for an explanation.

Have you ever wondered how long craigslist postings last? See www.craigslist.org/about/help/posting_lifespans. The key is the main cities versus the "free" cities where it doesn't cost to place jobs ads. Classifieds last 7 days in "pay" cities, while resumes, jobs, gigs, and brokered housing postings in New York City stay up for 30 days. In the "free" cities all listings last 45 days. Postings for events expire according to the date range of the event.

If you don't want to keep writing an ad every time you need to hire someone, or if you've lost the file on your computer, you'll have that listing saved for you by craigslist if you have a user account. For more info, see www.craigslist.org/about/help/repost.

It's highly advisable to check out the **what are "flags" and "flagging"** link under **frequently asked questions** on the **help** page. The site offers a long explanation of how craigslist postings get flagged for removal, but the following paragraphs summarize it pretty well:

Millions of postings are removed through community flagging each month, and of these we consistently find that 98–99% are in violation of the craigslist terms of use or other posted guidelines.

No moderation system is perfect, and 1–2% of ads removed through flag-ging are within our terms of use—but without the flagging system, craigs-list would quickly become unusable.

That's not hard to believe, given some of the statements on the craigslist factsheet about site traffic:

- More than 12 billion page views per month

- #8 worldwide in English-language page views

- 50 million users each month, with more than 40 million in the United States alone

So if you find that what you think is a perfectly legitimate posting is getting flagged and removed, save yourself some anger and headache and explore the options available at that page. There's a **flag help forum** linked there that is staffed by knowledgeable volunteers. If you visit the page, you find on the right side a link to the Unofficial Flag FAQ: Answers to Frequently Asked Questions about flags and your craig-slist ad at www.eskimo.com/~newowl/Flagged_FAQ.htm. You might want to check out the latter page first; it's a much simpler page to read through and could just solve your problem. You'll find some very interesting infor-mation, such as how craigslist basically turns down making $12,000,000 a year (which will give you more reason for supporting them as mentioned earlier).

> **Skip's Tips**
>
> If you feel like you're just not finding the answer you need anywhere on the site and/or it's not cov-ered in this book, contact craigslist via the email form (organized by category) at http://sfbay.craigslist.org/cgi-bin/emailForm.cgi.

You might get tired of reading this, but it really is worth reading through all the links on the home page. For example, at www.craigslist.org/about/help/search you'll find some choice advice about finding things more quickly.

Let's say you want to locate a used Honda or Toyota with low mile-age, but you don't want one from certain years, and you hate the color red. The examples of advanced searches given on that help page explain exactly how to do it. This short bit of education can come in very handy. Let's say you wanted to get into business importing wine from another country and using craigslist to find sellers in France or Chile. Assuming you knew the legalities of that type of importing, and you knew what wines were good in what years from those countries, you might save a good bit of time by using the "delimiters" explained under **Advanced Searching** on the search page.

And speaking of legalities, those are covered very well under the last category on the help page. You'll find an online form to report harassment, the entire craigslist Terms of Use (TOU) statement, what to do about spam (including a forum and an address at craigslist where you can report it), an address and fax number and what to do about legal issues, and two separate linked pages on what to do if your email is being rejected by craigslist email servers.

In summation, craigslist goes to great pains to be as helpful to their mostly free-of-charge users by providing a great deal of explanation and educational material online at the main site and the Craigslist Foundation site. Despite the astonishing amount of traffic they deal with worldwide, they also remain very open to contact by all traditional means of communication.

So read the rules and don't abuse it. It's a darn good bet that you don't want to lose it.

The Least You Need to Know

♦ Not everything is free on craigslist, but the cost of placing paid ads there is extremely low, compared to other media outlets.

♦ Not only does craigslist do most things for free, they provide a great deal of online information to keep you from getting scammed or defrauded.

♦ At the **personal safety tips** link on the home page, you'll find important information about ensuring you're safe when making transactions, as well as other sites with a lot more great advice.

♦ The Craigslist Foundation, linked from the main site, offers even more educational material at no charge, including downloadable podcasts pertaining to setting up a web-based business.

◆ If you make money via craigslist (and we hope you make tons), give back to the site. You can make a donation via the Craigslist Foundation page.

◆ All the links accessible in the six categories on the **help** page of craigslist give you a complete education in everything you need to know to do business on the site. Most people don't realize this.

3

Profiting Across the Listings

In This Chapter

- ◆ Knowing your community
- ◆ Perusing housing
- ◆ Searching for jobs and gigs
- ◆ What's for sale
- ◆ Checking out the services area

You'll do most of your business on craigslist in **housing, for sale, services, jobs,** and **gigs,** but as you might have gleaned from discussion in the previous chapter, how you go about posting and responding to listings can be directly proportional to your degree of success. Anyone building a business of any size knows or quickly learns that the most powerful way to increase customers is by word-of-mouth. Opinions about good products and trustworthy merchants or service providers travel almost as fast as bad news in a community or around the world. So let's start out by looking at how you can use one particular area of the site as your own private public relations headquarters and source of many more valuable resources.

Community

The community area is a catchall in the middle columns; the various categories under the **community** banner. In case you didn't already figure this out, know that you can click on the word in each banner and have access to *all* of the listings in all of the categories under the banner, at once. In the case of community, that would be:

activities	lost+found
artists	musicians
childcare	local news
general	politics
groups	rideshare
pets	volunteers
events	classes

It may or may not be noteworthy that the categories are not in alphabetical order. That could speak to the popularity of each category, or not. It can change by location. For example, click on **caribbean** under **countries** and you'll find that **artists** becomes the top category under **community.**

Time-Wasters, or Not?

For the most part, you won't find many money-making activities under most of the categories in **community,** but there are so many "except" possibilities here, it bears a good deal of discussion.

Let's say you need to get the word out about a new product or business. How are you going to do that? If it's something you can do in person locally, the **activities** area might seem logical, but you'll find that the listings are mostly about things that people do, like softball or other sports or fitness activities. If you happen to be a fitness trainer, however, this is probably your best place on the site for placing a listing.

If you're looking for an artist for your promotional material, book, or anything else, you're likely to find them under the **artists** category here. Similarly, you could look under the **creative** category under **services,** but that's not as specific as **artists** in **community.** If you are an artist looking for work, you'll find ads for that here. This is also the most popular area in urban areas for photographers, for both finding models and offering photographic services.

The **general** category is the Wild West of the **community.** If you can't find what you're looking for anywhere else, or don't know where else to post something you need, such as "kangaroo wrangler needed," post it here. After all, if someone searches craigslist from the main page in the search box provided there, it will show up no matter where it's posted. If you're an astrologer, or have a new network marketing company or franchise, post an ad about it here. With the latter, you might choose **sm biz ads** under **services,** it's your call. Note there is no "general" category under **services,** so if you don't know where to post, use **general** under **community.**

> ## List Notes
>
> Remember the general craigslist philosophy of being community-minded and helpful when posting under the **community** banner. If you're a small business posting ads about something that might not necessarily contribute to your community, your ad might belong under **sm biz ads** in **services.** Otherwise you could get flagged.

In the **groups** category, you'll be fine as long as you're offering a group activity or looking for a group where you might meet potential customers or business partners. Let's say you offer walking tours and provide history and knowledge of edible plants in a national forest near your home. While that might fit under **travel/vac** under **services,** the keyword here is "community." People look for ads under **groups** that they associate with a lot of people who share similar enjoyments and aspirations.

The **pets** link is where you would sell any pet-related items. (You'll notice there is no such category under **for sale.**) If you sell pets or provide a pet-related service like dog walking, this would be your category, too.

To find people that you think could be like-minded with regards to business opportunities you offer, it's worth a look under **events** to see whether or not you want to list there. Whether you sell Avon or time-share condominiums, if you're throwing an event to talk about your business, you'd place a listing here. If you're looking for entertainers or other personnel for the event, you're also likely to find them by *searching* here in the search box on the page.

You might think there's no money to be made in a **lost+found** category, but that's not true. Particularly in large cities, you'll find a great number of ads offering a *reward* for lost things. Thousands of dollars for a missing dog isn't unusual, or a nice bonus for returning someone's missing passport. Give it a try if you've found a pet or something you think might be of value. Click on the category, enter "reward" in the search box, and see.

Under **local news** you'll usually find a hodgepodge of posts, kind of like the box of chocolates in *Forrest Gump*; you never know what you'll get. Since you can narrow it down by "tabs" in the menu of large metropolitan areas, it might be worth a search there if you need something specific, like someone to clean your house while you're working in your home office. (Hey, some people think that when they're looking for a job, that's news.)

Skip's Tips

When you click on the **local news** category, it expands to "local news and views." If you have a regular activity for people in the community, like Karaoke Night at your restaurant, or if your church has a regular bingo night, placing regular listings here in advance will often boost your patronage.

And under **politics,** good luck. You probably won't find any moneymaking opportunities at all, except at election time when campaign workers are being hired. If you want to laugh at people's political rants while taking a break, though, you'll be right at home on this page.

Where Musicians Get Work

Ask yourself a question. If you wanted to hire someone to play at your wedding but didn't know anyone, would you look at the **creative** category under **services,** or under **musicians** at the top of the page under the **community** banner?

Thought so.

This is a very active posting area, particularly in larger areas. If you want concert tickets, you'll find them here. You'll also find equipment and other musical items for sale, as well as people who give music lessons of all kinds. The key to posting depends on whether you're hiring or want to get hired. If you want to hire someone, write something like:

> Band *wanted* for corporate event

If you would like to get hired for that kind of job:

> Excellent band *available* for weddings, dances, and corporate events

Note the *italics* emphasis on the keywords you should use. Obviously, the reason you do that is because people use the search box. Sometimes they'll go to the category and search (better idea) or often enough they'll simply use the search box on the home page. The more *specific* you can be in the title line of your listing, the more successful your posting will likely be. Remember, at the top of a *category* page, there's a box to check **only search titles.** That box is not available on the main page.

If you're selling musical equipment, it's probably better to place your ad here than under **electronics** under the **for sale** banner. The same is true if you are training people in software like ProTools that is used by musicians. Shouldn't that service be listed under **classes?** Maybe, but musicians using craigslist tend to look for everything musical under the **musicians** category. The one difference might be old recordings and things that would appeal to people generally, in which case **collectibles** under **for sale** might be best.

Child Care Help

We discuss this in a book about moneymaking opportunities because in addition to many working people needing child care, providing it can be a lucrative business. In addition, this is the category where you'll more likely find tutors for your children, which can come in handy if your workload is so heavy, or your own education lacking. You can also use delimiters in your searches. If you would prefer day care in a Christian environment, simply search for "daycare + Christian" and you'll find listings that include both those words. Similarly, if you're concerned about the credentials of a nanny, add the word "licensed" to your search. You'll find products for kids, companies that help you find the right child care provider, and if you want a job in child care, this is a good place to post.

And if a person or a company makes a claim in a listing and you're not quite sure, in addition to checking with the Better Business Bureau or local government for complaints, you should also check in the **parent** category under **discussion forums** to get to the parenting discussion. You'll find plenty of people discussing child care. There are also other forums there, like the **parents' giving forum,** where you'll get help as well as opinions and advice.

Finding and Sharing Rides

Occasionally under **rideshare** you'll find special offers that are worth checking out, like new transportation companies that are competing with taxis. If you'd like to carpool to cut down on expenses and be able to drive in the diamond lane of the freeway, this is where you would post. Be forewarned, though, that most of the postings in this category are by people *wanting* rides from place to place. It's up to you whether you find them trustworthy or not.

Online Heat

Downsized at your job and lost your health insurance? Freelancing and can't afford it? If you think you have a specific medical problem, do a search under **volunteers.** You just might find a medical study that will help you for free, or even pay you to participate.

Volunteering and Profits

A famous filmmaker named Robert Rodriguez got the money he needed to make his reportedly $7,000 feature film *El Mariachi* by answering an ad to be a medical testing volunteer. Although some craigslist users hate the idea and try to flag the postings, focus groups and medical research studies repeatedly post in the **volunteer** category to find subjects. You'll find people who will pay you for your opinion (hint: search with the keyword "cash") and companies doing clinical trials. How do you know if they're legitimate? If they point you to a company website, that's a good indicator. If they're listed in the phone book, better yet. We can only advise you on what's out there.

Life isn't always about making money, though, so if you're the type of person who believes in "giving back" and helping those less fortunate, particularly in tutoring, you'll find plenty of opportunities here, and give yourself another kind of wealth.

Improving Your Skills

In the **classes** category you'll find a very crowded page, with people trying to stand out with classes they offer. That's why so many type their headline ALL IN CAPS, which apparently they don't realize is considering *shouting* in cyberspace. The best listings use normal fonts and list the area where the classes are available in parentheses at the end of the line; for example (Los Angeles).

If you teach classes, you might get a little confused figuring out where to place your ad at the **post to classifieds** link on the main page. The hint can be found when you click on **classes**. At the top of the resultant page you'll see **event calendar** not something about classes. So when you **post to classifieds** about a class you're teaching, scroll all the way down to event and click on that. That takes you to a page with two choices:

Please choose a category:

- ◆ *classes*

- ◆ *events (no tickets please!)*

Clicking on classes takes you to a page that lets you pick the area where you're teaching (if there is more than one available in your city). Make your pick and you'll be ready (finally) to create your listing. It expires in 30 days, so if you teach the same class each month, you need to create a new listing as necessary.

Housing

Most of the categories under the **housing** banner won't apply to making money for you, unless you're a landlord or selling real estate. Oh sure, you'll probably be able to find an apartment, room, sublet, or temporary housing. You might get a deal on parking or storage, or find reasonably priced office space. Using craigslist, you'll find it easier to locate people interested in a vacation rental you own, too. As in real life, however, your moneymaking opportunities under **housing** will likely come from the categories **office/commercial** or **real estate for sale.**

As you look through housing ads, you'll find that some pages will have much more sophisticated ads than you're used to seeing. They'll have special fonts, elaborate pictorials and layouts. While you can get a bit of an education in HyperText Markup Language (HTML) by clicking on **help** and then the link **what HTML code does craigslist support?** under **frequently asked questions,** that won't help you make those sophisticated ads. Those are created using tools like those available at www.postlets.com or www.vflyer.com. Give them a try, you might like them.

For Sale By Owner

If you're selling your house on craigslist, it's fairly unlikely you're working with a real estate agent. That's true in many suffering markets in a down economy, with credit tight or frozen and real estate sales slow. Additionally, some areas in cities like Detroit, Michigan, may be highly undesirable even for bargains. Still, opportunities abound if you have money to spend, and you might find that 25 percent of people selling their homes are operating on their own and using craigslist as a tool.

 List Losers

Criminals can copy craigslist ads. They use your information and represent themselves as the owner. They may say they're away from the property and con people into sending them money, or they may get keys made and falsely represent themselves at the property. Remember the craigslist admonition: "Deal locally with folks you can meet in person." If your property's distant, you'd better use an agent.

If you plan to sell your property on craigslist, you'll have to get an education about real estate on your own. There's no craigslist "for sale by owner" page to help you out. The only thing remotely connected to the subject is a **posting guidelines for NYC housing ads** link under **help.** (Remember, you have to pay for placing housing ads in New York City.)

There are numerous sites to advise you on this, however. Just do a web search of "for sale by owner."

You'll find that on the **real estate** page the search bar offers you many choices in searching and that a user can select **real estate—by owner** or **real estate—by broker** and that there are links to the **housing** forum and off-site links to protective groups (depending on what craigslist area you're using) like the Better Business Bureau. So craigslist does a lot for a mostly free site. We'll cover tips on writing effective listings in the next chapter. Meanwhile, let's look at the difference in the **office/commercial** category.

Commercial Possibilities

No matter where you look in the craigslist sites around the world, **real estate for sale** ads specify whether the property is for sale by owner or broker. On the office and commercial page, people are renting or leasing, not selling, and the type of person placing the ad is not mentioned in the title line. If you're sophisticated enough to own commercial property, you'll probably know what the going rate is for tenants, either per month or by square foot, but in case you don't, you can easily find out. Just do a search by location. Because people search in that way, most listings in this category reveal both monthly and price per square foot prices in the title line for the ad.

We'll get into more ideas on how to profit in real estate (and other things) in latter chapters. Meanwhile, just know that the basics in ads in the housing area are roughly the same worldwide. And sometimes, a simple idea can turn into a goldmine. There was a time when spaces beneath freeways and overpasses were not used by rental storage facilities. If that's true in your city, it might be a business you could get started, and the **parking / storage** category would be a great place to start advertising.

For Sale

There are over 30 categories under this banner area, and it's meaningless to try to cover them all in a book that is about using craigslist more effectively. Still, you don't need a degree in marketing or business to learn to how to profit by selling on craigslist. What you do need to keep in mind, though, is what you should *not* attempt to sell on craigslist. Under each category, the page you open will have a **partial list of prohibited items** link to www.craigslist.org/about/prohibited.items. It's a long list and it's highly advisable to read it. Doing so will quickly disabuse any ideas that you might have about craigslist being an "anything goes" sales tool. You're also admonished to not sell recalled items. Will you get busted if you violate the rules? Maybe, maybe not, but your computer could get banned from using the site.

Selling in the Right Place

Click on **for sale** in the banner and you'll get a site with everything that's for sale and a search bar where you can select your category. A glance at all the available items there will show you what the "big ticket" items are under **for sale.** The two big categories are **cars+trucks** and **furniture.** In both categories you can choose "all" or "by dealer" or "by owner." In other words, if you're selling a vehicle or furniture, you're competing with businesses.

Akin to the real estate ads, you'll find an identifying phrase *in italics* at the right of each listing if you're on the **all** page. Enter **dealer** in the box and click on the search button, though, and you'll get all the dealer listings. In the furniture area you'll find incentives in the title line, such as "free s&h" (shipping & handling) or to the right of the listing (FREE DELIVERY)—that's a choice that can be made when creating the listing.

Skip's Tips _____

Don't be intimidated if you think you're competing against a dealer. There's no "craigslist licensing" criterion. You might be dealing with someone who operates in volume, or not. If you study their posts, though, you can learn something, and who's to stop you from asking about their business methods? They might answer, and you might learn some hot tips.

On the **cars & trucks** page the listings are pretty much the same whether they are placed by owners or dealers, with the subject lines jammed with information. An owner example:

1991 Mercedes Benz SL Second Owner Beautiful - $3950

A sample dealer ad is more likely to stress the type of incentive you'd expect if you need financing:

Do you want a Volvo but have bad credit?

If you're into finding auto or truck bargains and reselling them, you can search through the listings, or you might visit dealer auctions. You'll sometimes find those auctions on craigslist in the dealer listings.

Whatever you choose to buy or sell via craigslist, you'll develop your own methods of building a business. The keys will generally always be: knowing a) who your competition is; and b) where to place the most effective ads, which might include which craigslist site to use, worldwide.

The Areas Explained

Only you know what type of merchandise you want to market, if that's your aim on craigslist. With that in mind, remember that each category under a banner expands into a larger phrase on its resultant page. So here's an explanation of each of those and what they cover.

barter—not just item for item, if you want to trade services for same, or products, this is the place

bikes—it's the pedal kind, as well as accessories and other things, with a link to the bicycling forum

boats—every type and price

books—*and* magazines, in case you have a collection you want to buy or sell

business—while there are some business opportunities, it's mostly about items used in business

computer—anything and everything, with links to the Linux, Apple, and PC forums

free—you might be surprised what people give away, and garage-sale type resellers could do well here

furniture—as mentioned earlier

general—anything you can think of, from a rabbit cage to a cemetery plot

jewelry—both buyers and sellers post here

material— "materials for sale" is with some exceptions, this category is mostly about construction items

rvs—recreational vehicles can include anything from a Seadoo to a Gulfstream trailer, parts, and accessories

sporting—not tickets to athletic events, but items for use in athletic activities

tickets—it's easy to spot the tickets from scalpers and dealers as they often advertise the tickets for $1

tools—from hammers to lawn mowers, you won't find dealer ads here

arts+crafts—it's "arts/crafts for sale" on the linked page, so if you've turned a hobby into a business or are importing this type of item, post here

List Notes

If you find your carefully crafted listing has been removed and you just don't know why, see if it is because of one of the "normal" causes at www.craigslist.org/about/help/reasons. If that doesn't cover you, inquire further at http://sfbay.craigslist.org/cgi-bin/emailForm.cgi.

auto parts—what it says but you may find an occasional ad for auto insurance or other odd listings

baby+kids—mostly recycling of baby items

cars+trucks—covered earlier

cds/dvd/vhs—usually not much different than what you'd find at a yard sale

clothes+acc—clothing & accessories, some new

collectibles—the category with the most potential, but it pays to browse in places other than major metropolitan areas where these items might be better bargains

electronics—the category most likely to have stolen items listed, caveat emptor

farm+garden—this "farm/garden for sale" category isn't tools and seeds, as expensive livestock listings are found in this category

games+toys—"games/toys for sale" is the second most likely category to have stolen items listed

garage sale—if you're holding one of these sales or looking for bargains at one, list and look here

household—it's "household items" and all that implies

motorcycles—"motorcycles/scooters" at the page can include things like dune buggies, and accessories

music instr—the prices here are always cheaper than retail, and it certainly beats browsing pawnshops, but watch out for stolen items

photo+video—the "photo/video for sale" page is best browsed in major metropolitan areas because of the competition and thus lower prices

wanted—if you have something for sale and want to potentially save yourself the hassle of posting an ad, do a search at this "items wanted" page first

The Services Area

Professions advertised in this area can be broken down into those that are usually limited to local performance and those that can be done via telecommuting. The former would include: beauty, event, financial, legal, automotive, household, labor/move, skill'd trade, real estate, sm biz ads, therapeutic, and travel/vac. The latter would likely involve: computer, creative, lessons, and write/ed/tr8. Obviously there is overlap in those categories.

Determine where your particular service should best be advertised, because you'll often find that products are offered as often as services. The **beauty services** page is a prime example. You're as likely to find a listing for nutritional products from the Amazon as you are an ad for a local beauty salon. Under **computer services** you'll find listings from all over the country (or world) for things like web design; it's not just computer repair and the like. Creative, event, financial, and legal tend to only be local service providers, but if you offer a service that is applicable all over the country such as tutoring, you might place a variation of your ad on many craigslist sites and build up your business.

Craigslist often links helpful sites in connection with its categories. At the Los Angeles site, when you click on **labor/move** and reach the **labor/moving** page, you'll find a **before hiring a mover** link that opens on a page of advice from the California Public Utilities Commission. So if you're providing a service that should be licensed, or where trust is a major factor, you'd better have your legalities in order because craigslist is watching you! That would definitely include the **therapeutic** category; just look over some of the listings and you'll see why.

The most likely areas for offering services and making money outside your own geographic area are **sm biz ads** and **write/ed/tr8.** The "writing/editing/translation" category is discussed in Chapter 14, which is all about the benefits of craigslist for people involved in the literary arts. Under "small biz ads" people will find you to get involved with your small business. At the same time, if you need someone with a particular talent like a private detective, you'll likely find his or her ad here. It's a bit of a catchall category, so it's best to use the search box to see what's there before posting.

Jobs, Gigs, and Resumes

The last three categories of the middle columns on the craigslist page are such heavy-use areas, they have their own chapters in Part 3 of this book. The basic thing to know is that the jobs listings are meant more for people who are looking for a steady occupation, with benefits like health care, pension plans, and the like. The word "gig" comes from the world of musicians and performers and by the nature of those occupations refers to something more temporary. The "resumes/job wanted" category is even more wide open. Rather than posted resumes grouped by category, you'll find listings from people wanting jobs to people looking for investors. (Hint: pay attention to your title line when posting in resumes, because people wanting to hire will often search on the page with the "only search titles" box checked.)

Good luck!

The Least You Need to Know

♦ The more you learn about the **community** area of craigslist, the more likely you are to reap its benefits, because craigslist is very community orientated.

♦ Under **housing,** you are most likely to make bigger profits via craigslist from the **office/commercial** or **real estate for sale** categories.

♦ In the **cars+trucks** and **furniture** categories under the **for sale** banner, you have mere owners competing with dealers.

♦ The key to competing with dealers in selling things like a car is in knowing how to construct your ad, particularly the title line.

♦ While most of the categories under **services** are meant for people living locally, the greatest chances for profits outside your geographic area are **sm biz ads** and **write/ed/tr8.**

Chapter 4

Effectively Placing and Responding to Ads

In This Chapter

- ◆ First you'll need an account
- ◆ Writing a great ad
- ◆ Saving a thousand words
- ◆ Knowing the can and can't do's in listings
- ◆ Maintaining your listing

Since craigslist is all about listings, which are also referred to often in this book as ads, and sometimes as posts, this chapter should help anyone who plans to do more than make occasional use of the site. And since we doubt you'd read this book unless you wanted to find ways to make money using craigslist, we hope you'll let us know if you find there's something left out, because we're always eager to improve.

You'll Need an Account

We say "need" because things are simply easier for you when you have one. You can create, edit, and repost ads much more easily with an account.

List Notes

At www.craigslist.org/about/help/user_accounts, you can get all your questions about setting up an account answered. Get there by clicking on **help** and at the resultant page click on **craigslist user accounts** or click on **my account** on the top left of the main page, then **Click here for additional information** at the bottom of the next page.

When you set one up, consider the email address you use. You won't suffer from spam as a result of posting on craigslist because unless you place your email address within the body of an ad, when you're posting you're given the choice of having an anonymous address for responses, one that craigslist creates specifically for that post. Response emails are routed to you at the address you provided to craigslist when posting your ad, or to the one you used when you set up your account.

It's probably a good idea to create a special email address of your own specifically for use with craigslist business. That way, if anything happens to your regular address, your business on craigslist won't be affected. For example, **bobslist@gmail.com** or **sallyslist@yahoo.com** would let you set up a separate folder in your email program and direct all your craigslist traffic to that single address.

Casual users of craigslist simply choose **post to classifieds,** then follow the prompts, picking the type of posting (like "for sale"), then a category (like "boats"), then an area (if multiple areas exist from your home page), and finally you're able to post, only needing to enter your email address twice, with the choice of "hide" or "anonymize (will show as: **sale-xxxxxxxx@craigslist.org**)" with a small question mark after the parenthesis. Clicking on the **?** takes you to **www.craigslist.org/about/ anonymize,** which explains why you should choose to anonymize your address in a listing.

You're probably aware how email addresses with active links (you click on them to send an email) are "harvested" by software robots. That's reason enough to use an anonymized email address; it stops you from being victimized by those spammers. Also, it's no longer active after your posting expires or is deleted from craigslist.

One catch to this: if someone wants to respond to your listings and sends an attachment such as a picture or resume, if it's of a size the craigslist servers consider too large (over 150 kilobytes), it will bounce back to the sender. It might not if you use a regular email address in your listing. On the other hand, once someone responds you'll have his or her email address and can respond from yours. So if you have to choose, we suggest the anonymized choice at first.

Go ahead, set up your account. Click on **my account** at the top left of the home page and follow the prompts. Maybe they should have a "set up an account" link but they don't, so pretend you have one. You'll go to the **Account Log In** page at **https://accounts.craigslist. org.** (Note the *https;* the "s" means the page is "secure".) Click on the next to last line: "Don't have an account? Click here to sign up." You'll go to **https://accounts. craigslist.org/login/signup** and all you have to do is type in the email address you're going to use and the verification word (a.k.a. "captcha").

Skip's Tips

Craigslist wants money for abuse. The Terms of Use (TOU) states: "If you post Content in violation of the TOU, other than as described earlier, you agree to pay craigslist one hundred dollars ($100) for each Item of Content posted. In its sole discretion, craigslist may elect to issue a warning before assessing damages."

You'll then be sent an email containing a link to verify your account. When you click on it, you'll get a web page where you'll be prompted to choose a password when you log in. And you'll have a craigslist account. You know the drill; write down the password, but craigslist will take care of you if you lose it. (It's easy to change.).

When you choose your password and enter it, you'll be taken to the **Terms of Use** page. Don't forget to read it. If you do you'll save yourself a lot of "I didn't know that" time later on. When you accept them, you'll get a page that you probably want to bookmark because it will say:

home of bobslist@gmail.com (the email address you provided)

From that page you'll be able to search through your past posts, up to 180 days. From the menu bar on the right, you can change the city where you want to post a new ad. (That comes in handy when you're reaching out across the world.)

By clicking on **[settings]** at the top of the page, you'll be able to reset your default home page, change your password, and set the amount of time you'll be logged in (up to one week). You can also change your email address there.

Wasn't that easy? Try it. You can do the whole thing more quickly than you read these instructions.

Welcome to your craigslist account!

How to Write a Great Ad

For someone who is simply trying to sell a used couch, or bicycle, or appliance, it might not make a lot of sense to study listings of similar items. If you're actively trying to make regular money via craigslist, though, you'll put a little more thought into it. But before we get into that, let's do a little test. Which of the following posting titles would more likely prompt a click response from you?

Like new Apple computer - $1000

2 Ghz PowerMac G5 with 20" Apple Cinema Display - $1000

It's fairly obvious which one is best. People don't just browse through listings; they use the search box. Quite often, they know exactly what they're seeking, like a PowerMac Apple with Intel inside (meaning it can also run Windows programs) as opposed to a PowerPC (meaning it can run both OS9 and OSX but not Windows without a software emulation program). Obviously from the two previously mentioned title lines, there's at least one extra step needed to know about the computer for sale. Unless someone used the word "Apple" in a search, the first computer wouldn't turn up in a search for "G5" (the latest model Apple), even though it might be one.

So the first step in an effective listing is the title line. Maximize the keywords here. Keep in mind that people will not only search on craigslist locally, they might use a search engine. Let's say someone is looking for a turquoise-colored car. While that might sound odd, they're popular in the southwest United States. With none available locally, if they search with the words "craigslist turquoise car" (the phrase in quotes just like that), they might turn up one in another part of the country. With **collectibles,** this type of searching is even more used. After all, the search engines look first at the title line of craigslist listing pages, just like people. Which would you be more likely to look at:

> Silver coins for sale

or

> American 2009 Silver Eagles - $39

Time is money for just about everyone, so try to save people time, and you'll make more money.

Specificity is the key to a good title. It might take some practice getting it right, but the more you think through what it takes to make someone click, the better you'll do.

Online Heat
Newer posts appear at the top on craigslist pages. If you're running a business that delivers meals to businesses, try posting about 10:00 in the morning, after people have gotten their work going and start thinking about lunch. Whatever you're selling, think about when people might be looking for it online.

If you set up an account with craigslist, by clicking **posting to classifieds** you'll automatically be directed to the Account Log In page. You don't have to log in, however. You're offered the option of going to the posting process without logging in, the one occasional users choose. On that page you're offered the following options:

What type of posting is this:

- ◆ job offered
- ◆ resume / job wanted
- ◆ housing offered
- ◆ housing wanted

- for sale (please review this partial list of prohibited items)

- item wanted

- gig offered (I'm hiring for a for a short-term, small, or odd job)

- service offered

- personal / romance

- community

- event

If you're offering an item for sale, it really is smart to review the partial list of prohibited items. If you want to sell your son's old BB gun, you can't; it's a prohibited item. Let's say you want to promote your business. That means you are required by craigslist to post in the **services** area. Click on **sm biz ads** and you'll see the kind of ads in your area. Search for your occupation and see if any competition comes up. Let's say you're a caterer. It shouldn't take long to review the competition's ads.

So now we're back to your ad. After choosing **services** as a category, you'll click on **small biz ads** on the next page. And then, guess what? You'll need an account.

Assuming you took our advice, you have an account, so you log in. If it's your first time, ads in certain categories like this one may require phone verification of your account. You'll be taken to a page to enter your phone number and once you've given the information, you'll get an automated phone call with a code. Enter that, your account is verified, and you can continue with your post.

Brevity Is the Soul of Success

The default email address for an ad is the anonymized one provided by craigslist. If you want to hide your email or show it, you can click that choice instead. After that's taken care of, you simply need to enter your Posting Title and the Specific Location in the box to the right. If you're selling an item, or if you want people to come to you to buy a product, list your neighborhood or town. If you don't, people might be reluctant to pick your ad over one more specific. "Let's see, I only have to drive 5 miles for this computer. With the other one, hmmm ..."

Now you're onto the Posting Description box and that's the heart of the matter. How much verbiage do you need? Look at the *size of the frame of the box.* It's about one third the size of a 15" computer screen. If you can't describe your item or service within that space, something's wrong.

If you find you're just not very good at writing or designing ads, you can opt for a professional service like www.craigslistaddesign.com, but it doesn't have to be complicated. If you're selling a service, it helps to link to your own website after briefly describing it. If you're selling a product, it's best to have a picture (more on that later). Mostly, you simply need to give the potential buyer the information they need to prompt them to contact you.

In the newspaper business, journalists are taught to write articles containing "the five Ws"—who, what, where, when, why, along with the how of the matter in question. (See http://en.wikipedia.org/wiki/5_Ws.) That works well in a craigslist ad, with a different sequence as follows:

> **List Notes**
>
> If you've wondered how people get colors and other things in their ads, it's through the use of HTML. If you don't know HTML basics, you can learn them quickly courtesy of craigslist at www.craigslist.org/about/help/html_in_craigslist_postings.

What—Whether you're selling a product or service, people want to know what it is in the title line.

Where—Your location is on the title line and next in importance. The email you use, a website, and a phone number are also "where" and you can place the location at the bottom of your listing when placing the ad.

When—People's schedules determine their availability in connecting with you, so mention when they can reach you.

Who—You can simply give people a number to call, but it makes an ad more personal and inviting if you give a name.

Why—If you're selling something that should still logically have a lot of use left, people will inevitably want to know your reason for letting it go, so be upfront.

How—Although craigslist advises against any payment but cash, that's not practical if your transaction is not local (for example, you might create websites). If appropriate, mention in your ad something about payment options.

Here's a sample ad using the aforementioned criteria:

Apple MacBook Pro 15" 2.4ghz w/Applecare - $1500 (Burbank)

Mint condition 15" MacBook Pro 2.4GHZ Intel Core 2 Duo, Penryn processor, with aluminum body, glossy LED screen and multi-touch trackpad, with Applecare warranty and tech support covered until June 2011. 256MB of video memory, 2GB RAM, 320GB/7200 RPM drive, 8X dual layer Superdrive (burns DVD's & CD's), built-in iSight camera, Airport Extreme WiFi card built-in, Firewire 800 & 400 ports, USB 2.0 ports. Includes all equipment that came in the original box including software and system disks.

Have upgraded for newer model. Selling for $1500 cash, firm. Contact Ron at (818)555-1212 after 4:00 p.m.

* Location: Burbank

* it's NOT ok to contact this poster with services or other commercial interests

PostingID: (this is provided by craigslist)

You may also wish to use capital letters to emphasize certain words in the title, so that the listing catches the browser's eye. But sometimes too many capital letters come across as "yelling."

Including a picture will help, or in the case of this ad, a link to a dealer website where that computer is being sold (for more money than you're charging). As you can see, our ad gives the important specifics and all the Five Ws and How. You wouldn't have to scroll to read it all on a screen. If you can make your ads that succinct, you'll have a much better chance of success.

Things craigslist Won't Allow

If you're at all unclear about what craigslist doesn't allow you to post, read through #7 of the Terms of Use, which covers "Conduct." Things unlawful and abusive are out as is anything discriminatory. If you're looking for workers and employ four or more employees, the antidiscrimination provision of the Immigration and Nationality Act comes into play. You may not misrepresent craigslist and/or its employees, and you cannot include "personal or identifying information about another person without that person's explicit consent." So if you had a celebrity's address book, you couldn't sell it on craigslist. You can't infringe "any patent, trademark, trade secret, copyright or other proprietary right" so forget pirated CDs or DVDs. No "affiliate marketing" means multilevels like Amway. Commercial advertisements (like print ads) are a no-go, and links to commercial services or websites are only allowed under **services.** And if you try web tricks like spamming ads to addresses in ads, you'll end with a banned computer. See http://craigslist.org/about/prohibited.items.html if you have any questions. Of course, people violate the rules all the time, but they're policed, both by the employees of craigslist and the community-minded users of the site.

Saving a Thousand Words

As stated at the bottom of the **craigslist factsheet,** "eBay acquired 25% of the equity in craigslist from a former shareholder in august of 2004." Anyone who's used eBay much knows that one of the keys to its sales are pictures. That also helps greatly on craigslist and the site makes it easy to upload photos, but there are a few tricks worthy of considering, to make your listings more attractive.

Skip's Tips

Want to browse craigslist via pictures? Check out Ryan Sit's site, which lets you take a visual tour through craigslist listings. It's set up like craigslist but not affiliated. Read about it at www.listpic.com/about.html and have fun using it.

Picking the Right Picture

The instructions for uploading pictures on craigslist couldn't be any clearer. You'll find the info at www.craigslist.org/about/help/pic. As you'll see, you can upload up to four pictures with any ad. You'll see numerous types of pictures used including gif, jpg, png, and tiff but the standard you should try to use is jpg because of file size. As you'll see when you try to upload a picture, anything larger than 150 kilobytes is taboo. The site will display the message:

Images taking too long to upload? Try reducing their size with image editing software.

You'll also find that if you're responding to an ad and trying to send someone a picture through the craigslist address, it also has to be 150kb or less.

You can find ample advice on the web about how to fix up your pictures. Here's a good article specific to craigslist: http://www. howtodothings.com/computers-internet/how-to-enhance-and-resize-photos-for-craigslist.

The main thing about any picture used in an ad is that it should be clearly visible, with good lighting, with the object of the picture positioned against a simple background. If a cell phone camera is all you have at hand, fine, just don't photograph your item (or yourself) in poor lighting. If there's a dent on something and you're disclosing that in the ad, take a close-up picture of the dent and include it.

Other Types of Images

Those pictures you've seen in emails that are made up of keyboard characters are called ASCII images. You can make up fancy images with text in different fonts by using this site: www.network-science.de/ ascii. If you find an online image that you want to convert to ASCII art for something a little different, check outwww.degraeve.com/img2txt. php. You'll need an online image to start from with the latter, like something you can find via Google images. There are also software programs that will generate ASCII images. We can't promise that any of these will help your ad stand out or get you more business, but some people like them.

Can and Can't Do's in Listings

Other than things that craigslist won't allow as discussed earlier, the main thing to remember is that the site is all about *community* and craigslist wants to protect the community, wherever it may be located. That's a lot of communities, with over 500 craigslist sites. Again, you'll fully understand if you read #7 through #9 of the Terms of Use. Generally, don't contact anyone who doesn't want to be, don't use automated computer programs to download data from the site or post to it, don't post the same item in more than one category or more than one site, don't "flag" the posts of your competitors, and unless you get permission from craigslist, don't let others post on your behalf. And if you start spamming craigslist addresses, craigslist might take it seriously because they consider you in violation of "the Computer Fraud and Abuse Act (18 U.S.C. § 1030 et seq.), Section 502 of the California Penal Code and Section 17538.45 of the California Business and Professions Code." (The quote is from #9 of the craigslist Terms of Use.)

Maintaining Your Listing

If you don't have an account and simply use the **post to classifieds** option to place an ad, you'll be sent an email from which you can manage your ad. As you will be told in the email craigslist sends you, *do not delete the email.* If you have your email program set to automatically delete certain emails when closing the program, save a copy of the email somewhere until you're done with the ad. You don't want continuing phone calls after you've already sold your boat. You can get the email back, though, by clicking on http://sfbay. craigslist.org/cgi-bin/resend and entering the email address you used to place the ad. If you no longer have access to that email, you'll just have to wait until the ad expires. You'll find that link at **resend publish/edit/**

List Notes
There is no method for removing an ad via the account page. It clearly states: *we are not able to offer a removal option at this time.* If you know that you're only going to want an ad up for a few days, *do not* log in to your account but use the **post to classifieds** option.

delete email under **classified postings** on the **help** page, www.craigslist.org/about/help.

If you have established an account, your options for managing your listings are much broader. The default in the search boxes you see when you log in to your account is the last 30 days, but you'll have the option of searching as far back as 180 days; six months can be a long time in the business world. This is good, though, because what if you have a dispute over a sale and your buyer claims something was in your ad that was not? With an account, you'll have the listing kept in place by craigslist.

The categories of maintenance on your account page are:

active   pending   removed by me   expired   flagged/deleted

Obviously, if you're actively using the site and placing numerous ads, it would be foolish to do so without an account. If you're selling imported items like pashmina scarves (a big fashion item some years back) and you want to reuse an ad from a few months back, and you can't find the file on your computer, if it was posted in the last six months via your account, you can find it under one of the latter three categories mentioned previously.

If someone flagged your ad and you need to reword it, you'll find it under **flagged/deleted.** Speaking of which, don't get terribly upset if you find your posts getting flagged by other users. Most likely, you've violated some rule in the flagging categories, explained as:

◆ *miscategorized—wrong category/site, discusses another ad, otherwise misplaced*

◆ *prohibited—violates craigslist Terms of Use or other posted guidelines*

◆ *spam/overpost—posted too frequently, in multiple cities/categories, or is too commercial*

Keep in mind that the flagging pane includes the admonition "please flag with care." If your competitor or some spiteful or misinformed person continually flags your posts wrongly, it's highly likely they'll be discovered and their computer blocked from accessing the craigslist servers. At **www.craigslist.org/about/help/flags_and_community_moderation** you'll find a full explanation of what should get flagged and what to do if you feel you've been wrongly flagged.

Who knows, your post might be nominated for **best of craigslist** if you have a "funny or memorable posting." That doesn't mean your ad will be effective (and it won't get deleted if nominated for best), but it's another 15 seconds of fame for you, and you can tell your friends, "Hey, go look at my crazy post."

The Least You Need to Know

◆ If you plan on using craigslist to do regular business, including offering your services, it pays to set up a craigslist account.

◆ The title line in your craigslist posting is very important, because it's the first thing that is searched by users, both on and off craigslist.

◆ Good craigslist ads are about the length of the size of the frame of the box on the page where you fill out your ad.

◆ The famous journalism dictum of "the five Ws"—who, what, where, when, why, along with how—works well in composing craigslist ads, with some variation.

◆ Posting pictures in your craigslist ads is a simple process that is fully explained on the site at www.craigslist.org/about/help/pic.

◆ If you study and understand the craigslist Terms of Use as well as the rules about how posts get "flagged," you shouldn't have many posting problems.

Chapter 5

Software and Other Shortcuts

In This Chapter

- ◆ software possibilities
- ◆ RSS feeds
- ◆ Using Crazedlist
- ◆ Google for craigslist Items
- ◆ You suck at craigslist (The Site)

Although craigslist has admonitions about what's allowed and not allowed, there are so many posts on the site(s) daily, if it weren't for the community-minded attitude of users, it would be impossible to police without adding vast numbers of staff and on-site advertising to support paying them. So for every rule you see posted, know that many people are violating them daily. That doesn't make your use of craigslist any more fun, but the point is, things are a bit more liberal than one might think. As such, there are all sorts of shortcuts and software available that allow you to make quicker and more efficient use of craigslist.

craigslist Software Possibilities

If you don't want to take the time to learn the minimal HTML language discussed in the craigslist help area, take a look at this site: http://craigslisteditor.com. For some reason, the instructions above the pane where you enter text is against a dark background and difficult to read. Basically, it allows you to:

- Easily insert bullets, numbering, and hyperlinks.
- Change text color, font, and size.
- Add bold, italic, or underlined text.
- Insert and resize your own hosted images.
- Adjust page alignment and more!

The problem is, I've found the site works sometimes and other times it doesn't. Maybe it's the traffic; after all, it's free. For that reason, we suggest you look into various software options that allow you to automate your interaction with craigslist. Since the makers of this software occasionally go out of business, you're best off searching for craigslist software on sites like www.download.com or www.versiontracker.com. It is often available for download on those sites even after the developers have abandoned the product. Please note: we are not responsible for any problems that may arise with your computer if you use such software and we are not endorsing it, merely alerting you to the fact that it's out there.

craigslist Software for PCs

CraigsPal at www.craigspal.com offers a free version as well as a paid Power version. It does a multisite search of craigslist across categories, with the content set by you, and you're instantly notified of new results. If will notify you by email or mobile phone. You can sort results by price as well, and there are free updates.

At www.craigslistnotifier.net you'll find Craigslist Notifier, a handy little tool that allows you to receive notifications on listings that interest you via email, text (SMS, cell phone), and onscreen. It's a Windows product that will automatically update itself.

Motion Technologies at www.motiont.com offers Craigslist Reader, a free application that gathers information off craigslist and notifies you about changes that you specify. There's also a pro version.

Craigslist Classified Ad Posting Utility is available at http://sam308.com/html/craigslist_s_classified_ad_pos.html. A Microsoft Excel-based utility, it lets you apply HTML formatting to your ads with "style, color, and character." According to the developer, you can also use the program to create ads for similar posting websites.

> ## List Notes
>
> If you ever wonder what proprietary system runs craigslist, have a look at that company here: www.f5.com/products/big-ip. The open source system originally preferred by CEO Jim Buckmaster eventually couldn't handle the flow of traffic on craigslist.

Craigslist Ad Extractor at www.craigslistextractor.com is a robust product that lets you to get data across all categories, cities, and countries on craigslist and extract all data and emails from the ads. Your results are saved in Excel format. If you have a problem, the software is backed up by 24/7 technical support.

See www.marketingpros.com/software/clg.html for Craigslist Genius, which promises to cut your ad posting time "to mere seconds!" The only thing that prevents it from being 100 percent fully automated is captcha verification image codes, says the site, "but we have even made that part super fast and easy!" (The site probably isn't crazy about this software, but people certainly use it.)

CL Desktop (Craigslist Desktop) at www.cldesktop.com lets you browse craigslist without saving the search settings. Your search results are presented in a visual way, so that you can search by images instead of only text. It's free software that requires the Adobe AIR platform available from Adobe Systems Inc. It runs on Windows XP/Vista.

craigslist Software for Macs

See www.marketplacemac.com for Marketplace, advertised as "Craigslist, without the ugly." With this software you can search any craigslist region around the world, across any category or subcategory, and "get all the results in one convenient window." Further filtering is available so that you can, according to developer Josh Abernathy, "Find the stuff you actually want."

CL Desktop (Craigslist Desktop) at www.cldesktop.com lets you browse craigslist without saving the search settings. Your search results are presented in a visual way, so that you can search by images instead of only text. It's free software that requires the Adobe AIR platform available from Adobe Systems Inc. It runs on MacOS X 10.4/10.5.

RSS Feeds and craigslist

Many websites these days offer RSS (Rich Site Summary) feeds to your browser. See www.whatisrss.com for a full explanation of Reader or News Aggregator software that grabs RSS feeds from sites like craigslist and sends them to you. If you want a craigslist RSS feed, see www.craigslist.org/about/rss for its rules. They've even started a blog to keep up with all the changes and options available with RSS. See http://rssblog.whatisrss.com for more details. Since RSS accommodates so many platforms and devices, expect it to gain even more steam in the future. For example, the RSS blog mentions the following outlets:

◆ Windows RSS Readers

◆ OS X RSS Readers

◆ Linux RSS Readers

◆ Web-based RSS Readers

◆ Mobile RSS Readers

◆ RSS-to-email tools

◆ RSS-related Firefox plugins

◆ RSS plugins for Wordpress

Mobile (see earlier list) would of course refer to cell phones. Wordpress refers to the free blog website at http://wordpress.com which seems to have become the site of choice for those who create high-traffic blogs.

Skip's Tips

If you have an iPhone, check out the apps CraigsMobileList ($2.99), Craigster (99¢), CraigSearch (free), or craigsphone from Next Mobile Labs (free). If they're not the iPhone App Store, do a web search. More are being developed all the time (and we can't guarantee their price). Some of these apps also work with the Blackberry and other devices.

As should be obvious, craigslist encourages the use of RSS:

> "We offer RSS feeds so that our users can embed a little piece of craigslist into their personal blog or home page, or watch the best-of postings come rolling into their desktop news aggregator. Look for this symbol at the bottom of each of our listings pages: RSS."

They also caution, in their normal antipredatory fashion: "craigslist RSS feeds are for your personal use only, and are not available for commercial use without first obtaining a license from craigslist."

How do you get a license? Send them a note via: http://sfbay.craigslist. org/cgi-bin/emailForm.cgi.

Using Crazedlist to Save Hours

This site at www.crazedlist.org, created by Andrew Payne in 2005, is a real boon to users of craigslist, and he goes to great pains on the site to ask people to not abuse the added capabilities they'll have when using crazedlist. (Note: some users have reported trouble with this site in Explorer but it worked fine for the author at press time.) At the time of this writing, Alexa.com reported that the site's traffic, based on a combined measure of page views and users, averaged about 63,571 per week, and reported that it was fast, saying "66% of sites are slower" and that it only took 1.5 seconds to load.

And speaking of fast, that's what it does for you as a craigslist user: makes the whole thing faster. As the title bar says, you can "search craigslist like a madman." Two tabs on the upper left offer the possibility of searching in the United States, or worldwide. On the right, you can get an RSS feed, once you've set up what you're searching for in a category. (You'll need an RSS reader for that, as mentioned earlier. Do a web search to find the right one for your computer, or check the previously mentioned www.download.com or www.versiontracker.com.)

Using an RSS reader helps reduce hits to craigslist. If you're new to RSS feed readers, you might have found them a bit complicated to set up, but entering your search at crazedlist and then using **Get RSS Feeds** will let you save an OPML file that your RSS reader will open. If all this sounds confusing, it's not. Click on the **[?]** next to **Get RSS Feeds** and you'll get a page explaining it all.

This site was actually made in the spirit of craigslist, and only intended to speed up searches. As Andrew Payne explains to craigslist at the link **dear craigslist, i love you, please don't hit me!** at the bottom of the page:

> "i know your mission is to create communities, and i totally love and respect that. the problem is, if i'm looking for a yamaha wr250 with a CA plate i'm willing to drive anywhere in CA to get it, or even OR or AZ. searching on 10 or more sites just gets tiring. you made craigslist because newspaper classifieds are limited, i made this search because i thought going to 10 different sites and re-entering the same search is what computers are made for."

If you have any doubts about Payne not being just some kind of hacker, read **what kind of loser builds this?** at the bottom of the page. It's pretty funny. Note: as of this writing, the site does not work with Explorer (PCs) or Safari (Mac). It works very well with Firefox and other browsers. This and other explanations for user questions can be found by clicking on **like it, hate it, want more?** at the bottom of the page.

So here's how it works. At the top left, the search bar has a button offering you the following choices:

all
west coast
northwest
mountain central

midwest
great lakes
midatlantic
south
southwest
north east
new england
none

Online Heat

Crazedlist comes in very handy in some searches because of its layout. Let's say you had just read the Forbes.com list of best cities for jobs in 2008. The top five were Salt Lake City, Wichita, Austin, Atlanta, and Fort Worth. Check those cities, type in a keyword, choose your job category, and go. You're more likely to find a job available in a great market.

As you'll quickly discover, choosing one of the categories will automatically select (with a check in the boxes) all the cities within a certain region, while choosing all includes all cities onscreen in the coming search. As of this writing, 332 cities were shown on the screen, so that covers a *lot* of territory. If you search worldwide, you'll get 159 cities and countries in which to search.

You may find that the first time you log on to the site, you'll get a popup screen that warns you not to try to search all of the United States or all of worldwide at once because doing so could get your computer flagged and banned by the main craigslist servers. Without getting technical as to why, it's good advice. You'll have to wait for the search results to come to you, anyway, so give yourself and your computer a break and search a region at a time.

In case you're wondering what the **none** selection is about, it clears all the locations that were checked automatically when you've selected a region.

So let's say you want to search in cities where horses are a business, like Dallas/Ft. Worth, Louisville, Phoenix, and Sarasota. You simply check those cities, enter something like "thoroughbred" in the search box, choose **sale/wanted** as a category, with **farm+garden** as a subcategory, check on the **pics** box and also on the **titles** box if you wish. (Try it, you'll get a lot of ads.) If you're in the horse business and want to make searches like that on a regular basis, you'll also want to click the **save search settings** link on the top right. Doing so makes the category and cities that you currently have selected a default setting. The next time you come back to crazedlist you'll find these items will be pre-selected, so if you want to search for different things at different times, don't click on **save search settings.**

If you have a small business and want to see what competitors around the country or world are offering or charging, you'd do that by choosing the **services** button, which will make a subcategories button pop up. One selection is **sm biz ads,** which is the one you'd want. Again, you can choose to save search settings.

If you're looking for a job, selecting the **jobs** category gives you a sub-categories button to the right, as well as the choices you get on craigslist:

telecommute   contract   intern   part-time   non-profit

Each of those has a checkable box, so if for example you're only looking for jobs where you can telecommute, this makes your search very nice.

When your search results are found, you will see a new page that shows frames within frames. The scroll bar on the far right of your browser will allow you to look through all your choices, while the inner scroll bars will allow you to examine listings from each area. You might find that when you click on an ad to open it and then try to click back to the page of search results, the page hangs up. If so, it's not much trouble to simply do the search again, compared to what it would be on the normal craigslist site. Of course, you can always use the **save search settings** option each time to circumvent any problems.

Hopefully, you'll use crazedlist judiciously and not get in such a hurry that you search with too many areas checked at once and end up getting noticed by the craigslist servers in a bad way.

List Losers

If you used craigslist, you've given them the right to block you, per #13 of the Terms of Use (TOU). Have a look at TERMINATION OF SERVICE at www.craigslist.org/about/terms.of.use#copyright and you'll see that the site, "in its sole discretion, has the right (but not the obligation) to delete or deactivate your account, block your email or IP address, or otherwise terminate your access ..." etc.

How Jobsites Use craigslist

Big jobsites like Monster, Careerbuilder, and Hotjobs don't comb through craigslist job listings and make links to their own sites, but a great many other job sites on the web do that. Prior to reading this chapter, you might have wondered, had you seen any of the craigslist ads linked from a jobsite, how people had the time to search through ads all over the United States or world and link them up.

Now that you know about all the software and other ways to "harvest" ads from the craigslist sites, it's obvious how they do it. In most cases, they just set it up on the computer, let it run, and then "massage" the results.

This kind of thing has been going on a long time. The big sites harvest jobs, too, but from newspapers and other sources. And when you're well enough known, people come to you with information. For example, who doesn't know about Monster.com? Still, that doesn't mean they're always the best. When the website consumersearch rated job websites, craigslist came out #1 in best online classifieds. See www.consumersearch.com/job-sites. It also said that craigslist's ads had a "large variety of freelance and part-time opportunities" with "little to no duplication on other job sites," but freelancers know better because they often find sites with opportunities linking to craigslist. The consumersearch site also stated that craigslist had "many unreliable or dubious job posts" but a quick search will reveal otherwise and you'll find that major companies now regularly post on craigslist for personnel.

And why wouldn't they? In times of economic struggles, job postings on craigslist cost a lot less than other sites, or newspaper ads.

A Google search during the writing of this book turned up about *3,110,000* hits when searching with the phrase "job sites using craigslist."

You'll find that "work from home" job sites and those that concentrate on telecommuting possibilities dwell a lot on craigslist. Also, short-term and part-time opportunities are often not that easily found using big jobsites, so an "aggregator" site might look to craigslist first to find those opportunities. You can post your resume on craigslist just like you can on Monster.com, and craigslist is much simpler to use with far fewer graphics. That might be another reason other jobsites link to its jobs.

In any event, now that you know how all those craigslist job links are gathered quickly by the small job sites, you might want to quit searching for those sites, and just use some of the craigslist tools shared with you already in this chapter.

Google and Other craigslist Searches

Whatever you happen to be looking for, the 800-pound gorilla known as Google can help. Of course, so can any search engine like Yahoo!, but before you start searching learn some search tricks, like Boolean searches and other subjects like those covered by craigslist at www.craigslist.org/about/help/search. As explained at www.internettutorials.net/boolean.asp a Boolean search consists of three logical operators:

OR

AND

NOT

And to limit searches to a specific site, say craigslist, just add site:craigslist.org to the search.

The search help page on craigslist tells you "Common words like "the" or "and" are removed from searches because they occur very frequently. If this happens, you will see a message at the top of the results telling you which words were ignored." This is not true, however, when you use a search engine in your web browser.

Let's say you're a freelance writer and editor. Sometimes you're hired as a writer, sometimes as an editor, sometimes both. If you Google search with this phrase …

>   writer AND editor craigslist

… you will get listing results that are on craigslist and listed as <u>writer and editor</u> as well as others listed at <u>writer/editor</u> and <u>writer & editor</u>.

If you substitute *or* in the previous phrase you'll get quite a different result, as you will with the word NOT.

If you substitute a minus sign for the word NOT, though, you'll get writer listings and not editor listings …

>   writer—editor craigslist

The latter search also works on the craigslist site. Under **jobs** there is a **writing/editing** category. If you open up the category you'll see all sorts of jobs: writing, editing, transcription, translation. If you narrow the search with the word "writing" it will still give you writer/editor jobs and other things. If you search within the category for "writing–editing" the editing jobs will not be returned in the search. Similarly, a plus sign in your search will change the results. Using "writer+editor" will give you only writing and editing combined.

You can use the plus and minus sign search both on craigslist and crazedlist and in Google and other search engine searches and get improved results, no matter what it is that you're seeking. Let's say you're speculating in real estate and you want to find properties for sale by owner. Use the phrase "house+for sale by owner craigslist" and you'll get very specific listings returned to you.

Note that putting a phrase in parentheses makes a search engine looking for that *specific* phrase, such as "for sale by owner", but in the search just mentioned it looked like …

>   house+for sale by owner craigslist

… in the search window. Also note that in such a search the plus or minus sign *does not* have a space between it and the word that follows. The operative item searched for was "house" and the words that followed; because of the +, all additional words were meant to be included within the text of the ad. Obviously, "craigslist" might not be within the text of the ad, but it was in the URL of the listing page.

Skip's Tips

In its continuing attempt to find and explain every single thing on the planet, Google has some very helpful web pages, including a thorough primer on effective searching. See www.google.com/support/websearch/?ctx=web. There's even a troubleshooting guide.

Narrowing a search further, let's say you wanted a house for sale by owner in a specific location, like east Texas. You could find the appropriate craigslist search page, or you could use crazedlist, but in the latter case you might find that the "buttons" available to narrow your search aren't always up-to-date with the latest on craigslist. So try Google with this phrase ...

house+east texas for sale by owner craigslist

... and you'll find that you'll get appropriate listings from craigslist at the top. You'll also find listings from real estate sites like www.forsalebyownercenter.com and http://homesineasttexas.com, but you'll still narrow down what you want to find.

Another thing you might try as you attempt to locate listings on craigslist is a metasearch, which can be accomplished on sites like www.dogpile.com. Dogpile combines four search engines—Google, Yahoo!, Bing, and Ask—in one search box and can be added to your browser's search bar with a simple click. The site claims: "The process is more efficient and yields more relevant results." You'll likely find this to be true. A search with the east Texas real estate listings on craigslist search referenced earlier produced much better results than simply using Google. Also, when you use Dogpile they donate a portion of the revenue generated to The American Society for the Prevention of Cruelty to Animals (ASPCA). Why not use a better search site and help the animals, too?

You Suck at craigslist

When you're in business for yourself, or trying to run or launch a side business while maintaining a full-time job, a little bit of humor helps. If the "best of craigslist" pages aren't enough, you should have a good look at www.yousuckatcraigslist.com. Its subtitle is "Exactly what it says on the tin." While that phrase might make you inclined to think the site was made up by someone in England (they use "tin" a lot there), it's all–American just like craigslist. It has a Twitter feed, a Facebook page, and a Livejournal feed as well. The statement about the site:

> "This started when I was trolling our local craigslist in my continuing attempts to find interesting additions to our furnishings. I've decided that people suck at craigslist, and I decided to provide illustrations to demonstrate this fact."

In short, they've done the browsing for you, with perhaps a little more humor than the **best of craigslist** pages flagged by craigslist users. For example:

Free couch Cream

Must pick up TODAY.

We have no idea what couch cream is, we just report the facts. You can laugh at the Recent Posts, or look through the categories and take your pick. Warning, some of the Personals listings are worthy of mention at a comedy club, but you'll have to find out for yourself. As you know, this book has nothing to do with craigslist personals.

If you ever wonder how well you're doing at writing your craigslist listings, just take a few minutes and look at the ones aggregated on this site. You'll discover that in comparison you're doing very well indeed. Also, the reposted listings have chat capabilities attached, so you can amuse yourself commenting on them with other users.

It's a whole different craigslist community!

The Least You Need to Know

- There are numerous simple software programs available, from free to reasonably priced, that will simplify your use of the craigslist site.

- You can automate receiving notifications of the types of listings you want to know about by having the site send RSS (Rich Site Summary) feeds directly to your browser or an RSS Reader program.

♦ Crazedlist.org is a free site that enables you to do craigslist searches in all the categories by a whole region at a time, or several locations at once.

♦ Increasingly, jobsites are aggregators of craigslist job listings, so it pays to know how they do it so you can use their methods for yourself.

♦ There are keys to searching craigslist worldwide that, if you understand them, enable you to find what you need in craigslist ads without initially going to your normal craigslist site.

Part 2

Getting Down to Business

Keeping your craigslist account in good standing, placing ads that work, and not being fooled by scams are things craigslist users battle with, worldwide. Learn some simple tips and learn how to keep yourself financially happy on the site. In addition, find out about the many other sites similar to craigslist and how you can use them in conjunction to give yourself an even more profitable online life.

Chapter 6

Keeping Your Account in Good Standing

In This Chapter

◆ How long your ad lasts

◆ Agreeing to the Terms of Service

◆ Getting the help you need

◆ Giving feedback back

◆ Whether to include your email address

Try to keep the community-oriented philosophy of craigslist in mind. Be respectful and conscientious, and should others not return the cordiality, know that the community will often take care of it. If not, the site administrators will.

When you're in business for yourself, the world is a lot different place than it is when you're working for someone else. You learn that you have to pay more attention to the community and its needs. When you do, and you deliver a good product and/or service, word of mouth brings you sustained business, while at the same time you learn what works in advertising and what does not. As your success escalates, you begin to see the potential in expanding your horizons, finding new outlets, perhaps even franchising your business. You may even be moved to give back to the community with charitable gifts and activities. And let's not forget a big one: you must learn about legalities and taxes and other formalities that never darken your door as a simple working person. Oddly enough, craigslist can help you with all these things.

Timing of Posts

Most craigslist users don't pay much attention to the life span of their posts, which are explained simply here: www.craigslist.org/about/help/posting_lifespans.

If you live in the big-city areas of Atlanta, Austin, Boston, Chicago, Dallas, Denver, Houston, Los Angeles, New York, Orange County, Philadelphia, Phoenix, Portland, Sacramento, San Diego, SF Bay Area, Seattle, South Florida, or Washington, D.C., it's simple: your classified ad is good for a week and resumes, jobs, and gigs ads are good for a month. Outside those areas all ads are good for 45 days, which is roughly six weeks.

Whatever site you're on as your craigslist home site, when you post to classifieds you'll see a line at the top of the page that will tell you how long your post will last, like this one from the Los Angeles site:

Your posting will expire from the site in 30 days.

Brokered housing posts in New York City expire on a monthly basis (30 days) but relatively few people post those compared to the broad craigslist community. If you wonder why there's a separate category for those ads, it has to do with sheer volume. You'll find that a great many housing ads, particularly real estate for sale in large population areas, are posted by brokers on craigslist, despite the site's focus on the individual. It's just a reality. With the site getting more than 12 billion page views per month of the more than 30 million new classified ads posted by users each month, it's hard to keep up with it all.

It's easy to keep a calendar, either in print or with a computer program or cell phone setting, to remind you when to place a new ad for your product. When you have an account, as previously mentioned you can simply borrow from your expired ad on the site and repost it.

By craigslist rules, you're allowed to post once every 48 hours. You're also not supposed to post in different communities, such as in Los Angeles and New York, but you'll find as you use the site in various communities that this is done all the time. While hardly anyone but craigslist.org onsite (in San Francisco) employees know exactly what things trigger their servers noticing your posts, your computer's IP address and the 48-hour rule is one of them.

> **Skip's Tips**
>
> If you're feeling frustrated about wanting to sell multiple products with multiple postings and being blocked, group them into categories and post every 48 hours. Sell all your computer items in a list in one ad, then two days later all your sporting goods in another.

In addition, regular craigslist users tend to frequent the same areas of the site and can be very diligent about flagging posts they think violate rules. So it pays to play by the rules, particularly with the 48-hour maxim. If you feel you need to change your ad because of some new policy or upgrade of a product you're selling, delete the original post before you make the new listing. That way there's no automatic block of your new ad by the craigslist server, as stated at www.craigslist.org/about/help/faq:

> *You may post to one category and in one city, no more often than about every 48 hours.*

> *If you are submitting a post that is similar to another currently active post of yours on the site, you will get a blocked message. Removing the active post will allow you to post the new ad, unless the active post is less than 48 hours old.*

Unless someone is operating under the mentality of a spammer, as in "throw a billion emails onto the Internet and see what sticks" it's easy to play by these rules.

It's Not Like They Didn't Tell You

If you get in trouble for violating the rules on craigslist, you don't have a lot of recourse because by using the site you've agreed to the Terms of Service (TOS). In #11 of the TOS, LIMITATIONS ON SERVICE, it states:

> "You agree that craigslist has no responsibility or liability for the deletion or failure to store any Content maintained or transmitted by the Service. You acknowledge that craigslist reserves the right at any time to modify or discontinue the Service (or any part thereof) with or without notice, and that craigslist shall not be liable to you or to any third party for any modification, suspension or discontinuance of the Service."

Once again, it pays to read and understand the TOS. If you've carefully constructed an ad with some of the software mentioned in this book, started an account, placed it on craigslist following the rules, and failed to back up the file on your computer because craigslist said they will, don't blame them if something goes wrong. Given the number of postings they deal with on what is mostly a free site, anyway, you're basically lucky the site is there, so try to be a good "citizen" of the community.

Who Monitors craigslist

Alf, Annette, Bill, Caleb, Eric, Jeff, Jason Leal, Jeff G, Jim Buckmaster, Joshua, Joshwitz, Josh, Leslie, Mabel, Pablo, Russell, Sean, and of course Craig Newmark and a few others keep track of all that's going on worldwide on craigslist. You can read about most of them here: www.craigslist.org/about/teambios. If you think we're kidding about how rules breakers slip through the cracks on craigslist, note that under "Mabel" we find the statement: "the CL crew can be a bit *ahem* disorganized at times." Of course, that doesn't mean you should ignore the rules thinking you won't get caught, because *other users* will probably nail you repeatedly and you'll end up banned.

You'll learn a lot about the team members if you read the bios, including the fact that Caleb is who greets the walk-ins at the front door of the Victorian house in San Francisco's Sunset District. It's no mansion.

See: http://en.wikipedia.org/wiki/
File:Craigslist01.jpg. Just don't go
jamming in there with a complaint
because joshwitz has "a black belt in
Kung-Fu (walk-ins take note)."

Craig has his own blog at www.
cnewmark.com. You're not likely to
find out anything there that will help
you make money using craigslist, but
the blog is entertaining and occasionally informative, as this note about
languages:

> **Online Heat**
>
> If you become adept enough
> at writing ads for craigslist,
> you can pick up some extra
> money doing it for others.
> Check out sites like www.
> getafreelancer.com and
> you'll see. They are usually
> listed there with titles like
> "EXPERIENCED Craigslist
> Poster wanted."

http://www.cnewmark.com/2008/03/multiple-langua.html

March 27, 2008

Multiple language support on craigslist

*We tend to do stuff without much announcement, but I figured you
might want to know that we implemented multiple language support for
craigslist in November. Just Spanish then, but last week we added more
languages. Check for yourself:*

- ◆ *http://quebec.fr.craigslist.ca*
- ◆ *http://venice.it.craigslist.it*
- ◆ *http://rio.pt.craigslist.org*
- ◆ *http://paris.fr.craigslist.org*
- ◆ *http://zurich.de.craigslist.ch*

*The programmers inform me that maybe Basque, maybe Klingon, are
next.*

Now, if you didn't read his blog on occasion, you wouldn't know about
those extra languages and the possibility of marketing in foreign languages, would you?

How to Not Get Flagged

There are many good reasons why the craigslist staff and the users of the site stay so vigilant about posting violations. You'll find some pretty wild stories on Wikipedia at http://en.wikipedia.org/wiki/Craigslist_controversies_and_illegal_activities_by_users. The site was sued in Chicago over supposedly discriminatory housing ads but the action was dismissed. Numerous suits and investigations have arisen over personals ads. Criminals have used ads to try to hire killers and to attempt to cover up burglary. And newspapers, which are in decline across the United States, have complained over loss of revenue from ads not placed in local papers due to free craigslist ads.

Keep the golden rule in mind—post as you would want others to post in the greater context of the community.

> **List Notes**
>
> On the help forums page, you have the option at the top of the right side column on the page of clicking on "subscriptions" for more help but you must be logged in to your account to use the option. Note: this is a forums handle, different than one for posting classified ads.

As situations like these arise, the site can only become more vigilant and strict, usually depending on the community of users to notify violations. Fifteen percent of the ads flagged are done so by the community. Only the staff know how many times an ad has to be flagged before it is automatically deleted, but craigslist maintains that most of the time the flagging and deleting is correct. At www.craigslist.org/about/help/flags_and_community_moderation they state:

"Millions of postings are removed through community flagging each month, and of these we consistently find that 98–99% are in violation of the craigslist terms of use or other posted guidelines.

"No moderation system is perfect, and 1–2% of ads removed through flagging are within our terms of use—but without the flagging system, craigslist would quickly become unusable."

Okay, so if 1 percent of the postings are removed each month, that's 300,000 unhappy posters (out of the over 30 million classified ads per month), but that's the cost of doing mostly free. So, if you don't want to get flagged, check and see if you can find anything that you are violating in the Terms of Use (TOU). If you think you're okay there but are still getting flagged, check the Unofficial Flag FAQ at www.eskimo. com/~newowl/Flagged_FAQ.htm (It's linked from the craigslist flag help forum.) If these things don't work, you still have some options, don't worry.

How to Deal with Being Wrongly Flagged

There are three reasons why your ad could get flagged off. They're listed in the upper right of each ad. Let's go over what they mean:

> miscategorized
>
> prohibited
>
> spam/overpost

You won't find definitions of those when you click on them at craigslist; you'll only see:

- *If you flagged by mistake—don't worry, it takes more than one flag to affect a posting.*

- *Over 15% of all craigslist postings are removed through community flagging.*

- *98–99% of postings removed are in violation of the craigslist terms of use.*

You'll find a full explanation of these at the Unofficial site: www. eskimo.com/~newowl/Flagged_FAQ.htm#000. If you've read the craigslist rules, though, it's obvious what they mean. If you carefully place your ad in the right category, you shouldn't have a problem. If you know the Terms of Use, you'll know what's prohibited, and what is considered spam. If you don't try to post the same thing before 48 hours is up, you won't have an overpost.

Seems easy enough, but people run into trouble. If the Unofficial Flagging FAQ site doesn't help, what do you do? You ask for help on the forum specifically for flags. Click www.craigslist.org/about/help/ flags_and_community_moderation and scroll down the page to the paragraph where you can click on **visit our flag help forum** and you'll go to a page staffed by volunteers *in your area*. In L.A. it would be http://losangeles.craigslist.org/forums/?forumID=3. At the top of that page you can click on **search cl—flag help** and you'll get a page with a number of clickable topics and a search box at the top to help you find solutions more quickly.

If you're still not satisfied, as long as the system status says the site is running properly, get in touch with technical support via the contact email form page at http://sfbay.craigslist.org/cgi-bin/emailForm.cgi. It might take persistence, but sooner or later you'll get an answer.

Using the Help Forum

At first the help forums might look a little daunting because there are so many "threads" started by people asking questions or making comments. Though some things are not explained up front, by using craigslist you'll find things will pop up to offer you explanations. For example, when you click on **help** under **discussion forums** you'll go to a page that offers you the option **compose new thread** at the upper left of the left side column. When you click on that, the right side column will change, with three questions at the top and a box for entering your question or comment (or "thread") and a place to register the "handle" (pseudonym) you'll use on the forums. Here are the questions underlined and the answers provided *in italics*:

Frequently Asked Questions—read these first!

Someone flagged my posting! Why?

Post the full title, body, category, and city of your ad in the Flags Help Forum

The unofficial flagging FAQ may be helpful too.

How do I post to multiple/all craigslist locations?

How do I search multiple/all craigslist areas?

You don't.

craigslist is for connecting with your local community, and most users seem to want to keep it this way.

Accordingly, craigslist is not the right vehicle to connect with folks who are not local to you.

If you want to reach a larger audience, we suggest you try another website, one that caters to more far-flung connections.

- ◆ *Be sure to read all the answers above before posting.*
- ◆ *Still have questions? search CL—help desk*
- ◆ *Search didn't help? compose a new thread*

While that's all nice in theory, as most people know people don't respect this "local community" philosophy, and craigslist isn't going to enforce it much, if they actually can, given the number of users worldwide. What it does tell you, though, is that if you're having trouble in a certain area, you'd probably be better off posing questions in *that* area. This means on the proper forum, and on the proper forum in the geographical area where you have a concern. If you're importing pashmina scarves from India, for example, get on a forum on an Indian craigslist page that's appropriate and ask "Is Raja Gupta a reliable merchant?" or whatever your question might be.

> ### List Notes
>
> You don't have to log on to the help forums to find the list of acronyms & slang used in craigslist ads. You can find them at www.craigslist.org/about/common_acronyms_and_slang. It's probably a good idea to read it before you being posting and reading.

When you click on a thread in the left column, the right column will change to reveal the text of the thread and above it you will have these choices:

reply to this post   email it   rate   flag

To use these options, you must have an account handle. A forum handle is *different* than your handle for posting, so you'll have to create one when you first attempt to post to the forums. You get there by clicking on **create a handle** top right in the help forum page. You'll see:

> *Please enter the new handle you'd like to create*
>
> *note—handle must be 18 characters or less, may contain A–Z a–z 0–9 _ and—but must start with a number or letter (you may create no more than 5 forum handles)*

It also offers other choices for using your handle when posting in the forums.

When you've created your handle, you return to the forums and can click on **subscriptions** in the top right, which gives you the following choices:

> *Subscribe to CL—help desk*
>
> *Email me:*
>
> *new postings to threads i've posted in (limited)*
>
> *all new postings to this forum (full) caution!*

Once again, it depends on what forum you're using. If you need help you can post your question, check the option to see only new postings to your thread, and you will be emailed all the answers. Pretty smooth, isn't it? Now, if you're doing business, like the sale of pashminas as mentioned previously, and you found a "scarves" forum in India, you could have all new postings about that emailed to you, but we'll get into things like that in a later chapter.

You can also click on **view all forums subscriptions** to keep track on what you've decided to follow.

You'll find that if you're not in the correct forum, you will most likely be told that by another user, and you'll get a reply that says something like:

> Wrong forum. This is help on CL problems. § < *user* >

You'll also find that if people don't respect the forums and use them in an attempt to place an ad, they'll get flagged there regularly. Here's an example. In the gift ideas forum, someone could ask a question about "Proper gift for 25th wedding anniversary?" which would be legitimate. Others might take advantage of having people on the forum who are interested in gift ideas and post an ad there like:

> save up to 40% on all your gift purchases < MyShop >

That one will likely be followed by something like:

> Spam, flagged, no ads allowed on CL! § < — >

So while you might be living in Los Angeles and reading forums in Mumbai, if you don't respect other people and why they're on those forums, you'll probably get your thread flagged and deleted.

Feedback to craigslist

At the far right on any discussion forum you will see the word **feedback.** Click on that and the right side column will change to read:

> we read all postings submitted here, but generally won't respond, especially if we've seen the suggestion many times, or just have nothing meaningful to say on the subject. please email serious abuse issues to abuse@craigslist.org rather than posting them here.

List Losers

It's a drag that there are troublesome people on craigslist and other places on the web, but once you figure out their mentality they're easier to deal with. A troll is defined at http://en.wikipedia.org/wiki/Internet_troll. That's the one craigslist uses.

Below that you can click on your choice:

> help desk flag help system status unofficial flag FAQ

And you'll also see:

> threads moved by staff ==> isle of misfit threads

please <u>flag</u> bad posts, rather than reporting them here

why did your ad get flagged? <u>flagging help</u>

feed <u>trolls</u> flags & red points, not replies

what's up with these <u>little red and green numbers</u>?

how do <u>forums subscriptions</u> work?

some <u>common acronyms & terms</u>

(Note: the things underlined are clickable links of the site.)

The "isle of misfit threads" is "Destination for threads that have been moved from their original locations by CL staff."

"Trolls" is the common term for people who are just there to cause trouble, used often in newsgroups.

The "little red and green numbers" that you'll see on the forums are explained as ratings points:

registered users can apply positive (green) and negative (red) points to posts.

rating points are a quick and easy way to respond to a post without actually replying …negative points are the preferred response to troll postings—they can help others know that someone is just making an ass of themselves, no need to bother with a reply.

positive points are a way to acknowledge an outstanding posting, w/o seeming sycophantic.

the longer you have been registered, the more daily rating points your account will receive, starting at 0 and going as high as 50, like so:

10 pts after 7 days
20 pts after 100 days
30 pts after 200 days
50 pts after 365 days

cumulative tallies of ratings received per handle are not kept at this time.

when a craigslist admin (degree sign after the name) looks at a given post, who applied what rating is visible.

admins can also look at how ratings are being used by a specific handle over time.

The Acronyms & Terms list gives you an alphabetical list of things like "ISO—In Search Of."

As you can see, although craigslist is laid out in a brilliant and easily navigable fashion, there is a bit of a learning curve necessary to master all the nooks and crannies of the site. The key is in exploring them all. You might think you're losing time in doing so, but you'll save a lot of time later on.

Give Out Your Email Address, or Not?

If you're selling an item locally, you probably won't get in trouble when someone responds to your anonymized craigslist with his or her own legitimate address. That's probably true even if they're across the country. Still, that won't stop people from wreaking havoc with your address if they're intent on using it badly. Get Safe Online, one of the protective sites recommended by craigslist, has a great discussion of this problem at: www.getsafeonline.org/nqcontent.cfm?a_id=1152. They suggest using Google, Hotmail, or Yahoo! for an address because they offer spam filtering.

They also explain how spammers acquire addresses including guessing, harvesting, online registration, supposed spam email cancellation services, and from other spammers. You'd only have to worry about the harvesting angle if your email address was listed in your craigslist ad, so why take a chance? Go with the anonymized option.

It's best that you create a specific email address for your craigslist business. If you build up a customer mailing list and then find someone is causing you trouble with that address, it's easy to simply delete it and send out an email to your full list advising them of the new address. You might even pick up some additional orders just because they heard from you.

The Least You Need to Know

◆ Understanding how long posts last and how often you're allowed to make a new post (no sooner than 48 hours) is essential in knowing when to post.

♦ Reading the Terms of Service, familiarizing you with craigslist staff, and even reading the blogs of Jim Buckmaster and Craig Newmark, can greatly improve your craigslist experience.

♦ The **help** forum may seem a bit complex at first, but when you get a forum account "handle" and read through the items in the right column, it's easy.

♦ Clicking on **feedback** on the top right of each page in a forum offers a virtual education in using the forums and learning the "language" of craigslist.

♦ It's a smart thing to create an email address that is specific to your craigslist dealings, but to *not* list it in your craigslist ad.

Chapter 7

Why Some Listings Work and Others Don't

In This Chapter

- Why the "Best Of" are
- Writing better ads
- What works on craigslist
- Good ads
- Ads outside your area
- Use the forums for better responses

It's not easy writing effective business advertising. Oh sure, you can write something simple if you're doing a yard sale, listing out your top items in prose that presents a little white lie about their true market value. After all, you probably know your neighborhood, and have a good idea of what people expect and find acceptable. But what do you do if you're trying to recruit people for your home-based business from another state? How do you describe the home you're trying to sell in a way that makes it stand out from all the others on the market? Are there cultural things you need to know about other countries that would affect the verbiage of your ad? And where can you turn for improvement if your ads don't seem to be working? We try to address things like that, and much more, in this chapter.

Why the "Best Of" Are the Best

One might think that something selected as "Best Of" would be an example of the type of craigslist ad you would want to emulate to get noticed above the competition. They're ads that get noticed, all right, but mostly only so people can laugh. If you start reading them, be prepared for anything; these are not for the faint of heart. When you get past the personals ads that people find funny, though, you'll occasionally see listings that are feedback on craigslist business experiences.

The "Best Of" ads are a place for public feedback on the use of the site. Most of the time people know that others read the "Best Of" pages for laughs, but they also know this area is like the public bulletin board of the site. You might find a post about posting effective ads, like "How to sell stuff on craigslist" that offered the following (edited) advice:

> *Pictures. Post a detailed picture of the item you are selling. People want to see what they are buying.*
>
> *Detail. Simply typing "For Sale" in the subject line does not give people any reason to click on your ad. Give a description … detail about the condition of item you are selling, why you are selling it, and why they should buy it.*
>
> *Price. People come to craigslist for a deal. People start seeing things as a deal when the price is set at about 50% of new or less. You would be amazed at how simply adjusting the price of an item you have posted for $285 down to $275 will make the difference between no responses and a full inbox just moments after posting.*
>
> *Courtesy. Be courteous! Make it easy for people to give you their money! Give a phone number (out of all my postings 90 percent of my sales were over the phone) … I cannot believe how many people thanked me, not for selling them something, but for making it easy on them, contrary to their previous craigslist experiences.*

So have fun reading the "Best Of" ads, but look for posts where people talk about the psychology of craigslist users, like the one earlier. You'll find that some people will also post sarcastic fake posts that get selected as "Best Of" that speak to people who are preying on people on craigslist, like scammers asking for free writers, artists, and actors with vague promises of future pay. If you plan to offer something similar in your area (let's say you're making a low-budget film), you can usually get an idea if other supposed filmmakers are scamming people, which will make your ad more likely to get nasty responses until you specify in the ad that you're completely above-board.

> **List Notes**
>
> "Best of craigslist" ads usu-
> ally run around two months
> behind the current date. If you
> want to warn the community
> about some scam, while you
> might find relief writing a
> sarcastic post and flagging it
> as a "Best Of," people won't
> see it for a long time. You're
> better off using a discussion
> forum to get the word out.

Getting Help to Write Better Ads

When you are creating a craigslist ad, that's copywriting. Given the number of ads being placed daily, even in nonmajor cites, you're dealing with busy people wanting to find what they're looking for quickly. That's true even if they're just looking for a business opportunity that you might be offering.

If you are doing more than selling an item or two or having some type of home sale, and you find that the ads you write don't seem to be very effective, you might want to look into hiring a professional. You can also find sites that offer free advice from professionals, so get searching.

When you're writing your ad, particularly if it's for something you'll be selling repeatedly, think like a "bricks and mortar" merchant in a store, preparing a print ad. You need to know what the competition is like, so study craigslist in the proper category and see what you can find amongst your competition.

If you don't have a digital camera for taking pictures, get one or borrow one, unless you have a cell phone that takes phenomenal pics. As you've already learned in previous chapters, there are some sites that build on top of craigslist and emphasize the pictures in the ads. To sell, successfully sell, on craigslist it often helps to take advantage of your ability to post four pictures with an ad.

Prepare to be haggled. Veterans know that craigslist is more like an open-air market than a merchant inside a shopping mall. Usually, people expect you to negotiate a price with them, so in writing your ad you'll need to know what others are *asking* for their items. If you undercut them too much and then have to haggle with your customer, you might cut too far into the profit margin you need. If you see others selling used computers for $500 and you think you'll beat them all by offering your desktop for $450, don't be shocked if you get offered $400 from a potential buyer.

One thing that craigslist stresses is that it is an online community intended for facilitating transactions that take place face to face. So in most cases, someone buying on craigslist expects to look over an item before they buy it, just as they would in a store. They'll look for scratches on used items, or mention they're looking at another product that's similar a few blocks away.

If you don't feel like haggling over prices, simply state "$500 Firm" somewhere in your ad. That signals your bottom line on the item and will discourage the negotiators.

Online Heat
You might want do some reading in the "PR University" at www.bull-dogreporter.com, a superb site for public relations pros. You'll learn facts like how women are America's #1 consumer group, influencing 85 percent of all consumer purchases in the United States and wielding $5 trillion in purchasing power. They also have a free White Paper library with great tips.

If you decide to hire someone to write ad copy for you, see if they know the tips you've just read. If they're not clued in to craigslist and the psychology of craigslist consumers, they are probably not the right copywriter for you. Don't buy into some claim about the great network marketing hard-sell ads they've written, unless that mentality makes sense for what you're selling. Usually, craigslist buyers are lower-key than those reached by "push" advertising like mailed brochures and magazines that mix a few health tips with ads for vitamins and books that tell you all the healing wisdom you supposedly need. Remember, craigslist consumers are there by choice.

Learning What Works on craigslist

You'll find for the most part that you don't need to get too fancy with pictures and copy to have an effective ad. In fact, given the overall feel of craigslist, it's usually advisable to use the format provided by the site, with four pictures and minimal HTML in use to change the colors and fonts. Some people like to put "clickable" pictures in their ads, and you can find a simple posting primer that includes that here: www.wikihow. com/Post-Ads-to-Craigslist. And in case you aren't sure what HTML is acceptable, see www.craigslist.org/about/help and click on **what HTML code does craigslist support?** under **frequently asked questions.** From there, click on the **HTML examples** page at www. craigslist.org/about/help/html_in_craigslist_postings.

The reason we don't go into detail here about too many technical steps like putting pictures and HTML in ads is because it's already covered on craigslist. For example, you can set up an ad that will display a picture that is "hosted" (stored) on another site. It's very simple to set up, and craigslist gives you an example at the page last referenced, under *"Externally-hosted images"* so rather than looking for the technical details here, stay current on the latest on craigslist. One thing is certain: if you do not have acceptable HTML coding in your ad, it won't make it onto the site.

The software mentioned in Chapter 5 isn't very expensive, so if you find that you're getting confused with HTML and/or doing anything but using the template for posting provided by craigslist, try the posting software that makes the most sense for you.

The main thing that counts about a good craigslist ad is the content, and that includes pictures, but the verbiage counts, too, except perhaps with guys looking through personals ads. When you're offering a product or a service, people can see by the subject line if you have a picture included or not, and in searching they can search only ads with pictures as well as searching only by titles. So the title is the first part of your content.

You are allowed 70 characters total in a craigslist title. Instead of trying to use eye-catching characters like typing in **ALL CAPS BOLD** or using nonalphabet characters, you should pay more attention to using words like "bargain" that evoke a powerful shopping emotion. Again, you need to peruse the competition. If you see "great deal" in every other listing, maybe your use of the phrase "fair deal" would get your ad clicked on first. Which ad would you be more like to choose from these two:

****\\\\\\\\\\FABULOUS COMPUTER DEAL, $400 LIKE NEW//////*****

Must sell well-maintained one owner Dell desktop, $400

Using a term like "must sell" could have a drawback in that the buyer would assume you're desperate for money and would take much less than your asking price. How about:

Dell Latitude D-620 Intel Core 2 Duo, $400

With that one, many buyers won't know what "Latitude D–620" means but they might know that "Intel Core 2 Duo" is a fast processor, so the memory of the computer might matter more:

Dell Intel Core 2 Duo 120GB hard drive 2GB RAM, $400

Note that the previous examples use at least 15 less characters than 70 for a reason. When a title line pushes the limit of 70, it's often less attractive to the eye than one that gets to the point. After all, the title line is something you click on to read the full ad. It's just a door, so to speak, not the whole house.

Ads will display the date of the ad in black letters, and the title line will be another color (usually default blue in most browsers). Once you've clicked on it, the next time you see the search results page, that link will be shown in another color (purple default in most browsers). Because of the lighter color, most people find

> **List Notes**
>
> A good place to find classy ads on craigslist, that use pictures well and have just the right amount of to-the-point eloquent verbiage, is in the **books** category under the **for sale** banner. People who read a lot and treasure books often have a nice sense of style.

that too much emphasis on ALL CAPS makes the ad harder on the eyes. Also, ALL CAPS is known to represent *shouting* in cyberspace, which some people either don't know or ignore.

One exception to this rule is that people don't seem to mind the asterisk (*) as much, particularly if it surrounds a *time limiter* in a title line, such as:

> ***ONE DAY ONLY*** Dell Latitude Intel Core 2 Duo, $400

In Hollywood movies, there is often a "time clock" so that the hero has to get to a certain place by a certain time or all is lost. Businesses use this psychology all the time, and it will work for you in an ad. Just be sure that you explain *why* it's one day only in the body of the ad, like:

> Leaving for college, need to move this computer today. No reasonable offer refused.

If you use a technique like this, don't do it too often or you'll be found out by regular browsers of the category and they might start flagging your ads. To give yourself a good out on lowball offers, make sure you say something like "No reasonable offer refused" to cover rejecting that lowball.

Good Ad Examples

A classy title line that provides vital information without "shouting" or looking cheap will probably work better for you. Keep in mind that when you have a title line you're happy with, the body of the ad should match it in tone. Using that criteria, let's take the same ad given as an example in Chapter 4, with the "Five Ws and How" variation given there, and see how to make a good ad better. To recap those elements:

What—Tell people what it is in the title line.

Where—Location on the title line is next in importance.

When—Share your availability in being contacted.

Who—Make it personal and be easily reachable.

Why—Share your reason for placing the ad.

How—Mention payment options if other than cash.

Here again is that sample ad from Chapter 4:

Apple MacBook Pro 15" 2.4ghz w/Applecare - $1500 (Burbank)

Mint condition 15" MacBook Pro 2.4GHZ Intel Core 2 Duo, Penryn processor, with aluminum body, glossy LED screen and multi-touch trackpad, with Applecare warranty and tech support covered until June 2011. 256MB of video memory, 2GB RAM, 320GB/7200 RPM drive, 8X dual layer Superdrive (burns DVDs & CDs), built-in iSight camera, Airport Extreme WiFi card built-in, Firewire 800 & 400 ports, USB 2.0 ports. Includes all equipment that came in the original box including software and system disks.

Have upgraded for newer model. Selling for $1500 cash, firm. Contact Ron at (818)555-1212 after 4:00 p.m.

* Location: Burbank

* it's NOT ok to contact this poster with services or other commercial interests

PostingID: (this is provided by craigslist)

If you're computer-savvy, some of those specifications might mean something to you. If you're a normal consumer, however, you'll probably be more interested in the continuing Applecare warranty and tech support, and the fact that it's a fairly new computer that can burn CDs and DVDs and has a built-in web camera. Since you're selling a used item, this is a good time to take advantage of the four-picture possibility of each ad and show the computer, the software discs in original packages, any nicks or dents, and perhaps a screen capture of the "system specs." You might find examples of ads like that on craigslist; you certainly can find them on eBay.

List Losers

Try to stay away from lines in ads like:

Please contact me ASAP this will not last long!

It's not very good reverse psychology and shows that you're anxious, not that you're looking out for the interests of your potential buyer.

If you're selling a computer model that is still being sold new by the dealer, Apple in this case, you're probably better off providing one picture of the computer and a link to the page describing that computer on the Apple website. We'll use a different computer for an example:

Title of Ad:

iMac 20-inch 2.66GHz Intel Core 2 Duo - $1000 (Burbank)

Body of Ad:

Only three months old beautiful iMac 20-inch 2.66GHz Intel Core 2 Duo (white) with 2GB memory, 320GB hard drive, 8x double-layer SuperDrive, NVIDIA GeForce 9400M graphics card, anodized aluminum frame, glossy LED screen. Built-in iSight camera and Airport Extreme WiFi card. Includes all equipment that came in the original box including software and system disks. Applecare warranty and tech support covered until December 2012.

More technical specs at http://www.apple.com/imac/*****

Buying new MacBook Pro laptop for more mobility. $1000 cash, firm. Contact Ron at (818)555-1212 after 4:00 p.m.

The ***** signifies a nonexistent link. Although an Apple link to your specific model might not be available, you might find a reseller site at the time of placing the ad that with the exact computer you're selling. Save yourself the hassle of describing an item perfectly when it's already pictured and described in full on a professional site, as long as your price is sufficiently inexpensive. If you have a good picture of your computer, put it in the ad as well as the type of link just mentioned.

As long as you're providing enough information either in the text and/or with a link, and you have a clear picture, the most effective craigslist ads are often simple because the ad can be seen in full more quickly. Students selling books that are used year after year in certain courses only need the title in the subject line, and in the ad a picture of the book, a short description, perhaps the ISBN number, and the name of the seller and contact info. The simpler the item, the simpler the ad can be. For example:

Title of Ad:

College Algebra 4th Ed Dugopolski - $95 (Burbank)

Body of Ad:

Like New College Algebra 4th Edition (Dugopolski Series) hardcover textbook. Paid $150 new, selling for $95 OBO.

[picture of book here]

Call Bob at (818) 555-1212 after 3:00 P.M.

There might not be another ad for the same book in the area, so you couldn't compare pricing when placing your ad. In the case of a book or another item available on Amazon.com, you could get a comparison price there, and if selling locally you'd have the advantage, as shipping might not factor in with you.

Placing Ads Outside Your Area

Just as posting the same ad in more than one location is considered spamming, craigslist also looks for certain words in titles and in the body of ads that alert them to their definition of spam. If you think you can write a good ad using the tips from Chapter 4 and other ideas given in this chapter, great. You'd better rewrite that ad before you post it in some other location, though.

Skip's Tips

If you're selling the same product or service repeatedly, keep in mind that using the same title over and over might get you rejected by craigslist. Once you know the content you want, try to vary the verbiage and come up with 10 or more variations to cycle through.

The craigslist prohibition on posting the same ad in different locations probably is a good thing, because the sensibilities and considerations of people vary from city to city, or even by neighborhood, much less country to country. Australians, for example, don't like a "hard sell" approach that might be fine for people in the United States. A bit of sarcasm might be considered funny in New York City but be seen as offensive in Atlanta. It pays to know your buyer, wherever they are.

Listings in North America

The craigslist main page is neatly organized but it would be impossible to list links to all the available sites in the United States and Canada on one page. So craigslist handles that with a **more ...** link at the bottom of the **us cities** column and another at the bottom of the **canada** column. Clicking on the former takes you to—http://geo.craigslist.org/iso/us—with areas from **SF bay area** to **yuma** (in Arizona). The Canadian **more ...** goes to—http://geo.craigslist.org/iso/ca—with a page of links from **barrie** to **winnipeg.**

It comes in handy to familiarize yourself with this list of cities if you plan on marketing a product in multiple places across the North American market. Let's say you have a product that uniquely appeals to both an English- and French-speaking audience, like a toy bear with a switch to change what it says from French to English. From the main craigslist page, if you click on **montreal** you'll get that page, and then to the right of the middle columns you'll see a banner for **canada** with a list of Canadian cities with another **more ...** beneath them. If you clicked on the Canadian **more ...** from the main page, though, you'd get the full list of Canadian cities and could locate other heavily French-speaking cities like Quebec City on the same page.

You'll also find that when you're on the page of a Canadian city, beneath the listings on the right of other Canadian cities, there is a banner **ca provs** (Canadian provinces). Clicking on **quebec** there gives you all the main cities in the province: Montreal, Ottawa-Hull-Gatineau, Quebec City, Saguenay, Sherbrooke, and Trois-Rivieres.

From the main page, when you click on a U.S. state, you'll also get a page listing the main cities there. Clicking on **michigan** gives you a page with links to Ann Arbor, Central Michigan, Detroit Metro, Flint, Grand Rapids, Jackson, Kalamazoo, Lansing, Muskegon, Northern Michigan, Port Huron, Saginaw-Midland-Bay City, South Bend/Michiana, Southwest Michigan, and Upper Peninsula.

Knowing these navigational realities helps in the science of geomarketing, which is used broadly by businesses. See http://en.wikipedia.org/wiki/Geo_(marketing) for more information. Let's say you're selling website design services and you know that in a certain region there is a recent injection of government money into expanding broadband

Internet into rural areas. (You can actually find information like that at www.rurdev.usda.gov.) Since many people in an area like that probably haven't been able to market their products as effectively via the web due to slow Internet connections, but have been able to access text–heavy craigslist, this might be the ideal time to offer your professional website building services to them via craigslist.

It's easier to develop entrepreneurial ideas to make money using craigslist when you fully know how to navigate it.

Listings Outside the United States

You'll probably notice that the geographical banners on the main page, such as **countries,** are not clickable like the banners in the middle columns are. Clicking on a middle column banner like **housing** will take you to **all housing** listings. So if you don't see an international city you're interested in under the **intl cities** banner on the right, look for that city's country on the far right under the **countries** banner. There's no particular scheme for how many areas or cities are listed under any particular country, however. Clicking on **Ireland** only gives you a page for Dublin with no list of other Irish cities. Choosing the **germany** link gives you the **berlin** page, and a column to the right of the middle columns offers links to a list of 13 German cities including Berlin. Clicking on the link to **brazil,** however, takes you to a **choose your area** page that lists: Belo Horizonte; Brasilia; Curitiba; Fortaleza; Porto Alegre; Recife; Rio de Janeiro, Salvador, Bahia; and Sao Paulo—only nine cities/areas.

List Notes
Don't forget the small "w" to the right of the name of a location page. Clicking on it takes you to the Wikipedia listing for that city or area, such as Calgary, Alberta in Canada. Knowing something about a city helps in calculating how to market there.

So it's just like navigating in the North American pages: there are quirks and you just have to learn them. The good thing about the international pages is that you have the choice between the language of the country or area (or several languages in places like Switzerland). As a native English speaker it's a boon to know you can post your ad in English all over the world, and if you speak other languages you can post that way, too.

And it's fairly certain that your ad won't get flagged as being the same listing in two places if it's posted in different languages.

Using Forums for Better Responses

Some forums can be quite helpful in gleaning the mentality of certain marketing demographics. One example is **over 50** that links to the **over 50 club** page. You'll find a forum explanation by clicking on **Boomers & Beyond R+** in the right column. The R+ means this is a Registered Plus forum, signifying that any post you make will always display your handle/alias. This discussion forum for Baby Boomers, those born between 1946 and 1964, is also for anyone younger or older, but the Boomers are a major market in North America. You'll find endless websites, articles, and books about reaching this demographic, which in the United States is second only to the highly desirable 18-to-34 males market in terms of purchasing power.

When you're putting together a marketing plan for your products or services via craigslist, take some time to browse through the discussion forums and see which ones might be beneficial to spend time exploring. Just don't forget that placing ads in forums is strictly *verboten*. If you think you've found a group perfect for your product, that's great. Learn from them on the forum, but advertise to them in the proper place on craigslist.

The Least You Need to Know

◆ The "Best Of" craigslist pages are for laughs, but they occasionally have posts with effective tips about using craigslist, and reveal psychology.

◆ Writing better craigslist ads depends heavily on fully understanding the psychology of the normal craigslist user.

◆ From allowing only 70 characters in ad subject lines to what HTML is allowed and what is not, all the standards of craigslist are available on the site, if you just know where to look.

◆ The most effective craigslist ads are often simple ones with just the right amount of text, a good picture, and perhaps a link, because such ads can be browsed more quickly.

◆ Placing effective ads outside your area requires some study, but by using tools provided by craigslist such as Wikipedia links, it's easy to learn.

◆ There are discussion forums where you can glean valuable advice and insight into the psychology of specific craigslist users such as Baby Boomers.

Chapter 8

How to Handle a Scam

In This Chapter

- ◆ Search for Certainty
- ◆ Keep it close to home
- ◆ Use Government resources
- ◆ craigslist Variations
- ◆ Other resources for victims

Nobody wants to get burned, but it's a possibility you can expect when you're doing business online. The main reason craigslist stresses the local nature of its site is so that people can personally inspect items bought in a safe space and do transactions in cash. There is a separation between "jobs" and "gigs" on purpose; gigs are meant to be lower-paying, intern, and no-pay listings. Since people search for jobs across the country (or world), and since you can post your resume on craigslist, it's obvious that some things take place on the site that are not local. People sell items to others, and services to others, around the world. So since most people using craigslist don't have the resources or even inclination to chase down a cheat across the state, country, or world, it's good to have some idea of solutions if such a problem arises.

Search if You Smell a Rat

The great thing about computers is that every single machine that connects to the web has an Internet Protocol (IP) address that is its identity, such as 192.129.2.176. Other computers connected to that computer, like those at craigslist headquarters, can identify a computer. Thus, when you post to the site, your computer signature is left behind. That makes it easier to locate you and suspend your account or ban you from posting to the site. Of course, there are ways to hide your IP address and post anonymously, but one look at the craigslist personnel list that they provide tells any knowledgeable computer person that they know what they're doing and are adept at stopping those with malicious intent. Nevertheless, if you are using the web for making money, you should know as much about protecting yourself online as possible.

Scammers Don't Just Live in Nigeria

In the left-hand column on the home page you'll see **personal safety tips.** Clicking on that brings you to www.craigslist.org/about/safety where you'll find a basic statement that begins: "The overwhelming majority of craigslist users are trustworthy and well-intentioned." That's true, but it's always the rotten apple that spoils the rest in the barrel.

List Notes
"Best of craigslist" ads usually run around two months behind the current date. If you want to warn the community about some scam, while you might find relief writing a sarcastic post and flagging it as a "Best Of," people won't see it for a long time. You're better off using a discussion forum to get the word out.

I don't know anyone who hasn't received a crazy email from some moron in an Internet café in Nigeria who believes there's someone stupid enough to believe an email that claims the recipient has several million dollars just waiting for them if they'll send a few hundred or thousand to clear up some basic administration necessary to get the funds released.

And of course there's the Microsoft Lottery that doesn't exist, usually with emails supposedly coming from England that say "your Internet address" won and all you need to is give them all your personal information and bank routing and account numbers and you'll be almost as rich as Bill Gates quickly.

While craigslist doesn't have any warnings about email spam scams on its warning pages, it does have examples of how a poster might be scammed by someone overseas. At www.craigslist.org/about/scams it provides examples of real scam responses to craigslist postings. At the time of the writing of this book, they included:

◆ A person wanting to buy a 1987 Toyota Celica who offered to send out a cashier check for *more* than the price of the car, with instructions to send the difference in a cashier's check to a person who would ship the car out of the country to the buyer.

◆ Someone in "the netherlands(holland)" who supposedly had a client "in ENGLAND who is owing me 5800POUNDS" who will send "a money order/certifiedcheck." The seller is to deduct his or her money, then send the balance to the "buyer" by "western union money transfer."

◆ An "auto dealer based in TAIWAN" wants to buy a 1989 Jetta GL 4 door and needs "your full name and address including your phone."

◆ An "auto dealer based in TAIWAN" interested in buying a comic book collection, again wanting "full name and address including your phone."

As evidenced by the sloppy typing and odd offers presented earlier, it would seem that any normal person would see right through these scams, but people do not. Just as people have lost tens of thousands if not millions of dollars in the Nigerian email scam, people are gullible. They don't keep in mind the old dictum that "If it sounds too good to be true, it probably is." In the examples given by craigslist, some posters will not realize that the "certified check" they will receive could bounce several days after deposit while the "difference" cashier's check they send will be lost, just like the item that has been "purchased." When someone wants a full name and address and phone number, they might simply be someone local intent on figuring out when you're not home so that they can slip by and steal your item. What to do? Keep reading.

Protect Yourself at All Times

As craigslist warns, "ONLY A SCAMMER WILL 'GUARANTEE' YOUR TRANSACTION." While there are protections in place on eBay for protecting sellers, and buyers using credit cards in the United States who get scammed have protection from their companies, with craigslist you're on your own. While you need to read everything the site offers to protect you, here's the seven scam warning headlines from their **scams** page:

1. *Someone claims that craigslist will guarantee a transaction, certify a buyer/seller, OR claims that craigslist will handle or provide protection for a payment.*

2. *Distant person offers a genuine-looking (but fake) cashier's check.*

3. *Someone requests wire service payment via Western Union or MoneyGram.*

4. *Distant person offers to send you a money order and then have you wire money.*

5. *Distant seller suggests use of an online escrow service.*

6. *Distant seller asks for a partial payment up front, after which he will ship goods.*

7. *Foreign company offers you a job receiving payments from customers, then wiring funds.*

Please go read the additional comments on the scam page for a better grasp of what to avoid, because no matter how badly you get burned in a scam someone transacts on craigslist, you'll have no recourse with the site. They state clearly at the top of the **scams** page, *CRAIGSLIST IS NOT INVOLVED IN ANY TRANSACTION, and does not handle payments, guarantee transactions, provide escrow services, or offer "buyer protection" or "seller certification".*

When you make a local transaction
(the type that craigslist prefers), the
site suggests the following at www.
craigslist.org/about/safety:

- *Insist on a public meeting place like
  a café*

- *Tell a friend or family member
  where you're going*

- *Take your cell phone along if you
  have one*

- *Consider having a friend accom-
  pany you*

- *Trust your instincts*

You can't necessarily do these things when you'd doing long-distance
transactions, but you can tell a friend or family member about the type
of transactions you're attempting to do. While you might get lulled into
thinking a person sounds reasonable over email or the phone, often-
times when we share our experiences with family or trusted friends,
they will have unfortunate experience or knowledge about things that
will cause them to warn you just in time.

Knowing that people are going to do long-distance transactions via
their site, craigslist suggests the following sites for online safety:

http://getsafeonline.org

http://wiredsafety.org

We've mentioned them more than once because they're jam-packed
with very good information. Also see www.haltabuse.org/resources/
online.shtml for some tips about dealing with people online. That site
offers similar email tips to those you've already read in this book,
such as:

- Select a gender-neutral username, email address, etc. Avoid
  anything cute, sexual, diminutive, or overtly feminine.

- Keep your primary email address private. Use your primary email address ONLY for people you know and trust.

- Get a free email account and use that for all your other online activity. Make sure you select a gender-neutral username that is nothing like anything you've had before.

If you use the anonymized address option when placing your craigslist ad and then an email address like the type described earlier when answering people who respond to your ad, you're giving yourself another layer of protection that most people think about. In today's world, "Safety First" is the motto to follow.

There is also a U.S. federal government resource that you can turn to at www.ic3.gov/default.aspx. As stated on the site, "The Internet Crime Complaint Center (IC3) is a partnership between the Federal Bureau of Investigation (FBI), the National White Collar Crime Center (NW3C), and the Bureau of Justice Assistance (BJA). IC3's mission is to serve as a vehicle to receive, develop, and refer criminal complaints regarding the rapidly expanding arena of cyber crime." You can file a complaint right on the site at www.ic3.gov/complaint/default.aspx.

Skip's Tips

If you want to get extremely serious about tracking down Internet fraud, take a look at The Ultimate Collection of Forensic Software at www.tucofs.com/tucofs.htm. You'll find software for every computer platform, even Personal Digital Assistants (PDAs). You'll be amazed at this resource.

When you take advantage of all these Internet and "real world" tools, you should find that your craigslist experience will be smoother than most.

Great martial artists believe that if you are well enough prepared, you never encounter conflicts, and that's what we wish for you.

Government and Other Resources

The IC3 is one of the organizations recommended by craigslist at www.craigslist.org/about/scams to notify about fraud or scam attempts. They also include the Federal Trade Commission (FTC) toll-free hotline at

1-877-FTC-HELP (1-877-382-4357) and their online complaint form at www.ftc.gov, but if you're victimized by a company doing business on craigslist (or elsewhere) a better site is https://www.ftccomplaintassistant. gov (accessible via the FTC main site) and the link to the complaint form is www.ftc.gov/ftc/cmplanding.shtm.

The Canadian PhoneBusters hotline at 1-888-495-8501 is provided by craigslist, but not the website at www.phonebusters.com. Other information you won't get from craigslist is the fax number 1-888-654-9426 and email addresses, info@phonebusters.com and phonebusters@efni. com. This is the central Canadian agency set up to collect information on telemarketing complaints in Canada to prosecute criminals in Canada violating telemarketing fraud laws.

In truth, craigslist would be better off posting the Reporting Economic Crime On-Line (RECOL) site set up by the Royal Canadian Mounted Police at http://www.recol.ca. Given the proliferation of French-speaking people in Quebec and throughout Canada, both the PhoneBusters and RECOL sites are available in both English and Français.

You'll also find this statement from craigslist on the site on the **scams** page:

> "If you suspect that an item posted for sale on craigslist may be part of a scam, please email the details to 'abuse@craigslist.org'. Be sure to include the URL (or eight-digit post ID number) in your message."

So there are some North American resources for you in addition to the option of dealing with your local police. The craigslist idea of dealing locally with people who pay cash is a great idea but if you are a buyer and don't keep notes on setting up the transaction, and get a written receipt for your money as well as print out and save the craigslist ad to your hard drive, you're setting yourself up for a loss if you need to contact the authorities, or if someone makes a spurious claim about your ad.

Sure, craigslist maintains ads for a certain length of time (six months if you have an account), but in most locales people have up to two years to file a small claims court action. You should also keep copies of email exchanges with buyers and sellers.

Let's say you're willing to take payments other than in cash, or must because you're selling a product or offering a service long distance. How can you safeguard yourself? On its **scams** page, craigslist points out:

> *Most scams involve one or more of the following:*
>
> ♦ *inquiry from someone far away, often in another country*
>
> ♦ *Western Union, Money Gram, cashier's check, money order, shipping, escrow service, or a "guarantee"*
>
> ♦ *inability or refusal to meet face-to-face before consummating transaction*

Obviously, some people do business legitimately long distance via craigslist. If you're a writer or artist or someone with unique computer skills, you'll find that you will often deal with clients and even hold jobs on a telecommuting basis.

We suggest the following methods for getting paid with less hassle:

1. Take a bank check (not a cashier's check). Even if you take a cashier's check or money order, deposit it personally at your bank, not at the ATM, and find out what their policy is on clearing the funds. If it takes two weeks, fine. Don't release the product until the funds are absolutely cleared.

2. Getting paid via Western Union is not a bad thing in some cases because in some countries outside the United States, that's the best international method. As you can see at www.westernunion.com its country list is huge, and you can find an agent for your customer if necessary there on the site.

3. Try www.paypal.com. PayPal is owned by eBay and offers secure transactions, the ability to send an invoice via email, and a customer can pay with most credit and debit cards. Like Western Union, funds from the person on the other end must clear and be proven legitimate before they will be transmitted to you.

In doing business of any kind, there are no guarantees. As we've learned in recent times, guarantees that we think are sacrosanct, like FDIC guarantees on bank accounts, may not be as certain as we think. Like the old saying goes, "You pays your money and you takes your chances." We hope, at least, that the recourse resources given here make any troubles you encounter a bit more bearable.

> **List Notes**
>
> If you feel you've encountered a specific problem in a craigslist deal, you can search for a word or phrase by going to the **help** forum, then clicking on **search CL—help desk** at the top of the left column. From there you can search for "fraud" and you'll see all the previous discussions about that subject.

How craigslist Can and Cannot Help

The site goes to great lengths to stay out of conflicts between users. If you do get into a legal battle, however, and for any reason need to determine the identity of a craigslist user, you'll find their policy on that at www.craigslist.org/about/help. Click on **law enforcement (subpoena's etc.)** under the **harassment, legal stuff, spam, email** banner, and you'll see the following disclaimer:

> *Official requests for release of records can be forwarded by email, fax, or mail.*

They ask that the request be sent as a PDF file. Here's the contact information:

> craigslist
> 1381 9th Avenue
> San Francisco, CA 94122
> attn: Custodian of Records
> fax: 415-504-6394
> legal@craigslist.org

They request that you indicate your preferred method of delivery for response—email, fax, or U.S. Mail—and that you provide a date range for the records you request.

For a site that does so much for so many on a mostly free basis, and tries to promote the idea of community spirit, it would behoove any user to go to equally great lengths to try to not involve craigslist in any problems that arise during your use of the site. It's obvious to any logical person that they're here to help, and should be helped in return.

List Losers

If you get frustrated in trying to get justice over a transaction, don't immediately try to contact craigslist via phone or fax or email to complain. Use www.craigslist.org/about/help/feedback and explain your problem in detail. It helps them get a more organized complaint from you. You'll hear from them more quickly.

You'll find that craigslist constantly assesses better ways to operate. They monitor the categories and forums constantly. As stated on the **feedback** page:

> *New categories are added when demand is demonstrated by posting patterns in existing categories, e.g. when we saw a lot of furniture ads in the general for sale category, we added a dedicated furniture category.*

You might not be able to get a new category added by contacting craigslist, because they're serving the community first and individual users second; but you might, by using the feedback page, prompt them to change some of their help pages, particularly if they need to update something. During the writing of this book, the Canadian Phonebusters information that you'll find in this book was lacking on the craigslist **scams** page. Chances are that by the time you're reading this, though, they'll have updated it. Remember, they intend it to be a community, so contribute to making it better when you can.

Other Resources if You're Victimized

In May 2008 a lawsuit was filed against craigslist, *eBay Domestic Holdings, Inc. v. Craig Newmark, et al.*, C.A. No. 3705-CC. You'll find it on the craigslist blog http://blog.craigslist.org/2008/04/

complaint-department. Two weeks later, craigslist counter-sued to reclaim the 28.4 percent of its shares that eBay bought from a former craigslist executive in 2004. You can download the complaint from the craigslist blog at http://blog.craigslist.org/2008/05/unlawful-and-unfair or see http://blog.craigslist.org/etc/cl.vs.ebay.html.

eBay was accused of "unlawful and unfair competition, misappropriation of proprietary information, deceptive passing-off, business interference, false advertising, phishing attacks, free-riding, trademark infringement, trademark dilution, and breaches of fiduciary duty." Part of that statement had to do with eBay starting a competing site to craigslist, Kijiji.com. As of the writing of this book, the suit was unresolved.

Obviously, craigslist with only 25 or so staffers in San Francisco has plenty to do. Even though there are a great many people online volunteering in the forums at any given time, ultimately you'll have to solve your own problem if you run into troubles with people while doing business via the site.

One way to protect your email and keep communications safe is to use Pretty Good Privacy, broadly known as PGP. The international version is PGPi, explained at: www.pgpi.org/doc/faq/pgpi/en/#What. In case you didn't know, regular email can be read by people other than the intended recipient. With PGP encryption, people can intercept your email, but can't read it. Of course, the person you're doing business with will also need the PGP software, which can be found at: www.pgpi.org.

If you find that you can't resolve a business problem with someone you meet through craigslist and they're local, you'll probably have to take legal action, and that will probably mean small claims court, because in most states any lawsuit $5,000 and under is a small claim. We'll cover small claims and other things in the next chapter.

We hope you never encounter the type of problems discussed in this chapter, legal or otherwise, but hopefully you now have some tools for handling them that you didn't have before.

The Least You Need to Know

◆ The info at www.craigslist.org/about/safety and www.craigslist.
org/about/scams and the links they mention will greatly help in
keeping you safe while using craigslist.

◆ Many people and organizations are available to help you with
problems encountered online, like Jayne Hitchcock's www.
haltabuse.org.

◆ Government resources listed by craigslist for dealing with scams
are skimpy, particularly with Canada, where www.phonebusters.
com and www.recol.ca help solve many problems.

◆ Information pertaining to people you've had trouble with on the
site will usually only be released by craigslist if served with a subpoena or search warrant.

◆ Many of your problems that seem irresolvable can often be successfully addressed by using the feedback form on craigslist.

◆ If you must take legal action, your proper venue will probably be
small claims court.

Chapter 9

Separating the Payers from the Painful

In This Chapter

- ◆ Barter possibilities
- ◆ Finding fair value
- ◆ Cash, check, PayPal?
- ◆ Common complaints
- ◆ Small claims court

In dealing with anything but cash transactions, the main problem in running a business that revolves around Internet interaction is ensuring that you are paid in a timely fashion with payments that are valid. Since craigslist offers minimal advice on this—namely, *deal locally and in cash*—there's a lot to be considered in protecting yourself and your reputation. Forewarned is forearmed, so let's look at some options.

The Barter Possibility

The first category under the **for sale** banner on craigslist is **barter.** You are liable to find anything there. You'll find ads that shouldn't be in the category, things that are simply for sale, and ads that say "for barter or sale" that are thinly-disguised classified ads, but you'll also find a great many items and services that are legitimate offers.

If you want to see what's available, use the **search** box on the **barter** page and see if a listing comes up. That comic book collection you want to trade for dance lessons might actually be a possibility. Don't count on the other person to assess whether what you're offering is equal in value to what they have to trade, though. Do your homework and be prepared to send them the links to other craigslist ads or items on eBay that have similar prices. If you're offering a service in trade, it helps to have references that will if necessary attest to your hourly rate or normal quote.

Many people believe bartering bypasses the tax system, and that makes it more popular, particularly when people are low on cash. That's not always true. If you trade cars or any other equal item on craigslist, you may have nothing to report, but other exchanges are considered taxable by the Internal Revenue Service (IRS). According to the IRS website under "Tax Requirements for Barter Exchanges":

> Barter exchanges, whether Internet based or with a physical location, are required to file Form 1099-B for all transactions unless certain exceptions are met. Barter exchanges are not required to file Form 1099-B for:
>
> ◆ Exchanges through a barter exchange having fewer than 100 transactions during the year
>
> ◆ Exempt foreign persons as defined in Regulations section 1.6045–1(g)(1)
>
> ◆ Exchanges involving property or services with a fair market value of less than $1

Search for "barter" at www.irs.gov for more information. If you've checked the barter ads on craigslist and seen prices listed at $1, now you know why. People should, however, according to regulations be listing for 99¢ or less, and even then they are probably violating the "fair market value" phrase.

Barter ads on craigslist escalate in slow economies, so if you find that normal responses for products or services have fallen off, try the barter area. If you can trade a functioning refrigerator in your garage for software that will automate designing your own website, why not?

List Notes
If you barter your products, items, or services on craigslist, be sure and click on "partial list of prohibited items" and "avoid recalled items" (defaults to www.recalls.gov) at the top of the page. You don't want to take the time to create an ad, only to have it flagged.

Note that the IRS holds you exempt for fewer than 100 transactions. That covers a lot of people, but some people do a lot of business bartering, and U.S. companies do billions in barter transactions annually.

If you find you're doing a lot of bartering, it's probably wise to keep a log of such transactions. That way, you'll be able to see if you went over 100 transactions, and you'll have proof in case you ever find yourself in a tax audit. If you're interested in bartering possibilities off of craigslist, investigate the following sites:

www.barterbart.com—auction-style barter and trade

www.barterquest.com—goods and services in many categories, locally and internationally

www.mytradeamerica.com—the world's largest barter marketplace, a barter and trade exchange similar to a chamber of commerce

www.swap-it-now.com—"the Internet's flea market" where you can "swap DVDs, books, automobiles, toys, compact discs, autographs, and everything in between"

www.swaptreasures.com—an online swap community where members can swap, barter, buy, and sell goods and services

www.swaptree.com—swap books, CDs, DVDs, and video games

www.switchplanet.com—trade books, CDs, DVDs, CDs, and video games http://titletrader.com—book, movie, and music swap club

www.TradeAFavor.com—trade anything with everyone on Facebook

http://u-exchange.com—largest free swap site that specializes in every type of trade

If you get heavily involved in bartering and go over the 100 transactions mentioned by the IRS, you might want to look into organizations, publications, and websites that can help. One good hub of information is Barter News at www.barternews.com. They have a digital magazine available at www.barternews-ezine.com and a daily blog at www.barternewsblog.com.

You might also investigate the National Association of Trade Exchanges at www.nate.org. NATE offers the BANC (Barter Association National Currency), a scrip that allows "independent barter exchanges to do business with each other, without the need for back-to-back reciprocal trading." According to the site, the BANC currently represents more than 50,000 trade exchange members throughout the United States and Canada, and is "a stable barter currency that promotes trading and goodwill among its members."

You'll even find a credit card for your barter trades at www.bartercard.com. According to the site: "Bartercard currently helps over 55,000 smart businesses in 10 countries around the world (over 23,000 in Australia) to increase sales, customer base, cash-flow and profit."

Skip's Tips

If you want to give things away or get things free, use the **free** category under the **for sale** banner on craigslist, or try sites like http://freegan.info or www.freecycle.org (6,537,000 members across the globe). Remember, it's better to give than receive!

Keep in mind that, per the Terms of Use (TOU) on craigslist, they're not responsible for profits you make while using the site. If you are doing large amounts of bartering and get into tax trouble, records of your transactions on craigslist could be examined by the IRS. So keep good records, pay attention, and watch yourself.

Determining Fair Value

In determining what to charge for something you're selling on craigslist, don't just limit yourself to your local area. It's not that much more work to switch to various areas on the page, or even use www.crazedlist. org to do a more complete regional search.

When you are offering a product or service on a regular basis, you have to factor in your cost of living, the profit margin you need to feel like your efforts are worth your time, and what your competition is charging. Entrepreneurs learn terms like "loss leader," those items on sale at the local supermarket each weekend that lose money for the merchant but get people into the store to buy other things as well. New businesses use loss leaders to attract new customers and to build business and reputation. See www.investopedia.com/terms/l/lossleader.asp for a full explanation of the practice.

In addition to checking your competitors on craigslist, people selling products or used items can also do comparisons on eBay, but take a look at the online auction giant's competitors as well. Some are also in competition with craigslist. They include:

www.amazon.com—Amazon often offers lower prices than other merchants on items like computers so you could use its price to gauge pricing your similar used equipment.

www.ecrater.com—A free web store builder and online marketplace where sellers can create a free online store and browse and compare between thousands of products.

www.epier.com—A bit of a cross between craigslist and eBay that puts an emphasis on featured sellers.

www.hopeiwin.com—Free listings and stores, with a $25 bonus for signing up.

www.ioffer.com—A San Francisco–based site that "allows you to buy, sell, and trade just like you would in real life by negotiating."

www.listitforabuck.com—List any item in any category for 30 days "for only a buck."

http://classifieds.livedeal.com—The Live Deal Online Marketplace lets you search by zip code, city, or state in the United States and in many product and service categories. It also offers Yellow Pages and City Pages searches.

www.onlineauction.com—Auctions with free unlimited listings.

www.oodle.com—Allows you to see "local listings from over 80,000 websites" and sends you email updates when new matches pop up.

www.tagsaler.com—Organized, modernized, and free classifieds.

www.ubid.com—"Your connection to excess inventory from the world's most trusted brands."

Obviously, on the auction sites you'll have to follow a few auctions to see what the final amount of the bids are that win, but when you're attempting to build a business you have to do that kind of due diligence. The good thing for you is that success breeds competition, and craigslist and eBay both have many. In many cases, listings are free, and though craigslist discourages posting your ad in more than one category in one area, there's nothing preventing you from posting the same ad on many websites like those mentioned earlier. While you're researching prices at these sites, you'll probably figure out which ones you want to use regularly.

> **Online Heat**
>
> Sometimes you have to be product specific in figuring out a price. For example, if you're selling real estate, look for newsletters that go out to realtors in print, by email, or are on the web. In southern California, The Kitty Letter at http://ads.thekittyletter.com goes out to 50+ realtor offices each week.

After all your research, you'll still have to deal with the market in which you're trying to sell. You may find that people are accustomed to offering 50 percent less than you want, or claiming they got a better offer at another site. If you've done your research on those other places, you'll know whether or not they're making a terrible offer.

Cash, Check, or Paypal?

When you're in business for yourself, you learn quickly that you'll get burned sometimes. That's why people buy insurance, why credit card companies provide relief from the use of stolen credit cards, and why some businesses will only take cash payments. Obviously, if you are only operating locally, the craigslist admonition to only take cash is the best idea, but would you know if someone handed you a $100 bill that was bogus, or $20 bill? Most people would not.

Have you ever wondered why clerks in stores hold a bill you've given them up to the light? They're looking for a thread imbedded in the paper that runs vertically through the paper halfway between the Federal Reserve seal and the left edge of the bill. Printed on the thread is a phrase about its denomination. On the $20 bill, you'll see "USA TWENTY" repeated. While a high-quality color copier might be able to reproduce all the inks on paper similar to that used by the Bureau of Engraving and Printing, the phrase on that thread will *not* be reproduced.

You can read about other counterfeiting measures such as the watermark, color-shifting inks, fine-line printing patterns, enlarged off-center portraits, and a low-vision feature at www.moneyfactory.gov/section.cfm/7/35 but the simple "thread test" will serve you best.

In case you're wondering, real bills are printed on 100 percent cotton rag containing tiny red and blue fibers. Counterfeiters know all these things, however, so do yourself a favor. If at all possible, when someone is going to pay you cash for something that costs a few hundred dollars or more, you'll probably get large denomination bills. Use the thread test, but also have a $100, $50, and $20 bill handy to compare, if you feel the need.

Implications of Payment Options

Should you take a check for a craigslist transaction, ever? Well, first, did you know that when you deposit a check in your bank and the bank "releases" the funds, it's making you a loan, assuming that the check you deposited will pose no problem? *You and you alone* are responsible for that check you endorsed and deposited. If it bounces, it's your problem, not that of the bank.

If you want to get an idea if a check is good, you can verify a U.S. bank routing number for free online at http://yourfavorite.com/checkwriter/verify.htm. If the bank name, address, and phone number that pops up doesn't match the one on the check, you're dealing with a crook, so call the police (but don't jeopardize yourself by letting the "buyer" know that you know it's a bad check).

List Notes
At www.craigslist.org/about/scams there is a paragraph about watching out for "fake escrow" or "escrow fraud" and the statement that "most online escrow sites are FRAUDULENT, operated by scammers." Take their advice and do a Google search on those terms. If a scammer ever proposes using escrow and you fall for it, you'll be sorry you missed the education.

If you decide to take a check, a cashier's check, a money order, or any other kind of financial draft, your best move is to contact the issuing authority, such as the bank or institution that issued the paper, *before* you deposit it to your bank. Should it be from an overseas institution or some entity that you cannot easily contact, ask your bank to collect the funds. They'll verify it, or try to, and will charge you a fee, but that beats assuming the draft is good only to learn a few days later that it has bounced.

A good place to get an education on the various types of scams out there and steps to take is www.fraudaid.com. It's a 501(3) nonprofit site devoted to fraud victim advocacy, offering law enforcement support.

Although people occasionally get fake PayPal emails, the site itself, which is owned by eBay is considered secure by most veteran users. There are competitors, such as www.alertpay.com, http://payments.intuit.com, and www.swreg.org, but PayPal is by far the most popular. According to a 2008 study, the site compared its processing fees to 100 other merchants and found out they were up to 16 percent less expensive to use. Since they let you take credit cards, echecks, orders by phone and fax, and give you clickthrough button tools for your website, as well as the ability to send out invoices via email that will walk anyone who doesn't have a PayPal account through the paying process online, it's safe to say that PayPal is a good bet to use when taking payments for your long distance craigslist payments.

If You Need to Pay Employees

If you hire people long distance for your business, via craigslist or otherwise, you'll have to work out the method in which they'll be paid. PayPal may be an acceptable option, but in some cases employees won't like the transaction fee that PayPal charges them when they receive money. You can pay that fee in advance by adding it to their payment, or you can arrange to pay them by check or some other method.

To make sure you're covered if questions or arguments arise in the future, *put it in writing*. Get a contract in place between yourself and the employee as to what they are expected to deliver, and when and how they will be paid. You can find free template employee contracts at sites like www.business.com and www.rocketlawyer.com, but if you have any questions, hire a lawyer. You'll be able to use that contract repeatedly, and you'll be glad you have a good contract in place if problems develop with that employee.

Common craigslist Complaints

On the web, you can find any number of complaints by people about craigslist; www.complaintsboard.com is one site, and www.consumeraffairs.com/online/craigslist.html is another. People complain about being scammed, products being defective, and their postings being deleted by craigslist with no explanation, even when they keep contacting the site. Most of the trouble that craigslist has had with city governments has to do with minors potentially being abused and/or prostitution taking place via the **personals** or **erotic services** part of the site.

If you've spent any time in the craigslist community, however, and particularly if you've spent some time reading the blogs of Craig Newmark and Jim Buckmaster, you'll see that they go to great lengths to correct any errors or offenses. Reading over the complaints about craigslist on various websites, it's obvious that the majority if not all of the complainers did not take the time to read through all the pages on craigslist that explain the rules. If they had they might consider the following items on the craigslist factsheet:

◆ craigslist uses a ".org" domain because it "symbolizes the relatively noncommercial nature of craigslist, as well as our service mission and noncorporate culture."

◆ craigslist gets more than 12 billion page views per month, #8 worldwide in terms of english-language page views.

◆ More than 50 million people use craigslist each month, including more than 40 million in the United States alone.

◆ craigslist users self-publish more than 30 million new classified ads each month.

◆ More than 2 million new job listings are posted each month.

◆ More than 10 million new images are posted each month.

◆ There are more than 100 million user postings in 100 discussion forums each month.

All this is administered by 25 people working out of "a victorian house in the Inner Sunset neighborhood of San Francisco." And might we add, *most of the listings, worldwide, are FREE.*

We suggest that anyone using craigslist take our advice and read through all the suggested pages on the site as well as the blogs, and keep in mind that you're using the site for free. If you have a problem, please try the discussion forums. All things considered, craigslist is an excellent contribution to us all, and it should be helped more than complained about.

List Losers

If you're on craigslist to make money, there are some discussion forums you should stay away from completely because they are social forums. For example, **p.o.c** is for "People of Color" and **rofo** is Romantic Advice. If you try to do business there, you might get flamed, and you might have to browse the **etiquet** (etiquette) forum to learn how to get people to watch their manners.

Using Small Claims Court

If you find you have to sue someone you're having trouble with, use this directory of courts in the Unites States: www.statelocalgov.net/50states-courts.cfm.

In California, claims up to $5,000 are handled in small claims court, which would usually cover a majority of craigslist transactions. Check www.legalzoom.com and click on **Small Claims** in the column on the left. Once you've selected your state you'll reach a page that features an Education Center offering Small Claims Education, an FAQ, and Glossary. Whether you have your claim filed via LegalZoom or not, you'll find out what you need to know about small claims in your area.

In most jurisdictions you cannot have a lawyer argue your case in small claims court. If your problem rises beyond small claims, though, you'll probably need a good legal eagle. While many aspects of Internet-related law remain somewhat unsettled, there are lawyers who specialize in such things. A good one is The Internet Law Center, founded in September 2007 by Bennet Kelley. With offices in Santa Monica, California, and Washington, D.C., the firm focuses on "helping businesses navigate the challenges of the digital economy," while providing "comprehensive solutions for businesses both online and offline." You can find them at: www.internetlawcenter.net.

We hope you never need to go to any kind of court over a transaction that began on craigslist. If you do, however, we wish you the best of luck.

The Least You Need to Know

- More than 100 barter transactions on craigslist and/or other barter-enabling sites (which are numerous) are subject to taxation by the IRS.

- You can determine a fair price for your item or service not only by checking competitors on craigslist but also eBay and its competitors.

- Cash, checks, PayPal, and other methods of payment all have drawbacks, but with some education and diligence, it's unlikely you'll get burned.

- If hiring employees via craigslist, it is essential that you keep your employment agreements in writing.

- Most common complaints about craigslist could be avoided completely if people simply read the warnings available on the site.

◆ When craigslist transactions end up in a legal battle, most of them will fall under the purview of small claims in most U.S. jurisdictions, so users of craigslist should familiarize themselves with how small claims courts work.

Chapter 10

Using Similar Sites

In This Chapter

- Backpage competition
- Kijiji from eBay
- If only placing an ad
- Sites for service providers
- Other explorations

While craigslist began as a hobby for Craig Newmark in 1995, the site's imitators and competitors that have sprung up are mostly geared toward making money. They often copy the craigslist style, with many offering more emphasis on visual. One that we cover in this chapter was most likely started because craigslist would not allow itself to be bought. All have something to offer you, because you can repost your ad from craigslist on each site.

Backpage, craigslist's Competitor

The site www.backpage.com is organized by metro area, with slightly under 100 of them listed on the home page. Most are in the United States, with a few in Canada, one in Puerto Rico, and another in a place you definitely don't want to go in person, Tijuana, Mexico. The slogan at the bottom of the page reads: "Place a free classified ad with photo. Find houses for rent, apts for rent, local jobs, and local for sale classifieds on backpage.com."

You see the categories only after you select a metro area. The column categories include:

community	musician	jobs	personals
Automotive	rentals	forums	adult
buy/sell/trade	real estate		services

On the categories page, the metro areas are listed in the far right column, above which you'll see **Post in multiple cities.** When you post a local ad, it's "mostly free" while posting in multiple cities is for paid sponsor ads only, which the site says is: "Ideal for employers with positions in multiple cities, or anybody looking to reach users nationwide or in more than one location. Sponsor ads stay on the top or right-hand side of the page." This gives you "the ability to post paid sponsor ads in over 100 cities with one posting form." Setting up an account is easy. You simply type in your email address twice, then your chosen password twice.

List Notes

In contrast to craigslist ads, a welcome difference on Backpage is an "enlarge picture" option on listings with photos. The enlarged picture is over three times larger, 640 × 480 pixels, while original pictures are 200 × 150. That's substantial, if you're inspecting details.

Backpage aims to make using its site as easy as sending an email, and more fun. It's owned and operated by the Village Voice Media, from offices in Phoenix and Dallas. They have partnerships with "local newspapers, alternative newsweeklies, and other media outlets." They approach craigslist in number of views. As of the writing of this book, they were receiving over half a billion page views per month, according to

Alexa.com, with the largest percentage of its users (11.5 percent) coming from Houston, Texas.

How It's Like craigslist

Backpage has a **Terms of Use** (TOU) link on the bottom menu. Its tenets are very similar to those of craigslist. The site is, like craigslist, heavily involved with New York real estate brokers, and offers them RSS feeds. See http://newyork.backpage.com/online/bulkupload/ Documentation for more information. Placing a local ad is about the same as with craigslist. You don't need an account. You simply click on a metro area, then a section (one of the items in the columns listed previously), then a category, and you're ready to write your ad. Next, you preview it, then you're sent an email with a link just like craigslist, and you're done. You may include up to four images, just like craigslist, and you can anonymize your email address, too.

The site favors the "all lowercase" format of craigslist for the most part. There is a **search** box at the top like craigslist, and you adjust it with a category button. The cities within each listed metro area are almost identical to those within craigslist areas, but generally you'll find more cities grouped together in larger areas, because there simply aren't as many listings as you find on craigslist.

How It's Different

There is a bit more verbiage in the Backpage Terms of Use agreement covering legalities and absolving the site against any abuses you think you might suffer by using it. The site gives a Phoenix, Arizona, address, a fax number, and an email address for redress on the Terms of Use page, but it singles out users in California, stating:

> If you are a California resident, you waive any rights you may have under California Civil Code §1542, which states: "A general release does not extend to claims which the creditor does not know or suspect to exist in his favor at the time of executing the release, which if known by him must have materially affected his settlement with the debtor."

The site also has a more succinct statement about its ability to terminate your right to use it, and throws in some legalities in that statement
as well:

Termination of Access:

*The Site has the right to terminate your access for any reason if we
believe you have violated these Terms in any manner. You agree not
to hold the Site liable for such termination, and further agree not to
attempt to use the Site after termination.*

While craigslist offers its site in many languages, a feature you'll find
only when you reach the pages of sites outside the United States (such
as the four-language option in Switzerland), Backpage offers only a
Spanish language option, but it displays "sitio en Español" on each
page.

Like craigslist, you have to register to post on the forums, but that only
consists of telling them your birth date (which they make no attempt to
verify). You choose a "handle" and password for the forums, and as on
craigslist, you cannot post ads in the forums. You also have to check off
that you've read and agree to abide by the backpage.com forums rules.

> **Online Heat**
>
> Backpage offers an affiliate
> program that can earn you
> 10 percent on referrals for
> 30 days after they sign up.
> As posted on the site blog at
> http://blog.backpage.com,
> you only need to post a text
> link or banner ad for back-
> page.com on your website
> or blog and the site does the
> rest.

The listings can get flagged just as
on craigslist but they call it a *report*,
and you have the choice of "inappro-
priate content" or "wrong category"
or "over posted."

When placing ads on Backpage,
you can also create a map link for
your ad (not offered by craigslist).
You also have the option of showing
links to your other postings in the
buy/sell/trade section, which is good
for anyone wanting to sell a lot of
merchandise.

These ads are also tied into the news outlets that are mentioned in the
About section on the site. For example, in Memphis, Tennessee, your
ad is tied into the *Memphis Flyer* online.

When you view an ad, you can choose a brief or full view, and within the ad you can choose Google or Yahoo directions to the seller if he or she has chosen this option.

To post a paid sponsor ad—which allows you to post in multiple cities—you click on **Post in multiple cities** at www.backpage.com/classifieds/central/PostNationalAd, then choose a section, then a category, and then you'll see a page where you can choose all the metro areas you want to reach. You can buy an ad to run for up to 52 weeks. Prices vary by area, from 15¢ for an ad in Tuscaloosa, Alabama, to $6.72 in San Diego, California. The prices are totaled, so that if you wanted your ad to run in both Tuscaloosa and San Diego, the ad would cost you $6.87. A line on the multiple posting page states: "Post expires in 45 days or longer, depending on sponsor ad purchase." You can also buy a discounted package:

- ◆ 4 weeks for 25 percent discount

- ◆ 12 weeks for 33 percent discount

- ◆ 26 weeks for 50 percent discount

Presumably, 50 percent is the lowest discount, even if you buy 52 weeks worth of ads. If you choose multiple city postings, the minimum purchase required is 99¢. After that, placing the ad is the same as a simple listing, with the exception of requiring company information "in case a customer service representative needs to contact you. This information will NOT appear in your ad." They also require a valid phone number for contact info in this category, and the phone number is displayed with the ad. You also have the option of automatically reposting your ad to the top of the listings every seven days. The cost is $1.50 for 4 times, $3.00 for 8 times, $4.50 for 12 times, and $9.00 for 26 automatic reposts to the top.

Backpage offers a **Popular Searches** link at the bottom of each metro area page, which can cut down your search time if you're seeking something specific.

All told, Backpage is easily navigable and should be attractive to people wanting multiple postings, as long as they're willing to pay for it, because it has the added attraction of being connected to local publications in the metro areas selected.

Kijiji, Challenger from eBay

Kijiji.com generally gets slightly less traffic than Backpage but has on occasion passed it in web traffic. On the United States home page at www.kijiji.com, the banner states that Kijiji is "Your Free Local Classified Ad Web Site" and that you can "Use Kijiji to buy & sell new and used goods, look for cars and pets, find local real estate, and more." You are prompted to click a local area, select a state (there's a map of the United States there), or enter a zip code. A link for Kijiji Canada (http://toronto.kijiji.ca) is at the upper right. Cities and areas are grouped under states, and at the bottom of the page is a list of countries/regions that have Kijiji sites. If you enter a zip code, the site will show another map and give you a list of nearby cities from which to pick. Once you've picked a city, the maps disappear and you reach the main Kijiji page. The categories you then see (each with many subcategories) are:

For sale	Jobs	Pets
Services	Resumes	Housing
	Cars & vehicles	Vacation rentals
	Community	Events

At the bottom of the page there is a place for success stories from those using Kijiji, along with links to other cities and the countries/regions.

> ### List Notes
>
> Kijiji offers no Personals or Erotic Services categories like craigslist. It's more graphic-friendly with picture ads on each page and pictures in classifieds, making it a much more family-friendly classifieds website.

On the right are links to other cities in your area, and below that an event calendar. (You can post an event if you have something coming up.) To the right of each category or section, the site shows you how many ads like it are posted. For example, at the time of this writing under Vacation Rentals there were (102865) listed with the subcategories being Americas, Europe, and Rest of World.

The site has an RSS feed feature and also a Widget: you copy the embed code for JavaScript, Flash, or MySpace and paste it in at your blog or web page.

At the top of your local page you'll find five tabs:

- ◆ **Browse Ads** (with a drop-down arrow for quick selection of a category)

- ◆ **Post Ad** (with an electronic Post-It reminding you the ads are free)

- ◆ **My Kijiji** (for those with an account)

- ◆ **Discussion** (the forums)

- ◆ **Help**

Below the tabs is a **search** box defaulted to All Ads, with a drop-down arrow to change it to one of the main categories.

You have the choice of setting up an account, or you can manage your ads using your email address alone. Unlike craigslist and other sites, you can Post an Ad, Promote your Ads, Edit your Ad, Remove your Ad, or access "My Watchlist" without signing up.

My Watchlist allows you to keep track of an ad and what's happening with it, much like a similar function on eBay, which brings up the origin of Kijiji. According to the About page:

> *The word "Kijiji" (pronounced key-gee-gee) means "village" in Swahili. This word captures the essence of what we are creating—a community where members can connect with one another to exchange goods, ideas, and services.*

The site lists a company address in the Netherlands on the About page, but the fact is, it was started by eBay to compete with craigslist, and run overseas for a couple of years before debuting in the United States in 2007. If you do the math, its easy to see that the 2004 eBay buy of a 25 percent stake in craigslist from a former employee, giving it a seat on the craigslist board of directors, gave it a deep look into the operations of craigslist before it began a competing service. This makes the legal battle between eBay and craigslist a lot easier to understand.

Registering on Kijiji requires only filling out your email address and choosing a password. You also have the option of choosing a Nickname and registering your Skype name and letting others contact you via Skype. Once you've registered, you get your own page with three tabs: **My Ads, My Watchlist,** and **My Profile** (where you can choose a Nickname and enter your Skype name if you haven't already). If you want to participate in the Discussion forums, you must have a Nickname. Also, if you are a registered user, your ads go onto the site immediately, instead of requiring you to deal with a follow-up email.

List Losers

On the Help page you'll see **Terms & Conditions** as the last category in the left column. At the bottom of the page there is a **Terms of Use** link. Clicking on either takes you to exactly the same page.

Kijiji has a **Terms of Use** link and a **Popular Searches** link like backpage.com. They offer a **Customer Service** page, another for **Policies,** and a **Frequently Asked Questions** page that covers everything you might need to know about the site in a cleanly presented manner.

Like craigslist, Kijiji does not want people posting ads in more than one location. You are limited to 25 Ads per person per day, and the site screens ads for "potentially offensive language." Ads expire 60 days after being posted. They are displayed by picture first if they have one, and you click on **View Details** to see the ad. If the poster does not provide an email address, you can contact them via a text box on the right, but you have to type in a "captcha" Verification Code to get the message sent. Ads can be reported for the following reasons:

◆ Fraud/Scam/Offensive

◆ Spam/Duplicate

◆ No Longer Available/Outdated

◆ Wrong Category

◆ Copyright or Trademark Violation

The forums include Suggestions & Feedback, a General Chat Forum, and areas for discussing Family, Pets, Vehicles, and Housing. There are also discussions in other languages, and a Who Is Online area. Like the listings, you will find in parentheses the number of threads in each forum, such as "General Chat Forum (48984)" which helps you get an idea of who is talking about what, and where.

Kijiji has a family-friendly, attractive look and is easy navigation, but it's still a long way from the influence of the site it set out to compete with, craigslist.

If You're Just Placing an Ad

Some sites in competition with craigslist don't try to get very fancy. They find their own way, and maybe a better way, to present what they have available in ads. Often enough, people come upon them by chance, or perhaps get upset with craigslist or another site and do a web search for similar sites. You might find one that you favor, or you might want to learn about the ins and outs of them all and take advantage of the benefits of each site.

Oodles of Ads

Founded by former Excite and eBay executives, Oodle at www.oodle. com keeps coming on strong. Its motto is "Oodle is reinventing classifieds." It advertises itself as the fastest growing classifieds service and the statistics back that up. Oodle is an aggregator. It pulls together and organizes millions of listings from all over the web. Have a read at http://www.oodle.com/info/about and see. Oodle is a very inviting site, with pictured listings right there on the opening page. There are three steps on Oodle:

1. Tell us what you're looking for.

2. See local listings from over 80,000 websites.

3. Get email updates when new matches pop up.

How simple can it get? The site has a Safety Center, a blog, a Prohibited Content area, and a long list of categories down the left side. According to the site, it adds "more than 600,000 new classifieds listings every day." You can search in the United States, the United Kingdom, Canada, India, and Ireland. Posting an ad is free, in four steps. Registering and getting an Oodle Account is very simple and gives you free email alerts about new listings and lets you manage the ads you post. Multiple posts are allowed. All told, Oodle is such a friendly site we think you won't have any trouble at all navigating it, so have a look and find out.

The Classified Ads Site

Classified Ads at www.classifiedads.com (did you guess?) invites you to "Post a free ad" at the top of the page, and offers nine categories:

> Jobs & Employment
> Vehicles
> Items for Sale
> Pets
> Real Estate
> For Rent
> Services
> Personals
> Community

At the top right you'll see the word "Earth" and underneath that, a link to change location. Your choices, you'll discover, are extensive: United States, Canada, United Kingdom, Australia and Pacific, Caribbean, and India. Clicking on any of those areas gives you an array of choices, and you can also set a location in a zip code box as well.

Skip's Tips

As you discovered in Chapter 9, there are many sites similar to craigslist. One in the United Kingdom ranks higher than any in this chapter for traffic, according to the web traffic site Alexa.com. Take a look at **www.gumtree.com** for classifieds in London.

When you arrive on the site, on the lower half of the page you'll see under "Today's New Classifieds" a list of truncated classified ads with a corresponding picture to the right of each. At the bottom of the page is a list of cities and areas under the label "Most Popular Communities." And beneath that, links to: Log In (for registered users); Locations; Legal stuff; and Questions? It's a very nicely presented and inviting opening page.

We advise reading www.classifiedads.com/info.php?help, the Questions? page, first, because it covers everything and provides links to all you need to know about how the site works. It even lets you know that you can post five pictures, not the four you're used to on other sites. Setting up an account is extremely easy, as is everything on the site.

You might wonder, how do sites like these make money? Well, sometimes when you click on a category, on the resultant page on the bottom half you'll see "sponsored links" (paid ads). When writing this book we even saw one for Kijiji.com on the Jobs & Employment page at Classified Ads. Posting an ad takes only three simple steps after entering your email address, name (you can use a nickname), location (city), how you found out about Classified Ads, and agree to the Terms of Use. You can edit your ad and attach images after posting the ad. All ads are 100 percent free but there is a link called **report abuse/ miscategorized** for site users to click if they think you've wrongly posted.

The Community category is like a big electronic bulletin board where you can post under the following subcategories: Announcements, Carpool, Churches, Free Stuff, Garage Sales, General Entertainment, Items Wanted, Lost & Found, Musicians & Bands, and Volunteers. Other than that facility, there is nothing like a discussion forum on the site.

It's a friendly site and although it gets much less traffic than Kijiji, it's not much of a hassle to post your ad and keep track of it.

Sites If You Offer a Service

Some people are smart. They figure out a need and fill it. They find a niche that is largely unserved and do a great job providing something people need, and fortune and fame follow. So while craigslist has had many imitators, those are mostly geared toward people who are selling products or seeking jobs. The two sites that follow concentrate on things that would be listed in the **services** area of craigslist and take that idea to a whole new level.

Angie's List

For anyone looking for a professional, Angie's List is, as they say in urban lingo, "the bomb." Founded by Angie Hicks in 1995 with 1,000 members in Columbus, Ohio, the site has become so successful it now pays for media ads to draw people to the site. You have to pay a fee to use Angie's List, which you can see at www.angieslist.com/AngiesList/Visitor/price.aspx. You have the choice of a Monthly Payment Plan, an Annual, or a Multi-Year Payment Plan. There are no refunds.

Membership fees are reasonable and determined according to your zip code. According to Angie, "More than 750,000 consumers use Angie's List to find high quality service companies and health care professionals in over 400 categories."

List Losers

You cannot pay to list your service on Angie's List. If you want to get reviewed and listed, urge your customers to join the site and rate you for others. It might even pay you in the long-term to pay for their membership for the first month.

Take a look at www.angieslist.com/SPDirectory to see all the companies rated by the site, by area. If you're going to spend hundreds or thousands of dollars hiring a professional, you should take advantage of this word-of-mouth network for consumers based on "homeowners' real-life experiences with local service companies." Angie's blog at www.angiehicksblog.com will keep you current with developments on the site.

Trusty's: Service You Can Trust

At www.trustys.com, Trusty's is similar to Angie's List but has a much more small-town feel. It's also different in that it's *free*. Service providers and small business owners can create profiles and get reviews and ratings from clients. According to the site, "Members can search, browse and sort for service providers based on a reputation, location, price, quality of service, and specialties. They can communicate, share advice, seek referrals, or build relationships across the community. Trusty's replicates traditional, small-town, word-of-mouth recommendations for help, but on a much broader scale."

You can search for a service, job title, or name and by city, state, or zip. (It's primarily a U.S. site.) Services are organized by category on the left side of the page, and the blog at http://blog.trustys.com offers excellent advice on doing business in general. You join the site at http://www.trustys.com/signup; it couldn't be more simple. The *Washington Post* favorably reviewed Trusty's as "Yelp Meets LinkedIn For Blue-Collar Workers." We like it a lot, too, and not just because it's free.

Others Worth Exploring

You can find a full list of similar sites ranked by traffic at http://siteslikecraigslist.com/the-ranked-list-of-sites-like-craigslist. As you'll see, it's a long list, and from that page you can click on each site and explore every one. You'll probably be exhausted, but by the time you're done, you'll be an expert in online classifieds. Happy searching!

The Least You Need to Know

◆ Backpage.com is a lot like craigslist, perhaps a bit more simple, and has the added advantage of tying into ads in local publications.

◆ Kijiji.com is a craigslist competitor developed by eBay that is more family-friendly and is more graphically oriented.

◆ Sites like Oodle.com and ClassifiedAds.com take a broader, aggregator approach in emulating craigslist and offer unique possibilities.

◆ If you offer a service, there's Angie's List and Trusty's and they each have individual appeal, with Trusty's being free.

◆ You can keep track of sites like craigslist and access them easily from your browser by reading http://siteslikecraigslist.com.

Part 3

Jobs, Jobs, Jobs

On craigslist there are two types of employment: jobs and gigs. In this part you learn the differences in all the categories on the main page, as well as how craigslist compares to other job boards on the web. Major companies use the site now, so whether you want to work for one, or become such a company someday, you learn what you need to know here about resumes, staffing, and even ways to make money as a writer!

Chapter 11

Understanding the Jobs and Gigs Categories

In This Chapter

- ◆ Placing a job ad
- ◆ Placing a gig ad
- ◆ Understanding job categories
- ◆ Keep those gigs coming
- ◆ Beating out other applicants

It's a maze out there trying to find a job, particularly in a lessened economy. On the flip side, while you might get a hundred or more responses to a job ad you place, if people are desperate they will ignore desired credentials in a listing and send their resume anyway, hoping for the best. With a gig listing for a position that could lead to something full-time, you might be able to screen people who are willing to work part-time and prove themselves. On the other hand, the more serious applicants might not look in the gigs ads, but concentrate on the job listings instead. In this chapter, we hope that you gain some tips to help you sort out where to look and where to advertise for maximum efficiency, depending on your needs.

Who Places a Job Ad

When you create a job posting at $25 per listing per category, you're asked to select where you want to post it. Therefore, it pays to review the other types of listings available. That is, the possible category or categories suitable for your listing. In general, people post a job ad when they're offering employment that is more long-term than temporary, so keep that in mind whether you're listing or browsing for a job.

If you're an employer and you're looking for someone with a particular skill, it might be wise to save your money and time and do some searching first. As craigslist advises: "Search the resume category, it's free!" The person you're looking for may be waiting for you there.

Legalities and regulations come into play when placing job listings, so it wouldn't hurt to familiarize yourself with that type of thing if you're an employer. Once you've selected the category for your ad and the area in which it will be displayed, you'll be directed to the page where you'll write your ad, and you'll find choices to check off (or not) that include a box for describing the compensation as well as selections for the time period for the job, the type (such as internship), if telecommuting is okay, and whether phone calls by the applicant and/or recruiters are acceptable. You can also choose to highlight the job opening for persons with disabilities, meaning that disadvantaged people can more easily find such listings.

Compensation: [please be as detailed as possible]

☐ telecommuting ok ☐ part-time ☐ contract ☐ non-profit organization ☐ internship
☐ direct contact by recruiters is ok ☐ phone calls to you about this job are ok
☐ ok to highlight this job opening for persons with disabilities [?]

Qualify the type of job you want.

While many businesses have a 30-day to six-month probationary period for new personnel before they're considered permanent, familiarize yourself with laws about such things in your area. At http://employeeissues.com/probationary_period.htm you'll find a wealth of information. It says about such trials: "… the underlying agenda is to have the right to fire the new employee without good cause, under the Doctrine of Employment at Will." When you hire someone from a craigslist ad and they believe it is a "permanent" position, there will be certain benefits required by law that you'll have to deal with. That's why it's important that you think through the particular choices available when placing your ad, because if you don't delineate them in the listing and then you have someone work with or for you beyond a period when the law considers them permanent, you cannot fire them without "good cause" (the Doctrine of Good Will which you can find explained at the Employee Issues link given earlier).

> **List Notes**
>
> Read about hiring persons with disabilities (and why that might be a good business idea) at www.craigslist.org/about/disabilities. It's a comprehensive page with lots of helpful links to things like how to earn federal tax credits.

In short, people who respond to a listing in the **jobs** category are expecting something that might become permanent, unless stated otherwise. If you are a job applicant, it also behooves you to understand your legal rights so that you don't encounter a situation where an employer hires people promising something permanent, then lets them go just before the legal time limit. Save a copy of their original craigslist ad, because if it was misleading and you've been defrauded, it might help you against the offending employer in court.

While most employers placing ads for employees on craigslist are small businesses, which are more likely to hire people as independent contractors that receive a 1099 tax form rather than the W-9 of the regular employee, there are major companies hiring from craigslist. They will know the employment laws, and so should you.

Recruiters are allowed to post job listings on craigslist if they follow a few stated guidelines:

◆ Please identify yourself and make sure you include this information within your posting.

◆ No resume fishing, no bait and switch, and no other dishonest or misleading tactics. We're here to help each other out!

◆ Please do not post in the resumes category—direct principals only.

You cannot post a job fair on craigslist, and they ask that you not post multiple jobs in one listing. Also, if you post a link that goes to your own website where there are listings, they ask that it does not link to a full page of jobs but to one detailing a single job description.

Everything is clearly explained and straightforward, so if you post a job listing and run into trouble, it might just be because you didn't take the time to read all the things that you should have.

Who Places a Gigs Ad

If craigslist ever did a study and posted it, it's a good guess that a majority of people trying to find personnel via the site wouldn't be sure about the definition of "gig." When you're placing an ad for a gig, you can offer people the choice of "pay" or "no-pay" so that might be a clue. Although "internship" is a choice in the **jobs** listings, that implies that if someone does well, it could lead to a permanent position. And that speaks to the basic definition of "gig" on craigslist; you expect it to last a certain period of time. After all, when you're creating a listing, "gig offered" is a completely separate choice and the site offers this explanation: **(I'm hiring for a short-term, small, or odd job)**. A lot of talent, such as photographers, models, actors, directors, musicians, and student filmmakers, use the gigs section to announce projects, such as student films and bands seeking musicians, which might not pay immediately.

> **Skip's Tips**
>
> If you have a strong competitor and want to discover ways to beat them, get some free help from the website Hitwise. See www.hitwise.com/info/us-competitor-report-offer.php for details.

That's why the gigs categories are far fewer than the choices in the jobs subcategories. When creating a gigs listing, you find the following choices:

◆ Adult gigs (modeling / talent / film / etc. for adult industry)

◆ Computer gigs (small web design, tech support, etc. projects)

- Creative gigs (small design, photography, illustration projects)

- Crew gigs (low budget film / theatre opportunities EXCEPT acting, which go under "talent")

- Domestic gigs (cleaning, babysitting, home care, tutoring, personal training, etc)

- Event gigs (promotions, catering, wedding photography, etc.)

- Labor gigs (includes moving & hauling)

- Talent gigs (acting, modeling, music, dance, etc.)

- Writing gigs (includes editing & translation)

"Adult industry" means exactly what you think it does, pornography, which we won't cover here. Just as craigslist offers "erotic services," it reaches out to that side of employment as well. What do you expect, from a site that was begun in socially liberal San Francisco? Such ads are dangerous, anyway. At the time of this writing, a "craigslist killer" was being sought by police in the Boston area. He answered prostitutes and "massage" ads and then killed them.

It's probably not too hard to find a potential gig category listed previously that will fit your particular professional talent. So you'd search under gigs if you're seeking employment, but if you want people to find you, you'll have to choose **service offered** when creating a posting. Just to make sure this is clear, if you click on **gigs offered** craigslist will ask you "Do you want to hire someone for a short-term gig, or are you offering a service?" and give you two choices on which to click:

- I want to hire someone

- I have a service to offer

If you click on the latter, you'll be taken to the same page you would have landed on if you had originally selected **service offered** when creating a posting.

So what do you do if you're looking for someone who is a bit of a jack-of-all-trades as many creative people are? What if you'd like to find someone who does web design (computer gigs) but you also have a need for other types of design and photography (creative gigs). You can post the same ad in different categories and alter the headline, but you never know if someone will flag that ad because they think you're spamming. That's why it's best to alter the ad, tailoring it to the specific service you need, in both the headline and the text of the listing itself.

Look at it this way—if you're looking for a specific gig, such as web design, wouldn't you rather find it easily with a simple search? As previously stated, success is all about specificity. If you look through the services offered or in the resumes area to find someone you need, you want to save time, so think about how it looks to the reader and post as specifically as possible. You could advertise for "versatile media expert needed" but that's so general you might get applicants that will waste a lot of your time. A headline like that could get you resumes from public relations people who have no layout or design skills.

Whether you're looking for a gig or offering one, if you try to think through what the other person on the other end wants, you'll probably end up with a much better situation.

Understanding Jobs by Category

Everything about placing craigslist job listings is explained at www. craigslist.org/about/help/faq-job.

List Losers _____

If you're involved in network marketing, forget listing on craigslist. The site very clearly prohibits listings including "any franchise, pyramid scheme, multi-level marketing, 'club membership', distributorship or sales representative agency arrangement." See prohibited jobs at www. craigslist.org/about/help/faq-job. Click on the line "What kind of job posts do you not accept?"

Most of the categories are self-explanatory and any normal person can understand them merely from the column on the main page. Have a look:

> accounting+finance
> admin / office
> arch / engineering

art / media / design
biotech / science
business / mgmt
customer service
education
food / bev / hosp
general labor
government
human resources
internet engineers
legal / paralegal
manufacturing
marketing / pr / ad
medical / health
nonprofit sector
real estate
retail / wholesale
sales / biz dev
salon / spa / fitness
security
skilled trade / craft
software / qa / dba
systems / network
technical support
transport
tv / film / video
web / info design
writing / editing
[ETC] [part time]

As with most things on the main page, you have to click on a line to get an expanded category, but it might not expand to what you think it will. For example, **sales / biz dev** expands merely to "sales jobs" not "sales / business development." So when you're placing an ad, if you have any uncertainty at all where it might belong, click on the various links and do some reading of the other listings there to see if it really fits.

The **ETC** category is a catchall of listings. You might find a need for sperm donors there, and listings for people to participate in medical research. It might seem more logical to put listings like that under **biotech / science,** but remember, this is the **jobs** category and jobs usually equate in people's minds with longer-term employment. So why wouldn't such jobs be listed under **part time?** It's because part-time implies continuing employment less than full-time (40 hours a week in the United States). You might think, wouldn't that be a "gig"? No, because a gig implies employment that lasts for a specific amount of time, because the term originated in the music industry to describe a booking.

If you're involved in the computer industry in any way, it could be confusing about which category to use, so let's cover that quickly with the categories in that arena:

arch / engineering—Yes, computers come into play here. If you're looking for a job in Computer-Aided Design (CAD) you'll find it here.

internet engineers—This area covers development and programming. You'll find things like "SEO engineer" and "Flash developer" as well as deeper programming needs.

software / qa / dba—The site doesn't define the latter two terms. Quality Assurance is **qa,** and a **dba** is a Database Administrator.

systems / network—You'll find all sorts of jobs here, including Network Administrator and Helpdesk Support. Think big networks and you'll have the idea of this category.

technical support—One would think that a Helpdesk Support position would be listed here, but as we've said, people don't always take the time to understand the categories before posting. You might find "Linux System Administrator" here even though you're sure it should be in **systems / network.**

web / info design—You'll mostly find web design jobs here, but you might see a need for a "Search Engine Optimization (SEO) Specialist" that might seem more appropriate under **internet engineers.**

Take some time to go through the categories studying the various listings. If you're looking for a job and you know the specific term that describes what you do, or want to do, it might be smarter to simply use the search box on the main page, set the category button for **jobs,** and look that way, so that you'll be shown "SEO Specialist" listings from all the job categories. After all, craigslist jobs are posted by humans, many of whom might not have thought through what they are doing, for maximum effectiveness.

Skip's Tips

Have your own website? If you're running a craigs-list ad under **Services Offered** post a link to it on your website, or use that link at the bottom of emails. Most people don't mind clicking on something like that even out of curiosity, and it might bring you some business or get you a job.

Keeping the Gigs Coming

The bane of the freelance life is having to promote for new work at the same time you're trying to deliver work already contracted. Some people handle it by blocking out a certain portion of the day, or days of the week, to devote to promotion and advertising.

For a small business there are similar challenges, and even if you have employees to take care of such things, even at the smallest level, the administration of the business, dealing with invoices, taxes, and scheduling, can often take up a great deal of time, leaving little for getting the word out. Ads in the Yellow Pages, flyers handed out, and bulk emailing can come into play, but those are expensive and also time-consuming.

There's a way to use craigslist more economically to save time and spend little money, however. Depending on your business, you might get onto other sites like Angieslist.com from a client referral, but other folks like computer personnel or creative types will have to get noticed in other ways. The first step you can take to stay noticed via craigslist is to keep a resume posted there. As the site says, it's free, and you can change the resume as your work history changes. The listings last a normal time but you can delete or edit them as desired, so take advantage of that. In addition, when you click on **resumes** you'll see on the top right a clickable link titled "success story?" If you go to that page, you'll be able to share with others. As the page says: "If you've experienced a notable or unusual craigslist success story, please let us know!"

At the bottom of that page you'll see two check boxes that you can check to allow craigslist to share your story on the site, or craig's blog, or with the media.

Tell craigslist whether or not they can use your story.

☑ it's OK to reprint this story on craigslist (or craig's blog)
☑ it's OK to share this story with media

Submit Story

Once you have a resume onsite, post an ad under **services** and put a note on your computer calendar to be alerted a couple of days before your resume and services ads expire. [Note: the services ads expire in seven days so you'll have to stay on top of it.]

Then, either spend some time each day or set aside a specific day or time during the week to search craigslist for more gigs. If it's appropriate, don't forget to use www.crazedlist.org to search the gigs across the country or around the world. It's a fairly simple system, and you probably wouldn't be able to rely on this for all your business, but it's a more efficient use of craigslist to keep gigs coming. And if you do have your own website and your success story gets mentioned on craigslist, or craig's blog, or in the media, you can link that on your site, and everybody wins.

Errors Replying to Ads?

If you respond to a job ad and your email bounces back, the ad could have been deleted by the poster. Other reasons it could bounce back are explained on these pages:

> www.craigslist.org/about/help/generic_DNS

> www.craigslist.org/about/help/rdns_failure

The former is a simpler fix, with explanations on the page, and if that doesn't work they suggest you contact postmaster@craigslist.org.

With the latter, it's more complex but well explained, and they offer you the option of using the help forum (with a clickable line) to get suggestions from other users.

If you try to send a large file when responding to a craigslist ad, you may find your email rejected because your attachment was too large and rejected by the filters on the craigslist servers. In that case, you'll get a rejection email from craigslist that explains how large of an attachment you are allowed. So don't fire off that PowerPoint presentation right away. Explain in your response that you have one available that you'd be happy to send along, and when you get an email from a nontemporary craigslist address, then you can send the file.

Usually, however, you'll have few problems when responding to ads. They work hard at craigslist to keep it smooth. Whether you're hiring, or looking for a job or gig, we're wishing you good luck!

The Least You Need to Know

◆ If you take the time to understand the various craigslist job categories and follow the rules in posting, you might be surprised at the responses.

◆ The more specific you are in writing your ad and selecting its proper category or categories, the more likely you are to get the desired result.

◆ A craigslist job listing is employment considered to possibly be permanent. A craigslist gig is employment for a short-term, or a small or odd job.

◆ When placing a gigs ad, you're offered a choice of that or listing under **services offered** so make sure you get it right or it could be deleted.

◆ Errors that occur when replying to job ads are explained at www. craigslist.org/about/help under the category **harassment, legal stuff, spam, email.**

12

Major Companies and craigslist

In This Chapter

- ◆ Craigslist's corporate reputation
- ◆ Other ad outlet costs
- ◆ You will be screened …
- ◆ Locating companies regionally
- ◆ Beating out other applicants

Never forget, craigslist started out as a hobby when Craig Newmark was just trying to help some friends. As long as he is involved with the site, though, it's our guess that the community orientation of craigslist will continue. After all, it really hasn't changed much in 15 years, and that means no banner ads like most sites. Still, they have to make money somehow to stay on the web. A great deal of that income arises from job listings, and that's what this chapter discusses.

The craigslist Corporate Reputation

There are 32 categories to choose from in placing a job listing. If you ever wonder whether your occupation, or desired occupation, is listed on craigslist, click on **create posting** and then choose **job offered.** You'll see expanded descriptions of the categories under the **jobs** banner on the main page. On the **create posting** page further down you'll see beside **gig offered** the explanation "I'm hiring for a short-term, small, or odd job."

The site differentiates between these two as a public service, so that people seeking full-time, long-term jobs don't waste their time sorting through temporary listings. Even though looking at the employment ads are free for users, if the listings are not well-sorted and policed, with scammers kept as far away as possible, people will surf to other job sites and ignore craigslist.

With the .com sites that are solely about jobs, like BestJobsUSA, Career, CareerBuilder, JobBankUSA, Monster, and Net-Temps, the listings are expensive for employers and often don't last much longer than those on craigslist. For example, one listing on JobBankUSA is $350 for 60 days. In contrast, it's $25 on craigslist for 45 days, and there is not really a template to use in filling out the listing as with many sites. So job seekers are likely to get a less "boilerplate-" type description in a craigslist ad. Whether you're offering a job or seeking one, that's attractive, and yet another example of how craigslist upholds a corporate reputation of being helpful to communities.

Cost Comparison of Other Ad Outlets

Let's take a brief look at what some of the top job site ad listings cost. This might help if you're offering jobs, and if you're looking for one, you might want to know how much a company pays to find you. According to the ConsumerSearch website (see www.consumersearch.com/job-sites), the top job sites on which employers pay to list are as follows:

Yahoo! HotJobs (deemed "best large job site" by ConsumerSearch) at http://hotjobs.yahoo.com lets an employer post a job in any U.S. location. The site "instantly recommends candidates" matched to a job post, so that the employer can choose the most qualified resumes and keep "up to 25." The price of one job post plus the HotHire option is $399.

List Notes
Inspired by craigslist, Chris McGarry created www.TheJobSpider.com, a free employment information exchange job board that is very good for either employers or applicants. He designed it because he was "looking for a network administrator and it was frustrating to not see an intuitive and nicely organized free job board."

Dice "The Career Hub for Tech Insiders" (chosen as best job site for technology fields) at www.dice.com offers a one- month basic job posting for 30 days starting at $459.

Monster ("most popular job site" according to ConsumerSearch) at www.monster.com is the most pricey. At the time of this writing it had a Special Offer of a two-week "Local Resume Search Plus a 60-Day Job Posting" for $790. They offered other options including posting a job for 14 days for "only $150!"

CareerBuilder (listed as "aggregator job site" with no mention of whether it was better than others or not) at www.careerbuilder.com offered job postings for "$419 each or less" for one month in three categories, and three industries.

Obviously, when you contrast these sites with craigslist listings that expire in 30 days but cost only $25 per category selected, you can easily see why even large employers seem to be gravitating toward use of craigslist. For the most part, jobs on craigslist will usually be listed in only one category. Even if someone was looking for a Chief Finance Officer, they would probably only list in the "accounting/finance jobs" and "business/mgmt jobs" categories at most. As you can see, at a combined $50, that's $\frac{1}{10}$ of what some of the other sites charge.

Obviously, with the worldwide reach of craigslist, selling points from other sites such as "post in any U.S. location" don't mean as much. What the other sites might have over craigslist is simply being more well known by employers accustomed to using a site with flashy graphics and templates that human resources personnel utilize in placing jobs on those sites.

If you are an employer with a small business, however, it seems rather clear that using craigslist makes more sense.

Since You Will Be Screened

According to the web-tracking site Hitwise, for the four weeks ending 03/28/2009 the top search term was craigslist, which should tell you how much the site is used. The next four in line were MySpace, Facebook, eBay, and YouTube. Taking those five in context, it seems people are heavily interested in web 2.0 social networking as well as being entertained, but the fact that eBay and craigslist are in the top five also indicates the people want to find specific things they want (like jobs), and to sell things.

Employers have specific needs, too, and in good times and bad, the less money they have to spend finding the right employees, the happier they will be. In the Internet Age, that means the first line of contact for job seekers is the resume, which is anymore mostly received electronically. Have you ever applied to a job online and wondered why you never even heard from anyone? You are certain you have all the qualifications for the job, but you aren't contacted. Baffling, isn't it?

What Most Applicants Don't Know

If you do some reading, you'll find books and articles on the skills that employers desire. If you read their ads on big job sites, you'll find something more interesting: *keywords* and *key phrases*. It's the resume equivalent of Search Engine Optimization (SEO). When resumes come in, particularly by email, software programs in large companies scan them to see if matches are found. Let's say that you see on an ad:

Flexible team player needed

You'll need to do a bullet point at the top of your resume to match that, though perhaps not in those exact words. A good variation might be:

Flexible team player successful at juggling multiple projects

Similar resume bullet points should be created matching up your real experience as best as possible with the needs expressed in the ad you've found. Employers want certain technical skills, including computer proficiency, but at the top of many jobs is something about communications skills. If you don't demonstrate that you're paying attention to what they're advertising, that doesn't demonstrate very good attention to detail, and you're not in their view receiving the job communication well.

If you don't have the software expertise necessary, list any you do know that are similar. HTML skills are often neglected; you might be surprised how simple they are to learn, yet so many people don't bother. Remember, craigslist has a rudimentary primer in HTML for those placing ads. Click on **www.craigslist.org/about/help,** then find the link down the page under **frequently asked questions** at the question "what HTML code does craigslist support?" Click on that for the HTML primer page, and also take a look at the **examples page** linked there, for even more examples.

If an employer alludes to employee values like "integrity," use that word in describing yourself, such as:

> Seasoned management executive with reputation of leadership integrity

It's not that difficult to read an ad, look for keywords and key phrases, and adjust your resume to suit that ad and keep your work history from being rejected just because you didn't type in the desired words.

Similarly, if you are placing ads for employees on craigslist, take this method into consideration. Not all hopeful employees are clued into the SEO-type approach to resume verbiage. Those who figure it out are probably ahead of the curve and might be those you want to hire first. So you'll make sure you know what your own keywords and key phrases are, won't you?

Getting Seen by a Human

While software might be the first line of review in a submitted resume, cover letters are much more likely to be seen by human eyes. Excellent instructions on writing good cover letters can be found on many websites. A key thing to remember (other than keeping the letter at less than a printed page in length whenever possible) is to use the keywords and key phrases you think are most important to a potential employer. Many experts suggest the use of the same type of bullet point style mentioned earlier within the body of your letter.

Just don't forget that you're dealing with a real person and don't get too informal just because you're applying via the web. If you know someone's full name, like Kim Smith, don't start the letter "Dear Kim." You don't know Kim, most likely, so a more formal "Dear Ms. Smith" is better. If you want to get noticed by a human, try to treat them like one; it might pay off with your resume going in the "consider" folder.

List Losers

Click on **job boards compared** in the left column of the craigslist home page and you'll find contrast data. The problem is, some of the reference data is very old, like "Job Board Effectiveness" from an April 2000 *Wall Street Journal* article. Check out other sites for yourself; things can change considerably in nine years.

Locating Companies by Region

If you search for jobs by using www.crazedlist.org you are not limited to search by one city or area at a time; you can search by region. Your choices are:

> west coast
> northwest
> mountain central
> midwest
> great lakes
> mid atlantic
> south
> southwest
> north east
> new england

If you select "west coast" you can simultaneously search 24 cities and areas in California, 2 in Nevada, 10 in Oregon, and 9 in Washington State. When you select the **jobs** category for your search, you can search in **all jobs** or select from 25 subcategories. You can also check off what type of job you want, such as "telecommute." And better yet, you can save your search settings for the next search and set up getting RSS feeds about the jobs you want. If you click the **search worldwide** tab at the top instead of the default **search usa** you can look for jobs by regions of the world, such as the major cities of Europe.

That's a pretty powerful tool to use in finding multiple employers in your region in one search. Once you have everything selected and click the Search bar on the far right, your next browser page will enable you to scroll through the listings from craigslist sites all over that region.

Whether there are tough economic times or not, people are often willing to relocate for a better job. Thus websites gear themselves more and more to accommodate a search by region. For example, the U.S. State Department website at www.state.gov offers a page for **Job Search by region and country** that has links for job searches across the world. One that it suggests in the United States is Going Global at www.goinglobal.com/countries/usa/usa_work.asp.

If you're willing to relocate or telecommute, or if you're looking for employees who are willing to relocate or work with you via the web, there are many resources for finding what you want, on sites based on craigslist and otherwise.

Beating Other Applicants

Sometimes it's the type of job you're applying for that counts more than your skills. It's been estimated that the Baby Boomer generation, for example, has had to change occupations three times or more during their lifetimes. The *USA Career Guide* available from GoingGlobal.com states:

> *Over the last few years, approximately one third of the US labor force has been employed in managerial and sales jobs. Growth in these occupations is expected to be strong and steady or in some specialties above average. Employment growth is expected to be much faster than average in management of professional, scientific and technical services, as well as in administrative and support services.*

You can purchase that guide, or you can use something already paid for by U.S. taxpayers, data provided by the Bureau of Labor Statistics. Its *Occupational Outlook Handbook* can be accessed at www.bls.gov/OCO. As an example of what you'll find on its web pages there is a PDF document titled "Finding and Applying for Jobs and Evaluating Offers" that can also be accessed on the web, covering these clickable items:

Where to learn About Job Openings

Job Search Methods

Applying for a Job

Job Interview Tips

Evaluating a Job Offer

For More Information

One particularly interesting page is "Tomorrow's Jobs" at www.bls.gov/oco/oco2003.htm. Studying the information on that site will most likely accelerate finding a job, or even a new occupation, whether you're searching via craigslist, a derivative of craigslist, or another site altogether. Whether you're looking to hire or get hired, we wish you the best of luck.

The Least You Need to Know

+ The craigslist emphasis remains, unlike commercial job sites, on communities.

+ Job ads placed on craigslist are as much as $^1/_{20}$ as expensive as other job sites.

+ Putting the right keywords and key phrases in your resume is the resume equivalent of Search Engine Optimization (SEO) for web searches.

+ Using www.crazedlist.org allows you to search the United States and rest of the world craigslist job listings by region.

+ The Bureau of Labor Statistics' *Occupational Outlook Handbook* at www.bls.gov/OCO offers a wealth of free information for job seekers.

13

Maximizing Your Resume

In This Chapter

- ◆ Resume category resources
- ◆ craigslist's employer mentality
- ◆ Tailoring to your audience
- ◆ Adapting your resume by ads
- ◆ Pros and cons of hiring a pro
- ◆ Forums can improve responses

There are many books on resume writing, even more articles about it available on the web, and an endless number of services online and otherwise that promise to help you shape a resume for maximum impact and results. There's so much advice out there it can be daunting. Since there is a resume section available on craigslist, our aim in this chapter is to give you some advice on resumes but more specifically, on getting a resume noticed and acted upon when posted to the site.

Resources for the Resume Category

Before you post your resume, which might contain your phone number, read everything on the craigslist page about personal safety at www. craigslist.org/about/safety. As this book was being finished, a man was arrested as "the craigslist killer." It's very easy these days to use even a cell phone number to find someone's physical location via the web, so you need to protect yourself.

You should also read the **Avoiding Scams & Fraud** page at www. craigslist.org/about/scams. We can't stress this enough. Particularly when unemployment rates are high, scams proliferate. You might hear from someone offering to rewrite your resume that they found on craigs-list, or a so-called recruiter might offer to help you find a job if you'll pay them a fee. That's one of the reasons why the site states that an "inquiry from someone far away, often in another country" is suspect. Recruiters are paid well by employers, sometimes a large percentage of your first few months' salary, so it's unlikely that a legitimate recruiter would need your money.

With those things understood, the next thing you should do is look through some of the supposed resumes that are posted. You'll find they are *not* resumes. Instead, they are short ads that per craigslist rules should be posted under **services** in the proper category.

You'll notice immediately that there are no categories listed under **resumes** like there are under **services.** What this means to you is that it's more difficult to find the right person in the resume category, so people who look there are more likely to use the search box to find you. If you have several skills that are mentioned in your resume (or listing if that's all you post), fret not. The craigslist search engine looks in both the titles and body of the listings for the words you insert in the search box unless "only search titles" is checked to the right of the search engine window.

List Notes

If someone has "only search titles" checked when looking through resumes, they might miss your ad if you use contractions. For example, if you list yourself as "Ofc Mgr/Admin Asst" and they search for "office manager" you might not be found as you would if the search reached into the body of your ad. Think about that headline.

Just as we advise when placing any other kind of ad, it pays to read what the competition is doing. You can use the search engine to look for your job category, or you can browse through the listings at your leisure. By doing so, you'll see the various types of listings, from a short description of what someone does and how to reach them, to a full-blown resume packed with information that you must scroll down to read in full. Which one should you choose? That will depend on you and what you're trying to achieve, so let's take a look at what employers are thinking when they search the **resumes** category.

The craigslist Employer Mentality

Since both the employees and users of craigslist police the listings, it's probably worth looking into the philosophy of Jim Buckmaster, the CEO of the site. An article was written about him in the *Financial Times* that the site reproduced at www.craigslist.org/about/press/ft.lucy. What's interesting is that Buckmaster first came to the company via posting his resume on craigslist. Quoting the article, "In 1999, he was an unemployed web programmer who posted his resume on craigslist, where it was spotted by the site's founder, Craig Newmark, who offered him a job." A year later, he was made CEO! If you have any doubt whether posting your resume on the site is effective, that might settle it for you. The title of the article is "CEO who puts profits second." Now, that may be true for Buckmaster and many of the craigslist staff, but it's not going to be true of most employers who use and list on the site. What should be noted, though, is that Buckmaster says the site has one principle—"to please users." If you've used the easily navigable site much, you know that's true, so keep that in mind when you're posting your resume. Make it *easy* for the end recipient, your potential employer, to find you. Following are some tips.

- If you post a simple ad, make it no longer than something that can be read without scrolling.

- If you post a short resume, use a declaratory statement at the top, such as "I am looking for a full-time tech position." At the bottom of such a listing, use a line like "Full version of resume available upon request." If you have a full resume posted on a web page, provide the link.

- If you post a regular resume, use the convention of a paragraph describing abilities and achievements, such as "Experienced accountant and full charge bookkeeper with managerial and leadership experience. Excellent record in implementation of cost-saving business and financial procedures. Team player with keen awareness of the importance of strategic business decisions and precise financial planning." That would be followed by the other details of your resume.

- Rather than listing out references, put the line "References Available Upon Request" at the end.

As you'll discover when you look through the listings, employers will find all sorts of postings, usually of the three types just mentioned. Like you, they'll want to find what they're shopping for as quickly and efficiently as possible. The next thing they'll be looking for is keywords. Let's say the last person they had in a position was increasingly late, had too many absences, and tended to be a maverick with regard to company policy. Accordingly, maybe the main thing this employer has in mind is "team player." That's another reason why you should look through a lot of resumes. You'll find that you'll continually come across key phrases like that, things that employers regularly seek. If you're interested in a position where you have more autonomy, though, "team player" is something you might want

Skip's Tips _____

If you have no idea what your competition is like, or if you're considering starting a business and wonder what kind of talent is out there and what they'll cost, place an ad and ask for resumes. Be truthful about it so you don't violate any laws. "Building talent base for new business" would work. You'll quickly find out who's out there.

to leave out. Some employers concentrate on finding the right person for the job, testing them for a short time, then leave them alone to perform their job. As Jim Buckmaster said in the article, people come back to craigslist repeatedly. They find housing, furniture, cars, jobs, and relationships there. It's a good bet that, for the most part, an employer or recruiter who regularly posts on craigslist for personnel knows the site well. You can "reverse engineer" their thinking by researching what they post and what others post as well. Use the old Boy Scout motto: Be Prepared. In the resume area, it will put you far ahead of the pack.

Tailoring to Your Target Audience

While craigslist has an admonition against posting the same ad in different categories, it does not prohibit people from placing similar ads in different categories. There's also nothing preventing you from responding with the same resume but adjusting it to suit particular ads.

If you're looking for administrative personnel, it's fairly simple to alter it slightly to fit in categories other than the one you'd normally place it in. Let's say you're a nonprofit company. The de facto craigslist category would be **nonprofit sector** but what if someone's never worked in nonprofit? They might assume there are things they don't know about it, and so wouldn't apply. What if you're a nonprofit involved in something to do with schools? You'd add the **education** category, but couldn't people in other businesses and customer service fit? They could, and maybe even someone in finance. So the following categories might be appropriate:

> accounting+finance
> admin / office
> business / mgmt
> customer service
> education
> nonprofit sector

If you're open to it, you might even promote helping someone learn something new. Some skills are transferable across industries, and the knowledge of new areas can greatly expand confidence and competence.

It is common practice for CEOs and managers in training to spend a certain amount of time working in all departments of a company to learn how it works. Someone working in administrative areas while going to college part-time for an advanced education degree might jump at the chance to work in a nonprofit involved in education. Since craigslist can be overwhelming to some people with all its categories and possibilities, people usually think about the ads they post and search for in a fairly simple manner, almost like a reaction. Making it easy for them by changing your ad for different categories might not prevent someone from flagging your ad as an offense, but it might mean you'll find the best talent more quickly than your competitors.

Adapting Your Resume Ad by Ad

Since the **resumes** banner has no subcategories, there's nothing to change once it's posted on your local site, and if you do something like post it every day, you'll probably get it flagged and removed by craigslist. If your situation is such that you can work with people across the country, or if you're willing to relocate to another location for a job, it might be worth considering changing your resume to suit each potential employer. While you might think, *my resume is my resume, I've done what I've done*, the way you present it can mean all the difference in getting what you want.

An interesting aspect of the Internet is that you can fool someone via email in ways you cannot in person. If you're looking for a job that can be done on a telecommuting basis, chances are you'll only go through an in-person interview via a phone call. Still, each employer is different, and each interviewer is different as well, so it pays to try to learn as much about that employer before applying, and tailoring your resume if necessary, to make yourself stand out.

> **List Notes**
>
> If you're looking for a job, don't count on an employer to place their listing in the correct category. If you're certain about the job title you're looking for, like "admin asst." use the search bar on the main page first, set to jobs.

Let's say you've found an ad for a company that lists its name and they're looking for customer service representatives that can work from home. Use that name. Do a web search and see what comes up. There are websites where people chat about companies that prey on those who work from their homes. The About.com Job Search Forum is one example. If a company lists their website, that's a good sign, because even if the site was put up by a single person, they are often traceable by using a "Whois" lookup. If you're not familiar with that, try www. samspade.org; it's free. Type in a site—like (we just made this up) www. possiblejob.com—and if the site has actually been registered you'll get the name of the site administrator and full contact information including address, phone number, and email. (If that information isn't present, they violated the rules.) If the site was registered via a site that has some protection regarding a Whois search, like www.godaddy.com, you might have to take another step and go to that site and find the Whois button and search by clicking on that. By checking out company websites and their registration information, you'll learn more about them in ways that can both inform and protect you. So how do you use that information? What if you learn via their website that the company is growing rapidly? Add that to the resume description of your abilities: Demonstrated ability to adapt to rapidly changing conditions while maintaining expansion

As you look for other ways to tailor your resume to suit employers, keep in mind the keywords present in their listing. You can't count on all companies and employers being savvy enough to concentrate on such things, but in tougher economies where jobs are scarcer than normal, employers are keen to get the very best people possible, so they take extra steps to make ads more specific.

Watch out for companies that stress your salary requirements too much, with disclaimers like "resumes without salary requirements will be disregarded." That's often a sign of a company in financial trouble with no flexibility on salaries.

Should You Hire a Professional?

If you have a spare $100 or so to spend, and you've simply never been a good writer, it might be worth it to get an expert to tool-up your resume. Given the amount of free web pages available on the subject, however, it might be better to invest some eyeball equity and surf around for some diverse opinions. One thing most professionals will tell you is that you must list your *job objective* so that employers know where you want to go with your career. They know something you don't: where their team is headed. If you don't state a direction, or if your direction doesn't harmonize with the company to which you're applying, often enough people won't bother to go any further in studying your resume. Professionals know how to present gaps in your work history, how far back to list your experience (usually no more than 10 or 15 years), and the general qualities that most employers want that should be stressed in the resume. (An open and willing nature is high on the list.) Before you hire a professional, try some of the following websites for information. Some also offer advice about writing a good cover letter.

◆ http://hotjobs.yahoo.com/resume—An excellent step-by-step series of articles about putting together a professional resume, connected to Yahoo!'s excellent job search engine.

◆ www.dailywritingtips.com/resume-writing-tips—Forty-four resume writing tips.

◆ www.damngood.com—From author and resume expert Yanna Parker, has free templates and advice.

◆ www.pongoresume.com—Offers paid services as well as thorough free advice.

◆ www.provenresumes.com—Comprehensive site that offers examples of resumes that were rewritten to get salary increases and jobs.

◆ www.resume-help.org—Examples and tips and pro services.

◆ www.rockportinstitute.com/resumes.html—Extensive site that offers a literal education in resumes including information on power words.

If you can't get together an excellent resume after studying the information at the above sites, you probably do need to hire a professional. If you find you're adept at it, and improve your skills as a result of consulting those sites and others like them, maybe you'll develop another skill, of writing pro resumes, and you can put an ad on craigslist to get business for yourself.

List Losers

If you have a knack for writing effective resumes, it's probably not a good idea to post an ad under **resumes**. That would be misplaced. Oh, you'll find them there, but they really belong under **services**, specifically the **write/ed/tr8** subcategory with the headline "Resume Writing Service" or similar.

Using Forums to Improve Responses

Under **discussion forums** you'll find several subcategories that might be places to discuss your job search, ads you place, and the writing of resumes. You can look up people by their regular "handle" on each forum, and also search for threads by keyword. The **jobs** subcategory expands to **job market** and offers chat threads about any and all aspects of job seeking. According to craigslist, it covers "hiring practices, job market trends, recruiters, career development, resumes, interviewing tips, you get the idea." You'll also find a link there to a **self-employment forum** that does not have its own subcategory under **discussion forums**. [Note: you must register and pick a "handle" to post in the forums, but you don't need to do that to read the postings.]

In the **feedbk** forum you can get discussion on anything you post (if anyone cares to respond). It's a catchall of topics, but comments on your resume or chats about how your job search is going are common themes in large metro area craigslist sites, so dive right in.

At **npo** you'll find the nonprofits forum for anyone wanting a job or interested in that sector of the job marketplace.

For anyone over the age of 50, a click on **over 50** (the "over 50 club") could offer a lot of help and commiseration about trying to find a job if you're a veteran in the workplace. The **writers** forum is more literary than business, so you might not get much help on a resume there unless you're willing to pay someone, but you can try. An additional benefit to using the discussion forums is that some people use them all the time, and know their way around craigslist to a greater degree than the casual user. When you're seriously trying to do business via the site, it can't hurt to make new friends like that. Happy surfing!

The Least You Need to Know

- ◆ Reading the **Personal Safety** and **Avoiding Scams & Fraud** pages on craigslist can save you a lot of trouble and headaches, so study them thoroughly.

- ◆ You can learn something about the people who use craigslist (both employers and employees) by studying the site's philosophy on the site.

- ◆ Changing a job posting ad to place it in different categories might get you the employee you want more quickly.

- ◆ Tailoring resumes to suit employers is likely to get your resume to the top of the pile.

- ◆ You don't have to hire a professional to write your resume. If you have any writing talent at all, there are many free resources available on the web.

- ◆ There are several craigslist discussion forums that offer free feedback for your job search concerns.

Chapter **14**

A Writer/Editor's Dream

In This Chapter

- ◆ Want a job, or a gig?
- ◆ Finding work that pays
- ◆ Smart searching craigslist
- ◆ Beating foreign competition
- ◆ Marketing your literary services

It used to be that the only centralized source for a writer or editor to find a job was the *Writer's Market*, a book that still comes out every year, with online search now available. When researching a similar book about selling to Hollywood, however, I learned from a *Writer's Market* competitor that some of the publishers listed by *Writer's Market* didn't want to be included in that book. In contrast, most craigslist writing and editing listings are there because someone wanted to hear from people. Similarly, if you want someone to find you, there's a place to post your resume. If you don't want that much information revealed and simply want to get people to contact you for your services, there's a place for that, too. And if you want to talk shop with other writers, editors, and even translators, you'll have a forum to vent and ask questions. What you might find amazing, though, is that your competition could come from halfway around the world. But even that can be turned to your advantage.

Jobs for 9 to 5, Gigs for Your Own Schedule

It costs an employer $25 to post a job offered on craigslist in over 30 categories. While that price is minimal compared to some online job list sites, in a tight economy you can bet that there will be fewer categories selected than in the past. For example, a writer/editor job for the federal government (there are generally thousands) might not be listed in "government jobs" but in "writer/editor jobs" only. If you need a writer, that's something to consider. If you're looking for a steady writing or editing job, it won't cost you anything to check in multiple categories, so don't limit yourself to searching only in the writer/editor category.

> **Skip's Tips**
>
> On Twitter.com you can get a question answered quickly, if you pose it in 140 characters. On the "writers" discussion forum on craigslist, you're not limited to your "tweet" list. You remember character names but not the source book? Ask and go on writing. You might get an answer on the forum within a minute or two.

If you're unfamiliar with the term "gig" it's a show business term usually meaning a temporary position for a musician or performer. Therefore, the freelance and temporary positions are more likely to be found in the **writing** line under **gigs** while more permanent jobs are usually in **writing / editing** under the **jobs** category. It *does not cost* to list a writing job under **gigs,** so you might find that more penny-pinching employers will save $25 and post their position offered there, or simply post there to make sure the job is seen by as many people as possible.

Let's say you're more interested in a full-time writing or editing job than finding someone to buy that screenplay you've been working on part-time for the past year. That's probably a smart decision for most people. Click on the **writing / editing** line under **jobs** and you'll land on a page where, at the top you'll find several choices.

search for:		in:	writing jobs	▼	(Search)	☐ only search titles
	☐ telecommute ☐ contract ☐ internship ☐ part-time ☐ non-profit			☐ has image		

Specify the type of job you want.

While those choices may be self-explanatory, let's go over them briefly so you don't waste your time searching on pages that you'll simply find frustrating.

> **Telecommute**—This is the freelancer or work-at-home writer/editor's dream, and increasingly popular even with major companies. If this is what you want, use it as an overall search term but *do not* click **only search titles** at the right of the Search button. Employers rarely put the word telecommute in an ad listing title.

> **Contract**—A norm for Silicon Valley, these jobs have set time limits and usually mean you will be an independent contractor for tax purposes.

> **Internship**—While there are paid internships, on craigslist this usually means you will need to be on the premises with an employer and getting little or no pay for *the "great privilege" of learning on the job.*

> **Part-time**—In contrast to a contract job, this category usually means you will be limited by the number of hours you're required to work each week or month.

> **Non-profit**—This can be a full-time job with full benefits. The catch is that it will likely be at a slightly lower salary because it involves employment at a tax-exempt, nonprofit organization.

The **writing** selection under **gigs** brings you to a slightly simpler page than the **jobs** link option.

| search for: | | | in: | writing gigs | ⊡ | Search | ☐ only search titles |

○ pay ○ no-pay ◉ all   ☐ has image

Do you want to be paid, or not?

Why, you might ask, would anyone choose "no-pay"? Well, let's say you're an aspiring writer and you're looking for a writing partner. That happens a lot with screenwriting. Or you might want to create a comic book or graphic novel and you're looking for an artist with whom to team up.

You'll find just about everything under **gigs**—typing, transcribing, translation, public relations needs, website writing, you name it. Most people looking for a writer, even in our Internet Age, don't have a clue where to look, other than on craigslist. So if you're looking for a not necessarily permanent job, look under **gigs.** You might find a ghost-writing job on a book that could last a year. Just make sure you found it while searching with **pay** checked, so you don't get involved with some-one who thinks they have such an amazing story that you should spend a major part of your life writing for them what they cannot.

Writers and Editors Hold Regular Jobs, Too

A great many people use craigslist, so some people will advise you that you can only secure a posted writing assignment if you respond within an hour of the posting. If that were true, the obvious question would be "When are they posted?" Answer: all hours of the working day, and even at night. The time and date is the next line down from the "Reply to:" line. The fact is, since major companies now look for personnel via craigslist job listings, they're highly unlikely to fill the position from the pile of resumes they receive within the first hour.

> **Online Heat**
>
> Check out the **job boards compared** link on the **jobs** search page. While the Careerbuilder.com site has more "Applicants per Job Ad" craigslist is #2 in replies. According to craigslist, quot-ing the *Wall Street Journal*, its ad effectiveness is #1.

In 2008, *The Hollywood Reporter,* one of the top two entertainment magazines in the city advertised for an Editor for THR.com. The posi-tion required "10+ years of writing/

reporting/editing experience, 5+ years of writing/reporting/editing experience at a national/international brand, 5+ years of digital editorial experience, and extensive movie and entertainment industry contacts."

Obviously, this came from a major entertainment company (the magazine is owned by Nielsen), but it says something about the company's perception of the quality of people reading craigslist job ads in the **writing / editing** category, at least in the Los Angeles area. An ad like this might be an anomaly, depending on the area of the country. Some large companies may be more likely to list jobs on sites like Careerbuilder, Monster, or Hotjobs, simply because they have craigslist mentally equated with a place that is the web equivalent of a local garage sale.

Like all "real world" job applications, writing jobs listed are usually more formal in nature than a need listed under **gigs.** That means you may be asked for a resume, which could be an attachment, or put within the text of an email. Read the ad closely; you'll find it's usually specified. Often enough, you'll find a link within the body of a listing that directs you to the company website to fill out an online application. Unlike the resume storage and coaching advantages on job-specific websites, there is no craigslist facility that allows you to keep a resume on file to be sent to prospective employers.

That's probably a good thing, because you have to think every time you answer an ad, and you're more likely to tailor a resume and/or cover letter to the employer.

And please don't forget this very important fact—there are *over thirty* possible job search areas. Let's say you are, for example, a technical editor by training. You do a search in the **writing / editing** jobs area and find nothing in your locale. Try moving the listing menu bar and searching under **engineering** jobs or even **etcetera** jobs.

Remember, most people placing substantial job ads, including people working in Human Resources at a big company, will not have the time or take the time to read a book like this one and gain a better understanding of the most effective use of craigslist. The beauty of the website is that it is laid out in such an easy-to-navigate manner. The secret to it, though, is learning to use all the various links and buttons to cover all the bases on where the just-right job for you has been listed.

You cannot count on it being in the place that you would think most logical. Often enough, valuable gems take a little digging to find.

List Notes

Some ad posters check "no phone calls about this job" even though no phone number is listed. Huh? Well, that's usually someone with a not-hard-to-find phone number, like a company listed in the phone book white pages. Also, it might be because a nonelectronic response cannot be electronically scanned for matching criteria like an email or resume can.

You Don't Have to Search craigslist on craigslist

You can use a search engine with the word craigslist and a phrase in quotes like "creative writer" or "ghost writer wanted" (or "ghost writer needed") and get a plethora of responses from across the country, or even the world. Google seems to be the search engine of choice, but you might also try Dogpile.com, which combines Google, Yahoo!, LiveSearch, and Ask in a metasearch. Clever writers who know how to optimize their ads for search engines will turn up in your search results, but it's easy enough to wade through them to find ads to answer. I've found that a Dogpile search turns up fewer results but what it finds are more specifically what you want, and you'll turn up far less ads on craigslist *by other writers advertising their services.* Plus, a Dogpile search, while turning up fewer pages, seems to pull not only craigslist job results but also those from other web pages.

If you simply search with the keywords "craigslist writer" (and by that I don't necessarily mean a phrase in parentheses, which narrows the search), you could end up with a bit of a mess. All sorts of article links will turn up, which you might find useful, but not if you're specifically looking for work right now. It's a good idea to try to think like someone placing an ad and consider what you would write if you had his or her specific need. It will shorten your search time considerably.

One excellent site for making the most of craigslist in writing and editing searches is the aforementioned www.crazedlist.org. Just don't take its "search craigslist like a madman" idea too seriously and try to search across the entire country at once, or the watchful computers at craigslist central (and/or some of the vigilant staff at headquarters in San Francisco) could flag your computer and effectively ban it from craigslist. That's a problem you don't want, so take your time and search by region. Let's say you start with the top listing, west coast, and use the phrase "editor wanted." You'll have two places to search, jobs and gigs. If you start with gigs, you can choose **all gigs** or one of nine other categories.

Once you've gone through all the listings that come up under gigs, switch to searching under jobs in the same region. In this case you'll have twice as many categories to choose from, 18 in all. Again, I'd suggest searching with **all jobs** selected, unless you have a track record in a certain area, such as **medical / healthcare jobs.**

The great thing about searching under the jobs category is that you get to choose between telecommute, contract, intern, part-time, and non-profit.

You can check the ones you want in a box, or leave them all unchecked and you'll have a default **all** search going on. Unless you're someone wanting to learn a specific job and don't need to be paid right away, I'd suggest checking all of them except **intern.** In the Hollywood entertainment business where I work sometimes, people are expected to take 10 percent less than they would normally make for the "privilege" of working in entertainment, and "intern" often means "we will exploit you mercilessly, make you work inhuman hours in violation of California law, and if you're clever enough to learn something while slaving for us and putting up with monumental egos, you're hired."

If you think I'm kidding about that, think again. In other businesses, I imagine it's a bit saner, and interning might be a smart choice for a student looking into a profession. In the case of working for a law firm, interns get paid and can develop great working relationships with the firm's partners, so don't let my Hollywood knowledge deter you from using the intern category. If you're an aspiring writer, you might end up with a paid intern job with a famous author, or at a literary agency— who knows?

Using crazedlist.org, you can cycle through 10 regions of the United States under both gigs and jobs, and all the various categories within those two choices. While it might take you all day to do a search using these criteria, you can factually cover every single writer or editor position available that is advertised on craigslist in recent weeks, in a relatively short period of time.

List Losers

Try to avoid listings like: "Writers and Bloggers Wanted—Great Pay—(Work From Home)." The "great pay" might only be 10¢ per word or less and involve reviewing adult websites. Look for a (Location) that's real; it's usually a better job. Also, if a company is okay with a telecommuter, they'll say so in the listing, not write a "Work From Home" headline.

With a template email that you can customize to fit your response to each ad, and a resume to paste it or attach at the ready, you can make yourself known to eager employers across the country in an amazingly quick period of time. To me, that's a wordsmith's dream.

Dealing with Foreign Competition

Here's the bad news for literary types selling their wares and expertise via the web. It's one word: **India.**

Freelancers who find work via websites like Guru.com have found out the hard way that it's not just call centers that have operators who sound like actors in *Slumdog Millionaire*. Indians (and I don't mean Native Americans) have an expertise with the language, usually have an excellent education, and likely know grammar better than you do. (I hope that sentence is grammatically correct.)

What they *don't* know, usually, is the North American audience, which remains the largest market for writing of all kinds in the entire world. They also aren't likely to understand the nuances of a society where knowledge of Hispanic phrases or hip hop culture fit into popular literature, film and TV scripts, and video games. A person from India trying to compete for a writing or editing job like that might be as tough a task as an American who speaks Japanese trying to break into writing in the manga or anime market in Japan.

Being clued into the subtleties of a culture is powerful stuff. You can use that to your advantage by finding work outside of North America in the international areas of craigslist. What many people don't realize until they investigate is that the ads at these links *are written in English*. While writing this book I saw a **writing / editing** ad on the Egypt page of a college student looking for someone to write "a 4 page research paper over the topic 'Michelangelo's David'." Of course, the compensation offered was only $20, but it just goes to show how you can find ads for writers in English around the world.

Obviously, you're not going to pay the rent by doing work for lazy students in Egypt. There are, however, people with a lot of money in many places around the world who want assistance in writing and marketing to the American and/or English-speaking market. It might be that the currency in their country is stronger than the American dollar, and hiring you could be something they see as a bargain.

> **Online Heat**
>
> *Ideas for smart foreign craigslist ads:* Travel writing about the United States or your local area could be of interest to editors in other countries. Similarly, info about bargains like housing foreclosures in California could appeal to publications for Chinese bargain hunters.

Even when their currency is at a disadvantage, your expertise might be sufficient to convince them to "bite the bullet" and hire you. I've done work more than once for people outside the United States that I found online, simply because they couldn't get my particular expertise in their home country. Cheap isn't always better or even sufficient, even in the Internet Age.

Marketing Your Literary Services on craigslist

There are 17 categories under Services on craigslist, with the most obvious one for writers being **write/ed/tr8**. That expands to **writing/ editing/translation** when you open the page. Oddly enough, you'll find that people don't always pay attention to proper categories and will place ads looking for writers in areas that should be reserved for writers advertising for work.

Usually, people looking for a writer or editor via craigslist aren't going to go into great detail. A great many people are not at all good at writing an ad. You'd be surprised how bad some read, if you haven't looked through many. Since most people are busy, what they're going to do first is a global craigslist search on the left side of the home page. Under the **search craigslist** box they'll click on **services,** then type in what they want, then click on the arrow and see what comes up.

Let's say they simply enter **writer** and search. That has a liability in that they'll get everything from resume writing, to tutors, to ads for sample contracts. What to do? If they're smart, they'll narrow the category at the resulting page, select **write/edit/trans** and search further. They'll have a choice of also clicking the **only search titles** and **has image** boxes (though who knows why a writer or editor would need an image).

This further search will turn up a lot more specific professionals with one-line statements of what they offer, but a searcher will still see ads that say things like: "Need a project that SINGS instead of… (mumbles)?"

Maybe that would arouse your curiosity, maybe not. If you'd been dealing with uninventive writers, it might prompt you to click and investigate. A more reliable headline, though, is one as specific as possible, with superlatives that can be backed up with fact, like:

> "Award-winning copywriter with references available"

One I found that really got the point across was:

> "Automotive Journalist / PR / Blogger & Ad Writer"

Why are such specific listings better? It's simple; it won't cost you anything to post your available services, you simply need a craigslist account. So why not *create separate service listings under different areas of expertise?*

Think about it—how many writers or editors do you think simply state "Professional writer available" in their ad and leave it at that? If you're no more inventive than that with your ad, how creative will you look to a potential employer? And remember, from the opening page they can search with a phrase. If you were a publisher of a car magazine suddenly without a writer, would you be thrilled if you searched for "automotive journalist" and got a qualified candidate, rather than having to sort through dozens of "professional writers" to find someone, or post an ad hoping the proper person would reply?

List Notes

There is no separate listing under **gigs** for writing films, TV, or video games. To avoid the freeloaders, once on the gigs page, search with "pay" or "no-pay." And don't forget there are a number of types of gigs. A need for a video game writer might be under "writing gigs," but it could also be under "creative gigs," or "computer gigs." Search thoroughly.

craigslist gives this warning about cross posting:

Please post to a single geographic area and category only – cross-posting to multiple cities or categories is not allowed

That does not state that you cannot offer multiple listings of different services you offer. Do some thinking. Try out some headlines on friends; get their opinions. If you stand out from the crowd, you might just get picked first.

And don't forget this category when creating a posting for work—**resume/job wanted**—because in the larger metropolitan areas you'll find this note from CL:

choose the area nearest you (or suggest a new one):

please note: your posting will also appear on the main los angeles site.

there is no need to cross-post to more than one area—doing so may get you flagged and/or blocked—thanks!

If you post under **service offered** you're more likely to hear from people who want a freelancer. Think of it as being listed in the craigslist equivalent of the Yellow Pages. If you post under **resume/job wanted** you're more likely to hear from serious long-term and/or contract employers.

And don't think you're all alone out there looking for work. Check in on occasion in the discussion forums under **writers**, which expands to **craigslist > discussion forums > literary & writing.** You'll find "The Moving Finger" quote from Omar Khayyam and, along with the usual flamers present in any web discussion forums, some laughs and good advice.

Although craigslist seems simple in its presentation, the intricacies can be elaborate for people looking for editing, writing, and other literary creation work. Just as in writing, the more thoughtful and creative you are in your posting and searching, the more likely you are to find great success. One thing's certain: there's never been a tool in the history of writing for scribes to locate other people to work with like they have with craigslist.

The Least You Need to Know

◆ Job listings on craigslist are more likely for people wanting 9-to-5 jobs. Gig listings are better for freelancers and those who work contractually.

◆ From telecommute to nonprofit, it's important to understand the job categories on craigslist and what they mean to employers placing ads.

◆ Since major companies looking for employees regularly use craigslist, it's very important to understand Search Engine Optimization (SEO) keywords when responding to ads with your resume.

◆ Using more comprehensive search methods like the Crazedlist.org website offers far greater results in find writing and editing work.

◆ Being physically located in the North American market can help you get work around the world.

◆ When placing ads for your services on craigslist, specificity can help you triumph over others.

15

Staffing Your Company from craigslist

In This Chapter

◆ Assess your needs

◆ Interns and volunteers

◆ Finding the right job category

◆ Writing the right ad

◆ Resources to qualify candidates

The users of craigslist around the world usually start using it to do things like buy used furniture or find an apartment and then often end up checking out the personals, meeting someone, and getting married, and another cycle of using the site begins that might even include buying a house. Given the size of the **jobs** and **gigs** category on the site, it's instantly obvious that people also use craigslist constantly to find employment and employees.

With the 570+ craigslist sites around the world, you're certainly not limited in demographics, and in going through the listings you can gain an education in people, sometimes from places you've never visited or will visit. Let's have a look at those possibilities with regard to finding the help you need.

Assessing Your Needs

Do you know your own best qualities in business? How about assessing the strengths of various employees? Most people don't know these things well, and in a company large enough, they depend on Human Resources to evaluate and recommend employees. You can learn more about such things with books like *Now, Discover Your Strengths* (The Free Press, 2001) by Marcus Buckingham and Donald O. Clifton, Ph.D. (For more info see www.strengthfinder.com.) Buckingham is the co-author of the bestseller *First, Break All The Rules* (Simon & Schuster, 1999) and Clifton is the Chair of the Gallup International Research & Education Center. Their StrengthFinder Profile was evolved from a 25-year effort that identified 34 dominant strength themes and combinations of the most prevalent human strengths. Psychological profiles of more than 2 million people were used in developing the information.

If you're curious about what the strength themes are, visit the site and/ or buy the book. As an employer, you need tools like this to make better choices in selecting personnel, and in determining how to better work with the personnel you have. If you know what your own strengths are, that will help you in finding personnel, because you'll also learn what weaknesses you have that employees can cover.

List Notes

Check out the blog of the Craigslist Foundation at http://blog.craigslist-foundation.org for helpful articles for your business. One in particular is "Networking That Matters," a video interview with web genius Seth Godin about how "sites like Facebook, LinkedIn, etc. can be either a tool for connecting with people in meaningful ways or can be a real time suck."

Meanwhile, do you have a solid idea of your staffing needs? If you're simply at the "we better get somebody in here" stage, it might pay to do some reading and take advantage of your tax dollars at work by perusing the website of the Small Business Administration at www.sba.gov.

The Small Business Planner there at www.sba.gov/smallbusinessplanner/ index.html offers a myriad of informative tools. The **Manage Employees** page has a link to "The Interview Process: How to Select The 'Right' Person" that is an excellent summary of what you need to do in finding personnel, and because it's from the federal government, it's a good bet that the information provided confirms to the laws of the land, which come into play when you hire people. To summarize the steps, they advise:

1. Determine your need to hire.

2. Conduct a thorough job analysis.

3. Write a job description and job specification based on the job analysis.

4. Determine the salary.

5. Decide where and how to find qualified applicants.

6. Collect and review applications and resumes.

7. Interview the most qualified candidates.

8. Check references.

9. Hire the best person(s).

Please read the full article because it goes into great detail about what to do and not do. You might also spend some time looking around the link it suggests at the end, the U.S. Equal Employment Opportunity Commission at www.eeoc.gov. In lieu of hiring legal help for your company, you can find the same federal regulations a lawyer would access there.

Of course, no one knows your business like you do, and you might know exactly what you need before you place an ad on craigslist. Forewarned is forearmed, though, so why not take advantage of a wealth of free information?

What many people in business for themselves might not realize is that there was once a work system in the United States that included apprentices who learned a trade. If you have a specialty that could turn into a lucrative career for an enterprising employee, you might consider using volunteers (particularly if you have a nonprofit or charity organization) and/or interns, particularly if your needs lend themselves to part-time employees. Let's look at that first, just in case it's something you haven't yet considered.

Using Interns and Volunteers

You won't find a category or subcategory for "intern" on the main craigslist page. You will find a category for **volunteers** under the **community** banner. Internship listings can be readily found, however, under the **[part time]** category under the **jobs** banner. If you plan to ask for volunteers, your organization had better be performing some service for the public, like a hospice, or feeding the poor, because that's the type of listings you'll normally see under **volunteers.** Then again, you might see something as odd as someone asking for a donated kidney (we kid you not, there was one on the Los Angeles craigslist when writing this book).

A tour around the Craigslist Foundation site should reinforce the "community activist" nature of craigslist in your mind, if you ever doubted it. To that end, the people who post under **volunteers** and look at the listings there are very likely to flag your post immediately if it seems like you are taking advantage of free help to make money with a for-profit business. Nevertheless, you'll see all sorts of postings that violate the spirit of the category. For example, when writing this book we saw "Strippers wanted for student documentary." Supposedly, it was placed by "three students in the School of Social Work" at the University of Southern California, but it looked a little suspect, and it got flagged later.

Skip's Tips

If you're doing a study of some kind and offer free services and pay for someone's time, put your listing in the **volunteers** category. That's where most of those are found and where people are used to looking. An example might be free teeth cleaning with a small stipend.

If you have a business and occasionally do charitable activities, like putting on a carnival for your church or a bingo tournament, there's nothing wrong with advertising for volunteers in the category. You should also do a listing in the **event calendar** on the main page, just don't use the same listing that asks for volunteers or you might risk the servers dumping one of your listings as duplicative, which is *verboten*.

When someone is an intern, it's pretty much a given that they are there to learn something. Their goals and aspirations for the future may come into sharper focus, and there is no classroom substitute for working in a real world job alongside an expert. In the field of entertainment, interns are common, often working for no salary at all because of the supposed glamour of the industry. Many interns in Hollywood don't need to make a salary because they are "trust fund babies" with rich parents, while others are people who somehow manage to support themselves while learning the ropes and attempting to succeed in a highly competitive business.

Along that line, if you're looking for an intern, it might pay to make the position you advertise sound as attractive as possible, particularly with regard to future income potential. Law firms use interns every summer, and the more prestigious the firm, the more applicants they get, from the top law schools. Interns who do well get hired after graduation, and those that do very well might get on a fast track to becoming partner.

So what do you have to offer? On many intern ads you'll see this line first: "Great opportunity for a student or recent graduate!" Translated, that means: "We're going to pay you minimum wage or as little as possible as you learn our oh-so magnificent business and put in as many hours as we can get away with." Applicants know "ad speak" because they read many listings that offer similar terms. Interns are often asked to work 20+ hours per week on a contract basis, meaning in the United States they will receive a 1099 form for tax purposes, and most likely they'll be held responsible for their own health, dental, and other benefits a normal employee would expect. Under **Compensation** on internship listings, you'll usually see the line: "Commensurate with experience" which translates to "We figure you don't have much experience so we're going to pay you minimum wage or as little as possible." And naturally, in many intern listings you'll see: "This is an unpaid position."

Get the picture? Maybe you wouldn't be that strict or demanding of interns, but most listings have similar language. So put yourself in the shoes of the intern. What could you offer that others won't? It's probably not a good idea to offer an unpaid position if you can afford anything at all. Try a line like "Please state what you would expect for working 15 to 20 hours per week when submitting your resume." By doing so, you're likely to get a sense for what is being paid by competitors as you compare responses to your ad. That can come in handy in placing future listings.

More importantly, emphasize what someone can learn working for you, and if you have success stories of people who have interned for you and gone on to successful higher-paying positions in your company or with another, say so. Offer to provide a reference if an applicant so desires. Even in tough economies, people looking for any paying job at all seek out the one with the most benefits for both their present and their future. You'll be interviewed, too, when you meet an applicant, so don't forget that craigslist is a community. If you don't believe that word could get around about you and your company, go take a look in the **jobs** category under the **discussion forums** banner. You might find yourself getting discussed.

Finding the Right Job Ad Category

Before placing a job listing, cycle through all the categories to see what they read when the contraction for the category is expanded on its respective page. For example, as previously noted, **sales/biz dev** expands to **sales jobs.** If you were looking for a Public Relations Manager, it wouldn't go under "business development" as you might expect the expansion would read; it should be listed under **marketing/ advertising/PR jobs** that reads exactly the same when you click over to that page. That might seem trivial, but if you read through enough misplaced listings, you'll see the wisdom of having a good working understanding of the **jobs** categories.

As a shortcut, use the **search craigslist** box on the main page, set the button to **jobs,** and enter the job tile that you plan to use in your ad. When writing this book, a search for "PR Manager" brought up listings from just about every **jobs** category, including nonprofit, food/

beverage/hospitality, marketing/advertising/PR, etc., tv/film/video/ radio, software/QA/DBA/etc, and web/HTML/info design. In many cases, the same ad was placed in three or more categories on the Los Angeles craigslist, in direct violation of the craigslist rules. So you can do that and get away with it, but if your duplicate ads get repeatedly flagged, it's a good chance the "craigslist police" will spot your offending behavior and do something about it. Even if you have a paid posting account, that doesn't exempt you from the rules.

There's a simple solution: don't be lazy. It's really not that much work to reword the ad slightly to more closely fit a different category. You'll pay for job posts in major cities anyway (and $75 in San Francisco), so it's puzzling why some people will take a risk and post the same ad. Maybe the normal $25 per ad fee is so low they simply don't care to take time to rewrite. It's your budget, so it's up to you.

List Losers

Don't overpost. Listings can be flagged and deleted due to "spam/ overpost—posted too frequently, in multiple cities/categories, or is too commercial." "Too commercial" would not apply to a job post, but multiple cities and categories would. Only craigslist employees know how many negative flags a post gets before it's automatically removed. Do you want to chance it?

Writing Just the Right Ad

On the **Manage Employees** page at the aforementioned www.sba.gov/ smallbusinessplanner/index.html there's a link to "Writing Effective Job Descriptions." The resultant page is a fine article that includes the following description of what a job description should include:

- ◆ Job Title

- ◆ Job Objective or Overall Purpose Statement—This statement is generally a summary designed to orient the reader to the general nature, level, purpose, and objective of the job. The summary should describe the broad function and scope of the position and be no longer than three to four sentences.

◆ List of Duties or Tasks Performed—The list contains an item-by-item list of principal duties, continuing responsibilities, and accountability of the occupant of the position. The list should contain each and every essential job duty or responsibility that is critical to the successful performance of the job. The list should begin with the most important functional and relational responsibilities and continue down in order of significance. Each duty or responsibility that comprises at least 5 percent of the incumbent's time should be included in the list.

◆ Description of the Relationships and Roles the occupant of the position holds within the company—Remember to include any supervisory positions, subordinating roles, and/or other working relationships.

Read the entire article. It's an excellent free resource that will help you formulate an employment listing for craigslist.

Using the previous criteria, let's have a look at a good job listing. The better the title of your ad, the more likely you'll be found in searches. Remember, you can select "only search titles" in the search engine under a **jobs** category.

Just as prospective employees are expected to describe their job goal at the top of a resume, the beginning of your ad should clearly state "Job Objective or Overall Purpose Statement" as mentioned previously.

The List of Duties or Tasks Performed almost goes without saying, but how many job ads have you seen where it seems there is so much territory covered that the responsibilities almost seem overwhelming? As a potential employer, do you want to read a three-page resume, or a much shorter one? Probably, you chose the latter. Accordingly, think about what your applicant might be thinking while reading your listing. If you give them some idea of salary (as many ads do) they might be evaluating everything they think you expect of them against the number of hours in a normal day or workweek.

Similarly, the Relationships and Roles in your ad are important because (if you write the ad well) they will speak to management and possible camaraderie within the company. If your business maintains a collegial workplace and ready opportunities for advancement, it's something important to put in the listing.

Lastly but importantly, keep in mind that job applicants who frequent craigslist get used to three general types of job ads akin to the three different types of listings that are found under the **resumes** banner. In **jobs**, these are:

◆ A simple job listing no longer than something that can be read without much scrolling, if any.

◆ A medium-size ad with a declaratory statement at the top, such as "Seeking full-time Director of Information Technology." If you have a longer job description posted on a web page on your company site, provide the link, but keep in mind the craigslist prohibition against a link to a multiple job listing page.

◆ If you post a long ad that requires a good bit of scrolling to read, a full job description using the items mentioned above would be acceptable.

Using accounting/finance jobs as an example, you might find a short ad for "Staff Accountant Needed," a longer listing for "Senior Accountant," and a long ad for "Director of Finance." Generally, the more complex the position, the longer the ad.

For an example of a good ad, simply study what they look like in your local area. We could provide generic examples here, but they might not speak very well to local idioms and preferences where you live. So study your local craigslist.

Resources for Qualifying Candidates

At www.leadingforloyalty.com/free_employee_assessments.html, you can find free downloadable employee assessment tools. There are similar sites across the web. Most employers these days research potential employees' credit history and other areas that reflect on personal behavior, and the $29.95 or so you might spend for web-based information is usually worth it. You can also find information about the current job scene at www.gallup.com/tag/Jobs.aspx, which might be a good idea to give you an idea of what people looking for jobs are up against.

Since people who use craigslist to look for jobs often use it for other reasons, it might not hurt to casually ask a job applicant if they ever use the discussion forums. If they do, ask how you sign up for the forums.

Most likely, they'll tell you that you need to pick a "handle" to use. If they'll reveal theirs, you can search the job market forum and see if they show up complaining much about potential or current employers. If so, maybe they're not for you.

If you have a larger business with many employees, but not large enough for a full-time Human Resources person, look into an Internet-based company such as Well Hire. See http://wellhire.com/Public/how-it-works.aspx for more information. With a service like that, you can include a job test in your craigslist ad, and Well Hire will assess and track job applicants for you.

If you've never placed a job ad on craigslist before, you might be surprised to find that you need some help in sorting through a flood of applicants. In a tough job market, a simple ad for a secretary could result in hundreds of responses. Would you know how to sort through all those effectively? Don't forget, according to the site more than 50 million people use craigslist each month, including more than 40 million in the United States alone. Good luck in sorting it all out.

The Least You Need to Know

◆ It's a good idea to assess your own strengths when you start looking for personnel because you'll know where you have weaknesses and could use help.

◆ The Small Business Planner pages provided by the Small Business Administration at www.sba.gov can be a wonderful resource for writing better job ads.

◆ Place ads for **volunteers** under the **community** banner. If you want an intern, list in the **[part time]** category under the **jobs** banner.

◆ You're more likely to get better responses if you place a job listing in the right category, so study the categories before you post.

◆ The **Manage Employees** page at the Small Business Planner area at www.sba.gov offers a link to "Writing Effective Job Descriptions" that can be very helpful in composing an effective job ad.

◆ There are free downloadable employee assessment tools on the web beyond the de facto credit check, such as test links to be placed in your ads.

Part 4

Buying and Selling and Profiting

Whether you're bartering, selling cars, recycling, or brokering real estate, there's something for you on craigslist. The opportunities are not just in the United States, either. You can make connections in China, India, and many other places, and all in English, thanks to the site. Also, you might be surprised to discover that craigslist and eBay can be used compatibly to create an even bigger business for yourself.

Chapter 16

From Recycling to Real Estate

In This Chapter

- ◆ Bartering
- ◆ Collecting
- ◆ Generally, don't waste time
- ◆ Bigger ticket items
- ◆ Vehicle advice
- ◆ Real estate bargains

It's still the same old story, the chase for bucks and glory, or something like that. If you have an entrepreneurial spirit, craigslist offers a myriad of possibilities, starting with barter, the oldest form of commercial exchange. This chapter is about **barter** and other items under the **for sale** banner on the main page, and ideas and possibilities about using them for fun and profit. With over 30 categories, there's something for everyone, including those who want things for free. We won't cover everything in this chapter, but hopefully we give you some profitable ideas.

Bartering in the New Economy

You can find just about anything in the **barter** category. You'll see a couple of cautions at the top of the page: **[partial list of prohibited items]** and **[avoid recalled items]**. The former covers a lot of ground, as you'll see when you click on the link. It's a page that's a legal protection for the site, covering all kinds of weapons, fireworks, medical devices, pets, various types of tickets, and "used bedding and clothing, unless sanitized in accordance with law," among other things. It's a good idea to review it before you post, because craigslist receives a lot of scrutiny by legal authorities these days, and if you try to bend the rules by using the site to trade something you shouldn't, someone just might be watching.

If you don't believe that, take a look at the weblinks provided on the prohibited items page. They include the Bureau of Alcohol, Tobacco, and Firearms; the Copyright Office; the Food and Drug Administration; the Fish and Wildlife Service; and the Patent and Trademark Office. Along that line, the **[avoid recalled items]** link goes to www.recalls.gov, a site providing information on consumer products, motor vehicles, boats, food, medicine, cosmetics, and environmental products. That site is the joint effort of six federal agencies—the U.S. Consumer Product Safety Commission, the U.S. Dept. of Transportation, the U.S. Coast Guard, the Food and Drug Administration, the U.S. Dept. of Agriculture, and the U.S. Environmental Protection Agency. The aim of the site is to provide better service in alerting the American people to unsafe, hazardous, or defective products in a "one stop shop"

> **List Notes**
>
> Sometimes, people have a service to offer that they're willing to barter. Or they might have a product but have no idea of a fair price. If you find yourself in that position, use "for?" at the end of your title line, such as: "Acting lessons from an experienced coach for?".

for U.S. Government recalls. So if craigslist would go to the trouble of linking a concentrated federal site like that, doesn't it tell you they mean business about the things they don't want advertised on the site?

Now to the actual business of bartering, because it can indeed be a business, according to the Internal Revenue Service. At www.irs.gov/businesses/small/article/0,,id=188094,00.html the IRS explains:

> Barter exchanges, whether Internet based or with a physical location, are required to file Form 1099-B for all transactions unless certain exceptions are met. Barter exchanges are *not* required to file Form 1099-B for:
>
> ◆ Exchanges through a barter exchange having fewer than 100 transactions during the year
>
> ◆ Exempt foreign persons as defined in Regulations section 1.6045-1(g)(1)
>
> ◆ Exchanges involving property or services with a fair market value of less than $1.00

Since you're making a legal transaction when you barter something according to the IRS, it is in effect a sale, whose legal definition is "transfer of something (and title to it) in return for money (or other thing of value) on terms agreed upon between buyer and seller" (see http://dictionary.law.com).

You'll find numerous items listed in the **barter** pages that will display a $1 price at the end of the title line. That's there to make the transaction legal, at least in some states. You might never run into legal troubles with listings in the barter section, but it pays to know the rules.

A web search for "barter sites" will provide a long list, from BarterBee to SwapThing. There's even an application for Facebook that facilitates trading (see www.tradeafavor.com). On craigslist you have the advantage of your trading partner likely being local so you're able to personally inspect the item in question as craigslist advises. Other than the $1 price mentioned above, when you see a price on a listing, such as $1,400 for a plasma TV, that's the owner stating what he or she thinks the item is worth. That allows you to gauge if an item you have to trade has equal value. Many posters will not bother to list a price, and will simply enter something like (Or Low Cash Price) or (Let's Make A Deal) in the **location** box when they create a listing, thus putting their phrase at the end of the title line. For example:

> *Brand-new furniture for computer - (Make An Offer)*

How you go about trading is your call, and possibly a subject for another book entirely. The barter area of the site is like a giant yard or garage sale, except that people usually trade items for items, instead of money for things. If you're a skilled enough trader, you could profit handsomely, just make sure you're not violating any laws.

Collectibles and Valuables

If you seriously want to make money in the **for sale** area of craigslist, you need to do what entrepreneurs do all over the country—buy low, sell high. Usually, the most easily moved items are those that have some emotional quality to them. That's why you find all the "impulse buy" items like candy and chewing gum and gossip magazines near the checkout lines in grocery stores. Under **for sale,** with this principle in mind you'll probably have the most luck on small items you'll find under **books, collectibles, games+toys, jewelry, tickets,** and **music instr.** For marketing, one group to keep in mind (and you may be in that group) during your searches are Baby Boomers, the second largest financial demographic in the United States As Boomers get older and retire, they grow reminiscent just like all generations do, and often collect things fondly remembered from their youth, whether it's a first edition of *Catcher in the Rye*, a Roy Rogers lunchbox, the first Beatles vinyl album, or a Stratocaster guitar like the one they had to sell when they ran out of money in college.

Think about it, what are their choices? They can go to music stores and pay a premium price, browse through pawnshops (very time-consuming), or search on craigslist to find that blonde Stratocaster. Which one do you think they'll choose? As with everything else, prices vary by region, so if you know guitars and live in a rural area, you might look for a valuable instrument in your town and then advertise it in larger urban areas. Okay, you'll have the burden of distance and proving the value of your item, but if they make it work on eBay, why not craigslist? Besides, people sell things when under financial distress, so if you have the cash and can pick up items for far less than their market value, you're probably still paying more than people could get at a pawnshop, so you're doing the seller a favor, and can resell locally later.

Working young adults will probably be your largest buying group for other items like furniture, computers, and tickets, but unless you're a veteran ticket scalper there's probably not as much room for profit there. (Besides, that's usually illegal.) They could, however, be a source of items you could turn around for a profit, because of fluctuating finances.

Skip's Tips

Don't forget retirees. According to a February 2009 article by the Center for Media Research, the largest increase in Internet use since 2005 is the 70-to 75-year-old age group. With 45 percent of that group now online, they might be a market for you, or a source of saleable items.

Estate Sales and craigslist

With gold prices high and going higher, people frequent estate sales looking for bargains and sometimes walk away with steals. You won't find those in **events** under the **community** banner, but under **garage sale** in the **for sale** bracket. On the **garage sale** page, search for "yard sale," "moving sale" (or merely "moving"), "estate sale," or "garage sale" and open up the links that result. Remember, you're allowed four pictures per listing, and since people want you to visit their sale, they'll usually portray the most valuable items, so a quick glance at the ad should tell you whether or not you want to take the time to visit.

With a moving sale, you're more likely to find larger antiques and other items of value, so you might want to look at those first. And don't forget that you can seek out exact items in the search box. If you're looking for antique watches to repair and/or refurbish, search for that. You probably won't get many links with "watch" in the title. Instead, the links will be to ads that have that keyword within the body of the listing. When selling, keep in mind that if people are moved emotionally to buy an item (like tickets to a sold-out concert or an antique watch at a great price), your profit can rise proportionally.

Pricing Resources

Do you know what your time is worth? If you're like most people, the hourly, weekly, or monthly income that you're currently making is usually the criterion in starting a new business to make money using craigslist. It helps to have a lot more information like that. At the "Marketing Teacher" site, you can find free resources on the topic of marketing. At www.marketingteacher.com/Lessons/lesson_pricing.htm you'll find definitions on various types of pricing such as "Psychological Pricing: This approach is used when the marketer wants the consumer to respond on an emotional, rather than rational basis. For example, 'price point perspective' 99 cents not one dollar."

On that page you'll find another link to setting an eMarketing Price. The pages go on and on, with lessons and exercises, all at no charge. Spend some time there; you'll know quite a bit more than the normal craigslist user when you're done.

Wikipedia also has a thorough description of different types of pricing at http://en.wikipedia.org/wiki/Pricing_strategies.

An excellent free resource for learning about pricing and marketing is Scott Allen's Entrepreneur page at About.com (see http://entrepreneurs. about.com). His article "Pricing Methods: Four models for calculating your pricing" should answer many questions. For example, cost-plus pricing is explained as including your production cost (both cost of goods and fixed costs), plus a profit margin. If it costs you an average of $30 to acquire an item from craigslist (gas and price), and you want to operate at a 20 percent markup, you would add $6 and need to sell that item for $36. How do you know what size markup to use? What the market will bear is one consideration, but the worth of your time counts, too. Using a simple formula like that will help you determine if what you're buying and selling is worth your time. There are many other types of pricing, so do some studying before you launch into marketing mania.

General Is a Waste of Time

The **general** category under **for sale** is the catch all of that section of craigslist. If you want to look through it and you have an idea of what you want to find, use the search box first. There tends to be a lot of collectibles in that category, so sometimes you'll come across a rare find. If people get gift cards they don't plan to use (like from Apple, yet they use a PC), they'll put listings in **general,** but you won't get rich buying and selling items like that.

Probably because people just don't know where to place certain ads, **general** is a popular category. When writing this book, we found over 5,500 listings in that category on the Los Angeles craigslist page, covering four days' postings. Since those listings expire in seven days, it's safe to say we would find around 10,000 listings in the general category on any given week on a major metropolitan area craigslist site. Of course, some of the ads were odd. One was for "Gluten Free All Purpose Flour for $2." Naturally, the title was mis-leading. When the ad was opened, it revealed that they were selling five 5-lb. bags (25 lbs. total) with a price per pound cost of $2.14, with a website listed. Like the title says, **general** is a waste of time in many cases, but if you are looking for something specific, or if you just have some time to kill, you might find something you want there if you're willing to take the time to look.

> ### List Notes
>
> As an added measure to keep pet sales off its site, craigslist adds the note "please flag pet sales" at the top of the page that results from clicking on the **general** category. It's right next to **[partial list of prohibited items]** but is not "clickable" to more information.

Bigger Ticket Items Like Electronics

The categories **computer, electronics,** and **photo+video** under the **for sale** banner all offer decent possibilities for making money, but unless you have some interesting legal connection to a supply of the items sold under this banner, it could become frustrating trying to make excellent profits. Let's go over these three categories briefly.

The **computer** listings (expands to **computers & tech**) almost without fail offer used computers, software, and accessories. On occasion, you'll find a dedicated PC user who was given a Mac as a gift and just wants to sell it, but you'll find it hard to get a bargain because Apple polices pricing of its computers in any stores that sell new Macs. Because these prices are so well known and easily found on the web, unless someone really needs the money they generally won't flinch much on the price. It's easier with PCs and not hard to work out pricing by simply comparing ads. PC or Mac, if you know prices and worth of equipment, sometimes you can score.

If you're adept at fixing computers, it's possible to find real bargains from people frustrated by nonworking equipment. The problem is, though, that there are scores of computer techs that make a living doing just that. One thing to try to avoid is falling for the "loaded" pitch about all the software on a given piece of equipment that doesn't have legal, accompanying disks. Pirated software known as "warez" could be present, something notorious for being redolent with viruses (yes, even with Macs).

Under **electronics** you'll find smartphones like Blackberry and iPhone, as well as iPods, the occasional computer peripheral, Xboxes, Playstations, Wiis, and assorted other things. Obviously, the big ticket items like smartphones and iPods might offer the most possibility for profit, particularly if you can repair such items, but you'll have a good deal of competition in any large metro area, and you'll also run into the likelihood of dealing with stolen items, so be careful.

The **photo+video** listings pose the "Is this stolen?" question and if you're contemplating buying from this category, you'd better do your research online about every item. You'll find film and digital cameras, camcorders, prosumer videocams, ad infinitum. Real bargains can be found, too, like $500 worth of Kodak film for $300. So can you profit buying and selling in this category? Sure, if you know what you're doing. You'll probably find very few listings from people who repair cameras and sell them, so if that's something you can do, a good business might result. If you plan to shoot your own low-budget movie, however, it's likely you could find every piece of equipment you need here, more inexpensively than anywhere else unless a movie company is selling everything.

In all three of these categories, it generally takes technical expertise and experience to build a business buying and selling. It can certainly be done, but you'll probably need to be described by your friends as a techie, or even a nerd.

List Losers

If a computer ad looks too good to be true ... you know the drill. "BRAND NEW APPLE MACBOOK PRO LAPTOPS FOR SALE!!!" might have impressive pictures but an email address within the ad that is *not* a craigslist address, so the site won't know if you respond. Get serial numbers, check them with Apple (or manufacturer of another computer) and verify before you act.

The Vehicle Connection

People who sell vehicles are usually the same breed: they love the vehicles they deal in, whether it's **bikes, boats, cars+trucks,** or **motorcycles.** If you know the difference between a 7-speed and a BMX, and spend your weekends peddling around on two wheels, you'll have a reason for perusing the **bikes** category and maybe will figure out a way to make money there. The same goes for **boats** and **motorcycles;** it's probably folly for us to try to offer tips on buying and selling vehicles.

The **cars+trucks** category is a different story, because so many more people drive cars than use all those other types of vehicles, at least in the United States. While there is a direct link to the **motorcycle forum** on the **motorcycles** page and there is not a similar link at **cars & trucks,** something else on the **cars & trucks** page bears mention. In ALL CAPS, in a font twice as large are normal, craigslist says:

[OFFERS TO SHIP CARS ARE 100% FRAUDULENT]

It's a clickable link, too, leading to the scams page at www.craigslist. org/about/scams, and you'll see the following highlighted in yellow:

DEAL LOCALLY WITH FOLKS YOU CAN MEET IN PERSON—follow this one simple rule and you will avoid 99% of the scam attempts on craigslist.

There's a reason for this, the supposed Out-Of-Area Buyer that has been a plague on craigslist. If you scroll down the page on that scams link given above, you'll find "actual scam emails sent to craigslist sellers" that cover car and motorcycle scams people tried to perpetrate. Study every word on the page and, if necessary, click on the appropriate links like the Federal Trade Commission (FTC) online complaint form at www.ftc.gov.

All that said, it's possible to make excellent profits buying and selling cars locally via this category, particularly if you have a knack for minor repairs. You'll find there are two types of classification of ads here:

<<cars & trucks - by owner

<<cars & trucks - by dealer

You'll see one of those designations at the right of each listing. Here's a catch. Clicking on **cars+trucks** expands to a page with **cars & trucks – all** at the top. If you click on an **owner** designation at the right of any title, you'll go to a page that reads **cars & trucks - by owner** and lists *only* cars and trucks for sale by owners. Similarly, clicking on a **dealer** designation brings up a page reading **cars & trucks - by dealer** and lists only cars and trucks on dealer lots. Try it, and you'll see that on the resultant pages the <<*cars & trucks - by owner* and <<*cars & trucks - by dealer* designations will not appear on the right side of listings on the new pages.

If you're intent on buying and selling cars via craigslist, take a hint from the dealer listings. More often than not, they're very well laid-out ads with clear pictures, with links to the dealer's website. While you might not need your own website, a classier ad on your part that competes with dealer ads will generally put you ahead of the pack in the **for sale by owner** category. Owners often do things like typing the text of an ad IN ALL CAPS, as if that will convince the reader. (ALL CAPS is considered shouting on the Internet, and rude.)

Online Heat
To browse vehicle visuals quicker, try the Listpic "Visual Classifieds Browser" at http://sfbay.listpic.com. [Note: The site might not work using Explorer.] You can change to cities all over the United States. The page resembles craigslist but is not affiliated. When you click on a category, you see pictures immediately, with prices above the thumbnails.

If you do start making profits with vehicles on craigslist, cover your business bases, because your identity can be determined via the site if necessary. If you sell someone a car that breaks down even though you sold it as-is, and they decide to make trouble for you, the laws about dealers in your area might come into play. If you're not legitimate but should be, you could pay the price. Take care of business, and your business will take care of you.

Real Estate Bargains Across craigslist

Under the **housing** banner you'll find **real estate for sale** and that's all we intend to cover here. If you're sophisticated enough to own office or commercial or even vacation rental property, you probably don't need our advice. Given the 2008 residential housing crash across the United States, however, with prices off 20 percent or more in some areas, that means bargains for those that can afford it.

Do People Really Sell Houses?

Yes, people sell houses all the time, even in a down economy. Similar to the way cars are sold on craigslist, you'll find real estate listed in two ways:

<<real estate - by broker

<<real estate - by owner

When you click on such a designation to the right of a listing title, you'll be taken to a page of listings only by broker, or only by owner. In most metropolitan areas, you'll find that broker listings are much more common than owner listings. Once you're on one of those pages, you can select a minimum and maximum price, number of bedrooms up to 8, and whether you want to search only titles and if the listing must have an image. Just as you find when comparing the owner and dealer listings in **cars & trucks,** the **real estate** broker ads are much classier, so take a clue from them if you're selling as an owner.

You'll also find a top of page link in the real estate ads: **[stating a discriminatory preference in a housing post is illegal]** leading to www.craigslist.org/about/FHA. You need to read everything on that page and probably the links given there if you want to play it safe. The site says:

> When making any posting on craigslist, you must comply with section 3604 of the Federal Fair Housing Act. This law generally prohibits stating, in any notice or ad for the sale or rental of a dwelling, a discriminatory preference based on any of the following protected categories:
>
> ◆ Race or Color
>
> ◆ National Origin
>
> ◆ Religion
>
> ◆ Sex
>
> ◆ Familial Status (more)
>
> ◆ Handicap / Disability (more)

The **(more)** offers a link to a page of additional information in each category.

You'll find that in the post-Bush market there are many grouped foreclosure listings *offered by brokers*. You'll see many craigslist ads by brokers that list no specific properties, just a link to their foreclosure listings. Obviously, it's not difficult to find foreclosures on your own, as well as Real Estate Owned (REO) properties that have gone back to the mortgage company after an unsuccessful foreclosure auction. As such, enterprising real estate entrepreneurs will probably want to spend more time looking through the owner listings.

If you're new to real estate, watch out for scams like rent-to-own systems and other things that sound too good to be true. Don't fall for the "We can do this because it's a down economy" pitch. You'll see ads with links to outside websites that offer to get you into a home with only a few thousand dollars. Thoroughly check out those sites with web searches, contact the Better Business Bureau, and use any other resource you can find before you spend.

It's entirely possible, however, to find amazing deals, even no money down with the owner carrying the note (yet more reason to look only in the **for sale by owner** listings). If you have decent credit, steady income, and cover your bases legally, you could easily get started in the real estate business and build after answering one craigslist ad. Other factors like a first-time buyer tax credit, and knowing about depressed areas that will rebound in coming years also come into play. In the latter case, the craigslist advice of dealing locally again applies. In real estate, you really need to know your area.

Variations According to Locations

Midway down the www.craigslist.org/about/FHA page you'll read the following: Click your state below for a brief summary of state Fair Housing laws in your state. Please note that not all states have additional Fair Housing laws.

You'll find links to applicable states; craigslist put in quite a bit of work rounding up all that information, and there are many more links to various statutes to give you the exact information you need in those locations. Study the craigslist FHA page referenced above and the state links in your state, if they're available.

A curious aspect of craigslist real estate listings in a struggling economy is that properties that are much cheaper in one part of the country will be advertised on craigslist sites in more affluent areas, which of course makes sense for the sellers. Whether or not you're interested in bulk real estate purchases in Detroit and other depressed places in Michigan is up to you. A three-bedroom all-brick home in Tennessee for $169,000 might look fantastic to someone living in the Los Angeles market where a similar home could cost four times as much.

Where you choose to live and what your real estate interests and resources are, only you know. If you do find yourself wondering about real estate in other parts of the country, there's a quick way to compare. Use the "search by region" facility of www.crazedlist.org and do some snooping around in the real estate category. If "time is money," we can at least save you some time with that shortcut, and whatever you decide to buy and sell via craigslist, we certainly hope you make a lot of bucks.

The Least You Need to Know

◆ You can make some great deals bartering on craigslist and other sites, but you're still responsible for taxes on those transactions.

◆ Knowing who to sell to, how to best sell to them, and how to price your items are some of the biggest hurdles to overcome in business.

◆ Making money on electronic items found via craigslist often depends on an ability to repair and refurbish those items.

◆ Of all the vehicle categories on craigslist, **cars+trucks** is probably the best bet for making money.

◆ Real estate listings on craigslist offer ample chances to turn a profit, even in a down economy—but only if you educate yourself, which craigslist will help you do.

Chapter 17

Opportunities Outside the United States

In This Chapter

- ◆ Dissecting the countries
- ◆ Chinese and Indian connections
- ◆ Business down under
- ◆ UK and Europe
- ◆ Navigating the other Americas
- ◆ Exchange rate understanding

Remember the phrase "Think locally, act globally"? You can do that with craigslist and make money, despite the site's repeated attempts to stress that you should only make transactions where you can pick something up in your own area and pay cash for it. That's a nice theory but people around the world are more sophisticated these days. The main issue, once you learn how to prove the value of something you are buying, and certify the worth of things you are selling, is how to ascertain that the person(s) you're doing business with are legitimate. As anyone who's purchased something locally only to later find it defective or stolen will attest, deception can take place face-to-face and with cash, with no recourse. So let's look into how to deal with that and other possibilities, worldwide.

Dissecting the Countries List

In case you haven't already noticed, the banners on the craigslist home page have different colored letters. The **countries** banner has black letters, meaning *it's not clickable.* The clickable banners and categories have blue letters. The three columns on the right on the main page all have banners that are nonclickable. The other four are **us cities, us states, canada,** and **intl cities.** At the time of this writing there were 55 countries and 17 international cities. The **Canada** listing (after clicking on **more …**) had 47 city and geographical area links. Three of those in Canada were listed in **bold: montreal, toronto,** and **vancouver, BC,** designating large metropolitan areas.

You'll find the same graphic scheme when you click on some countries. Choosing **UK** gets you to the London craigslist home page (http://london.craigslist.co.uk) and on the right under the **UK** banner there, you'll see the following heavily populated areas highlighted **in bold: birmingham, edinburgh, glasgow, leeds, liverpool, manchester, sheffield,** with a **more …** at the bottom of the cities column that will take you to a list of more areas, none of them highlighted.

If that seems quaint and quirky, it nevertheless fits with the English. The point is that you can recognize the higher population areas by looking for this scheme, but sometimes they ignore it. For example, clicking on **china** from the home page takes you to a new page listing the following cities:

beijing
guangzhou
hangzhou
hong kong
shanghai
shenzhen

The populations of all those Chinese places are *huge* by world standards, but none of them are highlighted in **bold.** And oddly enough, under **intl cities** on the home page, Beijing is not listed, while **hong kong** is listed. What's that about? Who knows; perhaps it's a craigslist corporate reaction to Hong Kong being much more of a democratic city than the capital of China. We say this because, if you click on **hongkong** under **intl cities,** on the resulting page—http://hongkong.craigslist.org—instead of a list of other Chinese cities on the right, you'll find a nonclickable **asia/pacific** banner that lists important cities across that region of the world.

If you click on any city in the **asia/pacific** column, you'll find that on the resultant page (such as **adelaide**), the **asia/pacific** banner is displayed. The funny thing is, on your personal main craigslist page (in the United States, anyway), there is no direct access link for **asia/pacific.** This is just one of the little road map quirks of craigslist, and why it's good to surf the site a lot to find them, so that you'll save time in the future.

List Notes
Banners on the home page with letterings that are blue in color default to an **all** page when you click on the banner. For example, click on **for sale** and you'll get **all for sale / wanted.** That's all the listings in the section, from all the subcategories, lumped together, which can be helpful in searches.

You will find a similar "grouping" banner when you click on a European city under **intl cities.** Clicking on Rome gets you to http://rome.it.craigslist.it and you'll find a banner that reads **europa.** And so it goes around the globe.

The nice thing for English-speaking craigslisters is that the new sites they visit provide a choice between English and the native language(s) of the new page area. To illustrate, if you click on **zurich** from **intl cities** you'll have the choice of **de | fr | it | en** (Deutsch [German], French, Italian, English).

There are a couple of other ways to find a craigslist page for a city. You can do a web search, or you can try typing in the logical URL. As an example, all Japanese sites end in **.jp** and every craigslist Japanese city site would have the name of the city (in English) after the **http://**; thus, Hiroshima would be http://hiroshima.craigslist.jp. This generally holds true around the craigslist world, but not always. While Athens would be http://athens.craigslist.gr, Brussels would be http://brussels.en.craigslist.org for the English version and http://brussels.fr.craigslist.org for the French. If a quick web search won't give you the site you want, you're probably better off doing some clicking from your main craiglist page to see if the city you are seeking has its own site. So now let's see how you might make your journeys there profitable.

Isolating Your Wishes

What is it that you seek to accomplish in international business using craigslist? Do you want to import electronics from Japan because they get new releases before they're available in North America? Sounds like a great idea but there are import/export laws about such things. The site www.ehow.com/how_2191334_import-electronics-from-japan.html explains the steps necessary to import Japanese items. You could use a site like www.pricejapan.com to order such items. Maybe you know people who would pay the premium on a tariff plus a profit for yourself, just to have cutting edge electronic "bling" that most people don't. It might occur to you to use craigslist in Tokyo. You can find "unlocked and jail-broken" iPhones on craigslist there, meaning iPhones that don't lock you into AT&T service because they've been modified against Apple's policy, but the prices will be about the same as in the United States.

> **Skip's Tips**
>
> You can shortcut an international city search on craigslist by clicking on the larger font **craigslist** in the upper left corner on the home page to reach www.craigslist.org/about/sites. That will give you cities in your state, the United States, Canada, and around the world.

If you're going to find someone to import and/or export to make a business of it, you'll have to narrow down what it is that you enjoy, what you're good at, and then see if you can find resources via craigslist to help. An "obvious" choice like "everyone wants that kind of iPhone" won't usually help you much. You have to get ahead of the pack to see what opportunities are coming up.

Matching Your Needs by Geography

In using craigslist or any other media to market to other parts of the world, it helps to know the cultures and what is currently cool in any given area. In the 1980s, for example, UCLA sweatshirts were a big deal in Paris, and Los Angeles residents would often carry a few extra to sell on trips to France. As 2010 approaches, L.A. Lakers basketball superstar Kobe Bryant is massively popular in China, so if you managed to get a photo or jersey autographed by Kobe, it might turn you a handsome profit in China. The key is in what you need to do to make a reasonable profit, and what will maintain your interest, in something legal that few others have caught onto yet.

Did you know that disco was long established as a cultural phenomenon in Europe before it exploded in the United States in the 70s? Were you around during the Pokemon trading card and cartoon craze in the 90s? The North American market is the most desirable in the world and its consumers are constantly looking for new and entertaining things. If you come across one, you could probably find business partnerships in an involved country by a simple ad on craigslist. After all, North American English is the de facto language of business around the world, which is another reason why all craigslist sites have English options.

When the U.S. dollar is low compared to other world currencies, many American items are cheap to foreigners. In 2008, people from China began snapping up second homes in southern California when housing prices fell rapidly. You can be assured that many southern California real estate ads were placed on the appropriate Chinese craigslist sites.

Understanding Cultural Differences

A big reason to study craigslist sites in countries where you'd like to do business is that you can pick up patterns and idioms. You can also keep from embarrassing yourself. When Honda scheduled the release of its Fit model from Asian markets into Europe in 2001, it was to be called the Fitta. Thankfully, someone pointed out that in Swedish and Norwegian, fitta is slang for female genitalia. They called it the Honda Jazz instead. Major corporations have used odd translations for decades, and the American meaning of the titles of American movies are regularly butchered in Asian countries. But some times, people can be clever when they seem stupid. In the 1960s, when Electrolux of Sweden began selling its vacuum cleaners in the UK with the slogan "Nothing sucks like an Electrolux" the howls of laughter in U.S. marketing circles were endless and the "error" was cited in books. People got the joke in the UK, however, and the campaign was considered effective.

Language differences aside, there's a simple way to find out about various cultures around the world. *The CIA World Factbook* is available online and updated with new material every two weeks. The newly redesigned Factbook website was about to launch as this book was completed in spring 2009. See https://www.cia.gov/library/publications/the-world-factbook. Five new category additions to the Economy category added in 2009 should be helpful to building business: central bank discount rate, commercial bank prime lending rate, stock of money, stock of quasi money, and stock of domestic credit. These were in addition to GDP ("Gross Domestic Product"—representing purchasing power parity), GDP—official exchange rate, GDP—real growth rate, GDP—per capita, and GDP—composition by sector. If you're trying to sell to other countries but aren't sure about their economic circumstances, this resource should help you. Remember, the information is updated every two weeks. To search the Factbook, surf on over to https://www.cia.gov/search?NS-collection=Factbook.

The Chinese Connection

If you merely look at the numbers in the Chinese population, the possibilities can make dollar signs roll in your eyes. The potential has been getting the attention of Hollywood studios for years. Co-productions in Shanghai are common, and major Hollywood movies have even premiered in China. Work.com has an excellent primer on business in China at www.work.com/doing-business-in-china-461 that links resources like the "Are You China Ready?" test at www.export.gov/china, the U.S. Government Export Portal. It's a *very* good idea to take that test and gather in the information on that site.

> **List Notes**
>
> The Beijing craigslist page is at http://beijing.craigslist.com.cn, but the rules aren't any different just because it's geared for folks in China.
> If you click on **help, faq, abuse, legal** on the left, you'll get the same help page that you'll see in San Francisco.

Your Own Private Wal-Mart

One of the reasons Wal-Mart can sell so cheaply across the United States is because of its buying power, and a lot of that money is spent in China. If you have a little money to spend, particularly in traveling to China to trade shows, take a look at www.made-in-china.com. It has numerous categories and with a bit of looking around you'll probably see the possibilities:

(a) Line up suppliers in China.

(b) Use craigslist and other sites to market products.

Want a plasma ball like Nikolai Tesla is often seen pictured with (he invented it), the type seen in old science-fiction movies? Check out that and other electrical products at www.made-in-china.com/showroom/jdouya. You can send an inquiry directly from the site. So how can craigslist help with this kind of commercial exploration? The forums are one way. Let's take a look.

Six Cities, Six Possibilities

Clicking on **china** under **countries** takes you to a page allowing you to pick between six cities: Beijing, Guangzhou, Hangzhou, Hong Kong, Shanghai, and Shenzhen.

You'll find that none of the sites have a Chinese option; all the sites are completely in English. What does that tell you? At the very least, that people outside China are using these sites as much as English-speakers within China use them. A little about each city:

◆ Beijing—The capital city, passing Hong Kong in financial influence in the United States due to the massive amounts of money that flow to the U.S. government from China.

◆ Guangzhou—The third most populous metropolitan area in mainland China. With its "Science City," Guangzhou is the high-tech center of the country.

◆ Hangzhou—A beautiful city in the Yangtze River Delta second only to Guangzhou in GDP among provincial capitals, this city is highly important for its manufacturing.

◆ Hong Kong—The city that, while under British control, became the economic powerhouse of mainland China and continues its dominance to this day.

◆ Shanghai—The most populous city in China and the center of commerce in the country, as well as the hub of culture secondary in impressiveness.

◆ Shenzhen—A major financial center that may be the fastest-growing city in the world, Shenzhen is headquarters to numerous high-tech companies and very sophisticated.

So are people actually trying to do business with Chinese people using craigslist? Well, as this book was being completed, one ad found in Shenzen under **business** in the **for sale** category was titled "New product to introduce in USA" placed by someone looking for new natural pills, oil, or lotion for men. Another ad in the same category came from a Canadian company "seeking volume buyers of wine in China." In the same category on the Beijing site, a small resort complex for sale by someone in the Hamptons on Long Island in New York was being advertised.

There were many more in other cities. If you're looking to set up business with Chinese partners, use that category. If you want to set up an import/export-type business, you'll have to do some more surfing around, but without a doubt the opportunities are there, and the people speak English. Check out the forums; you'll see.

> **List Losers**
>
> If you think that the Chinese are known for being polite and worried about losing face, apparently it doesn't apply in some forums on craigslist. In the **etiquette** forum on the Beijing craigslist, you'll find almost as many flames as you will in any American site. Nice!

One more thing: if you're a talented writer and/or editor, whether you speak Chinese or not, and you want to get some experience in mainland China, look into taking a job there for a while. You'll see ads for English instructors and English editors in all the cities.

The Indian Connection

Surprisingly enough, clicking on **india** under **countries** on the main craigslist page takes you to the Bangalore page. Most people would think it would be Mumbai (formerly Bombay) because that city is so in the news with the Bollywood film industry and the film *Slumdog Millionaire* (2008). From the **bangalore** page, to the right the following cities of India are in a column, and here's a little information about each:

- Ahmedabad—With a history as a textiles capital, it also has a booming chemicals and pharmaceuticals industry, and also exports gems and jewelry.

- Bangalore—Known as the Silicon Valley of India because approximately one third of the country's information technology income is centered here.

- Chennai—Ever worn *Madras* material? That's the former name of the city. It's the home of a large film industry known as Kollywood, and is also an electronics manufacturing hub and responsible for about one third of the nation's auto industry.

- Delhi—The capital of India is New Dehli, and the broader area is the largest commercial center of the north. Its English-speaking workforce is huge.

- Goa—This is the tourist capital of India, on the west coast, and has the highest per capita income of any other state in the country.

- Hyderabad—The multicultural center of the country, it also has a film industry known as Tollywood. With information technology and conferencing expertise, it's one of the most happening cities in India.

- Indore—The commercial capital of central India, it has a history of traditional industries like cars, garments, and steel, but has moved more and more into software and electronics.

- Jaipur—Popular for tourism and the home of many international banks, this city has so many thriving industries including textiles, it's hard to keep up.

- Kerala—With an almost 100 percent literacy rate, the city had a socialist history that has given way to free enterprise a bit, but a large part of its income is derived from residents who work outside India.

♦ Kolkata—Formerly known as Calcutta, and once the capital of the country, the city has the fastest-growing information technology sector in India.

♦ Mumbai—Once known as Bombay, this is the most important city in the country, and not just because of the film and TV industry known at Bollywood. It's the largest city and the financial capital as well.

♦ Pune—Usually considered the educational center of India, the former Poona known as "The Oxford of the East" is the center of India's entrepreneurial spirit.

Obviously, this massively populous country is quite diverse in places where industries are centered. Picking where you might do business in India might take more work than with China, but in India many more people speak English.

Resources for Understanding India

Perusing the forums on all the city sites mentioned above will help, but it shouldn't take you long to determine which cities might be more likely to contain people for the kind of business you want to do. Somewhat like China, you will usually find interesting listings in the business category under **for sale,** but fewer listings from American or Canadian folks looking to sell to Indians. It really depends on the city. For example, you'll see a lot of ads in the **business** category on the **kerala** page. The forums will be much more helpful on Indian pages, because of the high level of English literacy in the country.

If you think you might want to do business in India, before you do

Skip's Tips

Should you consider importing jewelry and other personal items from India for sale, try this link: http://search.ebay.com/ india. You'll get all the items being offered for sale from India on eBay by people in that country and elsewhere. It's a great way to learn pricing.

anything else, read the book *Think India: The Rise of the World's Next Great Power and What It Means for Every American* (Plume, 2008) by Vinay Rai and Willam L. Simon. It explains how this fastest growing of the world's free-market economies works and is recommended by the former editor-in-chief of the prestigious *The Economist* magazine.

Beating Indian Competition

If you've ever dealt with paying a bill such as a credit card on the phone in the United States, or tried to get technical support on some software, chances are you've dealt with someone in India. The country has major international submarine cable systems, and will continue to advance in telecommunications. Unfortunately, they have a problem in that Indian English simply does not always match up well with North American English. If you find that your business is in competition with one in India and the use of the language is a factor, you might be able to exploit that to get the business. Given the natural disasters that often plague the country, too, proving your reliability could help as well.

> **Online Heat**
>
> If you want to know what kind of get-rich-quick schemes are buzzing through cyberspace, check out the 1099 forum. Sure, that's a U.S. income tax form number, but the page you land on reads "self-employment" and that's where you'll find supposedly hot opportunities, worldwide.

Doing Business Down Under

Clicking on **australia** doesn't take you to a default city or area page like **bangalore.** Instead you get a page that offers you a choice of cities:

- ◆ Adelaide
- ◆ Brisbane
- ◆ Canberra
- ◆ Darwin
- ◆ Hobart
- ◆ Melbourne

♦ Perth

♦ Sydney

If you know much about this country that is its own continent, you know how diverse in feeling and activity those cities are. If you don't have much experience with Australians, the chat forums should be quite entertaining.

Similarly, clicking on **new zealand** results in a page with these choices:

♦ Auckland

♦ Christchurch

♦ Wellington

Going to any of those pages will give you the **asia/pacific** banner to the right of the middle columns, with many places you should explore, such as Indonesia, Malaysia, and Taiwan. Just as with other sites we've explored in this chapter, a look through the offerings at the **business** category under **for sale** will give you a decent index of what might potentially be available. Obviously, Taiwan with its free-enterprise societal history might seem like a better bet, but you could be surprised and find more entrepreneurism in other areas.

Speaking of which, in the larger cities in Australia, you're liable to find more listings eager to do business with people in North America. The **business** category is also a great one in Australia and New Zealand if you have a new product or business (but not network marketing, still prohibited by craiglist) that is starting to do well in your area. There are many similarities in the cultures of the United States and Australia, and in Canada and New Zealand. Check out the **money** forum under discussions on those pages and you'll get an idea of what we mean.

The United Kingdom and Europe

Despite the trumpeting by the media of cultural strife between the United States and some European countries under the Bush administration, an examination of business trends doesn't reflect much antagonism. That is, not on the level of business that most readers of this book will accomplish. One thing that did happen was an explosion in the number of U.S. corporations flocking to offshore tax havens. Now, for all intents and purposes, the European Union is virtually merged with the American economy, in a way not particularly favorable to the United States. That's important for you to know if you want to do business with people in the United Kingdom and Europe, because they have likely been living under a somewhat socialistic worldview for many years. And that usually means they might be even more eager to do business with you to boost stagnant realities in their own country.

European Culture and U.S. Popularity

If you're concerned about how the United States is perceived around the world, don't worry, be happy. In fact, quit watching television when they're talking about it. Instead, study websites like www.buyusa. gov/europe. That page is from the U.S. Commercial Service at U.S. Embassies and Consulates and it's designed to work with companies "to increase exports to Europe of U.S. products and services." While you might have in mind importing things from Europe and selling them in the United States, the vast amount of information on the site, country by country, could be invaluable to you. Let's say you have a new medical product that you think would go over well in Europe. Would you know where to start? Try www.buyusa.gov/europe/medical_pharm_contacts.html.

Skip's Tips

> Accepted presentation techniques can vary greatly worldwide. For instance, Australians tend to highly dislike anything that comes across as "hard sell." An ad that works just fine for New Yorkers might turn them off entirely. Check out the local etiquette.

After establishing a business connection, you could trade email, files, and talk on the phone, but what if you want to sound out Europeans independently? You could consult with the Commercial Specialist at the American embassy on Grosvenor Square in London, but why not look for opinions from the people in "health & healing discussions" under **health** on the London craigslist page? They're much more likely to tell you if a product like yours already exists in England and what they think of it.

And, given the European penchant for more natural and homeopathic-type cures, they might inform you of something in common use in Europe that no one's imported yet to the United States. It's all about communication, isn't it?

What They Admire About America

When you're dealing with Europeans, you'll generally find that they are very enthusiastic about American culture, meaning music, movies, television, clothing, and other consumer items. Even American football has been gaining popularity in Europe in recent years, thanks to clever marketing by the National Football League. Similarly, Americans often favor new trends from Europe. Keep that in mind as you figure out a business model between yourself and people "across the pond" (the Atlantic). There are a lot of opportunities out there.

Navigating the Americas

Click on any Latin American country on the main page, like **mexico,** and on the resultant page you'll see a column on the right entitled latin-america. Some of the links are to cities and others to countries. In navigating these pages, it would come in very handy to speak Spanish and even Portugese. On each page, you'll have the option of seeing the page in English, but just as in the United States, those who are bilingual in a Latin language have greater opportunities.

You might ask, are the economies in countries where you'd want to try and do business stable enough? That's up to you to answer. Not all those countries are run by press-hungry dictators. The Caribbean islands have a craigslist site at http://caribbean.craigslist.org. What if you decided to set up vacation tours? How better to make contacts in places you don't know than browsing around this page? Check out the travel/vac category under services, which expands to "travel/vacation services," and you'll see all sorts of resorts and hotel prices listed.

Developing business around the world applies much the same in all the locations in the latinamerica category. What you choose to develop depends on your own creativity, but as is demonstrated every day with border crossings, America has great appeal to people south of our borders.

Understanding Exchange Rates

It's imperative that you know the most up-to-date information on exchange rates when you're doing business around the world. There's a good article explaining it at www.ehow.com/how_2183450_calculate-exchange-rates.html. You might also want to use the Universal Currency Converter at www.xe.com/ucc.

Since you want to be paid in a secure fashion, however, it's probably wise to consider using PayPal.com for the transactions. Any normal debit or credit card works, and if you're selling products or buying them, the site provides protection. (It doesn't provide backup on payments for services.) PayPal is owned by eBay and highly secure. You may have received "phishing" emails trying to get you to give up information that will allow your PayPal account to be compromised, but if it works worldwide for eBay, shouldn't it be trustable?

Another payment method to consider is Western Union. See www.westernunion.com for details. Although they don't send telegrams anymore, they do send money all around the world, even from Russia. They offer an "advanced worldwide security system" and "a global information network for fast pay out." Unless you've used the service you might not know, but locations are in many convenient places, even in your local supermarket.

You have to stay on top of the financial details if you are doing business internationally, but with some adjustments it's not much different than making money right at home. And since you're using craigslist, you very well could be at home doing your business.

The Least You Need to Know

◆ There are hidden area groupings that lead to international craigslist sites that you can only access after the opening page.

◆ All craigslist sites in every country offer English language options. Most offer the country's native language(s), but not always.

◆ You can often gauge the potential opportunities in any given international city or area by studying the listings under **business** in the **for sale** category.

◆ It's as possible for you to exploit the resources of China as it is for Wal-Mart, if you know what to do.

◆ Understanding cultural differences is a major part of doing business with people around the world, such as not trying to "hard sell" Australians.

craigslist vs. eBay: Using Both Effectively

In This Chapter

- ◆ craigslist "non-profit" areas
- ◆ Using craigslist to find valuables offsite
- ◆ When eBay can be a waste of time
- ◆ eBay and craigslist comparisons

Although they are very different sites in many ways, there are many similarities between craigslist and eBay. You can use the sites in conjunction to your advantage. On the craigslist fact sheet it states that "eBay acquired 25% of the equity in craigslist from a former shareholder in August of 2004." You should also know that there is ongoing litigation between the two sites. Take note, however, of this bit from www.craigslist.org/about/help/faq#auction:

Can I put a link in my for sale posting pointing to an auction site like eBay?

No—craigslist is not an auction site. If you have something to offer, please post a set price. Please do not scalp or solicit bidding contests on craigslist, and do not link to offsite auctions on eBay or elsewhere.

It doesn't have anything to do with the litigation, as craigslist feels the same way about other auction sites. The main fact is, eBay ad costs add up rather quickly, while craigslist ads in most categories cost nothing. So let's look at how to maximize both for profits.

craigslist Areas That Won't Make You Rich

As enticing as it can be to explore every item on the main craigslist page, monetarily you're wasting your time with some banners and categories. If you raise exotic pets, you can't sell them in the **pets** category under **community**. You can, however, sell a horse and other farm animals under **farm+garden** under the **for sale** banner. (We know, it's odd, but read the rules and you'll understand why craigslist feels that way.) The **events** category under **community** often has ads for various services and things, but they're usually miscategorized. Basically, don't count on making money under the **community** banner. If you make money under the **personals** banner, you're probably doing something illegal in most locations, so that one is a nonstarter for legitimate businesses. People place ads all the time under **discussion forums,** but they shouldn't, and those listings get flagged by members of the community.

Do you really want to hassle with all that? Probably not.

That means that, basically, all the banners on the left column of the middle three on the main page—**community, personals,** and **discussion forums,** are a waste of time for making money, unless you're violating craigslist's rules. So how can you make money on the site, in the kind of way people cash in via eBay?

> ### List Notes
>
> If you think you're going to post a number of listings at any given block of time, it might be well to check the **system status,** which you'll find near the bottom on the left. If there are or have been issues in the system and they're ongoing, you might want to post another time.

Collectibles Around the World

Under **for sale** whether you're buying or selling, smaller items that can more easily be shipped across the country or around the world can be found in the following categories (with explanations):

- ♦ **arts+crafts**—If you know art and markets, you might be pleasantly surprised what you can find in this category. Many beginning artists don't have a lot of money, and use craigslist to make people aware of their work. Have a look around.

- ♦ **baby+kids**—In recent years there has been another "baby boom" akin in size to that after World War II. Young families often don't have much money, so if you found something like all-natural baby clothes from India and marketed them locally, you might win.

- ♦ **cds/dvd/vhs**—This might not seem like much of a possibility, but in some cases products are released in other countries that are not sold in the United States, as was once true about the old Disney movie "Song of the South" based on the "Uncle Remus" stories, which was available in Japan.

- ♦ **clothes+acc**—While counterfeit "knockoffs" are a consistent problem in all major cities, it's possible to find many bargains in this category to build an inventory for resale.

- ♦ **collectibles**—It is amazing what can be found in this category at craigslist sites across the world. While writing this book we found a replica mastodon skull with tusks cast from molds made using the original fossil skull, for $2000, in Riverside, California. How much might that sell for to a buyer in New York City?

- ♦ **free**—Yes, that's under the **for sale** banner. People just want to get rid of things sometimes. You'll find furniture, appliances, anything. Maybe you'll find something valuable. A valuable copy of the Declaration of Independence was found when someone bought an old picture frame (but not on craigslist).

- ♦ **games+toys**—If you think in terms of categories and you're adept at selling to people of certain interest groups, you might profit here, with everything from paintball equipment to video game players.

◆ **jewelry**—If you plan to deal in this category, you'd better know the difference between fake and authentic, because larceny can run rampant here. Your competition is often established dealers.

You might be thinking that everything you just read is obvious. It's a toss-up whether you can find something at a bargain on craigslist and turn a profit, right? Here's where eBay comes in. On that site, you can do something you can't do on craigslist; you can set up a *store*. If you're not familiar with how that works, take a look at http://stores.shop.eBay. com/_stores/hub. Major manufacturers do it, so why not you?

In any of the categories listed above that fall under the **for sale** banner, is there something that particularly appeals to you as a basis for a business? Maybe you have a preference for another category, like **tools.** The categories we listed previously are where you're most likely to find small, easily shipped items that people find valuable everywhere. The same generally holds true for those categories on sites around the world, if you're looking for bargains that can be sold in your area. You need to enjoy doing business, so trust your instincts.

Are Resellers Worth It?

You've probably seen storefronts of companies that capitalize on eBay by taking items that people walk in with and charging a commission for selling on the site. They handle the transactions and shipping and pay you after taking a commission. Price it out. If you find bargain items on craigslist, unless they're quite a bargain, the commission you would have to pay a reseller probably isn't worth it.

 Skip's Tips _____

If the idea of finding cheap items via craigslist and selling via eBay appeals to you, you're probably the kind of person who could take advantage of eBay's Reseller Marketplace. See http://reseller.eBay. com/ns/FAQs.html for all the information about that.

If you're regularly using eBay and are a PowerSeller, you get the added benefit of eBay's Reseller Marketplace. You can buy directly from manufacturers and wholesalers and sell at a profit. Conversely, if you have a great deal of inventory of some kind, you can sell in the Reseller Marketplace and do not need to be a PowerSeller to sell there. See http://reseller.eBay. com/ns/home.html for complete information.

It's easy to find eBay resellers, so do your research. You may find that dealing in certain items will allow you enough of a profit margin to farm out sales to a reseller, but since only *you* know what you want to sell, you'll have to work out those logistics on your own.

Using craigslist to Find Valuables off craigslist

If you study the postings in the **jewelry** category, you'll get a clue on how to get craigslist users to come to you with merchandise. You'll find ad titles like "Cash For Gold at Joe's Gold and Silver." Some people post on craigslist so that people will contact them to sell, and those buyers are present in many categories. If you know there's a certain type of item that you want to sell for a profit, find the appropriate **for sale** category and create a listing about what you're willing to buy.

You'll find that gold and silver and jewelry dealers who place these ads will often list (ANYWHERE) as their location. What that tells you is that they are placing these ads on many craigslist sites across the country or even around the world. The question then becomes how would you know as a buyer if gold or silver or jewelry is real if you can't examine it personally? You could be paying for something that's bogus. Well, you can follow-up on one of those ads and ask the poster how they handle it, or you can take the advice of craigslist and do only local transactions and pay in cash once you've ascertained you have real, nonstolen goods.

Keep in mind that actual dealers in places like Beverly Hills place ads on craigslist (check the Los Angeles site and see), so you could ask them how their transactions work. Who knows, they'll probably explain. If you're trying to sell valuables to them, know that in most states, just as you must do when taking something to a pawnshop, you'll have to fill out a form with your thumbprint, and there's a waiting period to see if your item isn't stolen.

Websites like www.goldfellow.com weren't subject to those rules at the time of this writing, so you might also check them out and see how they handle buying precious metal jewelry over the Internet. GoldFellow lets you print a Fedex shipping label right from their site so that you can track (and insure) the shipment. That type of reassurance makes people feel secure about you. You might also explore using the **wanted** category under **for sale.** Dealers continuously use this catchall category, so use the search box to cut down on your search time. You'll find people wanting to buy things as curious as American Express points.

Another moneymaking possibility is the **tickets** category, but that's generally a local thing and as people often find when they buy "scalped" tickets outside a sporting or entertainment venue, you're running the risk of buying phony items. If you follow events and want to be in a ticket brokering business, though, placing an ad to that end could get people coming to you. Just check the local laws first; some locales have strict ordinances against ticket reselling of any kind.

Whatever valuables you're trying to buy and sell, whether on eBay or craigslist, it should probably be something you're simply interested in, maybe even as a hobby. When you can build a business slowly around something you love anyway, you're less likely to get disappointed if you don't become a raging success overnight.

Similar to craigslist being started just to help people out locally in San Francisco, eBay was begun innocently. According to the site its founder, Pierre Omidyar, "was experimenting with how equal access to information and opportunities affects the efficiency of marketplaces. As a test he posted a listing for a broken laser pointer, which to his astonishment sold." See http://news.ebay.com/history.cfm for full details.

Online Heat

Remember Beanie Babies? If you want to sell collectibles and are wondering what's hot at the moment, search for the phrase "hot collectibles" at http://shopping.yahoo.com or a similar site. Whether they're actually hot or just have the word "hot" in the title line, you'll learn a lot about what's for sale out there.

When eBay Is a Waste of Time

Any time you're getting paid for an item or service over the web, *even if using PayPal,* make sure that you are paid before shipping the item. While that might sound like a silly statement, consider the following.

You ask someone to pay you via PayPal but, instead of using a credit or debit card that is deducted immediately, they use their bank account and an "eCheck" is generated. Here's PayPal's policy on how that works:

> *PayPal sends the request to your bank immediately. It can take up to four business days to complete an electronic funds transfer.*

So let's say someone uses PayPal, a subsidiary of eBay, and pays you on PayPal via an eCheck. Only then that person goes to his or her bank, closes out the account, and the transaction has not registered with the bank.

If you sell an item on eBay but the buyer never pays for the item (as in the above scenario) but you ship it anyway, you'll be stuck. Here's eBay's policy per the spring 2009 update of the eBay User Agreement:

> *Buyers are welcome to contact eBay for any reason. However, eBay will not permit claims when the buyer has not paid the seller.*

While it may well be that you'll never get burned on an eCheck that doesn't clear or any other payment method, the best policy is to do nothing until you know you have the funds. If someone is in a hurry to receive an item, yet paid by an eCheck via PayPal that takes a few days to clear, don't fall for his or her explanations. Per PayPal policy, they can cancel an unclaimed payment. If a payment is complete, the recipient of the payment can refund it. If you're still waiting for an eCheck to clear your bank, that's an unclaimed payment, isn't it? If they're in a big hurry, tell them to cancel the payment and use a credit card or some other method, or forget it.

eBay and craigslist Price Comparisons

If you like the idea of accumulating items via craigslist and then selling them via an eBay store, before you launch into that, spend some time browsing for that type of item on eBay. You'll get a good cross section of prices for the item(s) you want to sell. Then check out prices for the same item(s) on your local craigslist. If you have or start your own eBay store, people usually pay for shipping on that site, so that won't be a cost for you. Buying locally, probably your only cost is that of picking up the item(s). The price differential between what you see on eBay and what you have to pay locally is one of the best indices of whether or not you're looking at a potentially viable business.

Don't forget the **shopping** area of **discussion forums.** Although you'll see a lot of ads there, in violation of craigslist terms, you'll also find people posing serious questions about prices and selling. And don't forget the Workshop/Discussion Forums on eBay at http://pages.ebay.com/community/boards/index.html. It's in eBay's interest for you to do very well selling via its site, so it has workshop events hosted by eBay staff or guests, and you can read through past workshops. Check the calendar for the latest schedule. The Community Help Boards and other links on that page are an amazing education in selling online and the problems that you have to confront in building that kind of business. They even have an International Trading Discussion Board. Know before you go, and you'll have a happier journey!

The Least You Need to Know

- In many cases, you can find merchandise at low enough prices, or even for free, that can then be sold on eBay for a profit.

- The most likely places to find profitable items for resale are the **arts+crafts, baby+kids, cds/dvd/vhs, clothes+acc, collectibles, free, games+toys, and jewelry categories.**

- eBay's Reseller Marketplace might be the best reselling medium you can find if you are dealing in a high volume of items for sale.

- Sometimes it's easier to simply create listings about what you want to buy on craigslist and allow sellers to find you with their items.

- Never assume you have been paid as soon as you receive notice about an eCheck from PayPal, and don't ship until you've verified everything.

- By comparing prices for items on craigslist and eBay, you can get a quick gauge on whether a contemplated business is likely to have the type of profits you desire.

Part 5

Covering All the Bases

Any business needs to cover itself financially and legally, and a craigslist-based operation is no different. From using government resources to dealing with the Internal Revenue Service, you'll need to know at least the basic steps. Whether you're hiring employees or independent contractors, or simply operating alone, there are things to learn. From shipping and handling tips to getting ideas and backup in the craigslist discussion forums, we're giving you the complete picture.

Chapter 19

Financial Safety and Legal Necessities

In This Chapter

- ◆ DBA …
- ◆ Net neutrality and your bottom line
- ◆ Government resources
- ◆ You and the IRS
- ◆ Keeping craigslist "free"

There's an old saying that "a rotten apple spoils the whole barrel" and to some degree that's true of craigslist users when things happen like the arrest of accused "craigslist killer" Philip Markoff in April of 2009. Prior to that debacle, the site had an ongoing struggle with attorneys general from nearly all the United States over the **erotic services** portion of craigslist, resulting in a joint statement solution. See http://blog.craigslist.

org/2008/11/joint-statement-with-attorneys-general-ncmec for Jim Buckmaster's statement about this on the Craigslist Foundation blog. The agreement resulted in a 90 to 95 percent reduction in problems, which you can read about at http://blog.craigslist.org/2009/03/cl-partnership-with-ags-ncmec-early-results.

After Markoff was arrested and the bad press continued, Wendy Murphy in the *Boston Herald* said:

> "The anti-Craigslist tirade isn't so much about protecting women as it is about protecting mainstream media. According to some experts, Craigslist has contributed to the demise of newspapers across the country because its free services led to a precipitous drop in classified ad dollars. (www.bostonherald.com/news/opinion/op_ed/view. bg?articleid=1169833 for the rest of the article.)

Ms. Murphy's comments point out something important—the huge impact of craigslist. She's right; craigslist ads are cheaper and they're very effective. As you'll see on the Frequently Asked Questions on the site, craigslist supports its operations "by charging below-market fees for job ads in 18 cities, and for brokered apartment listings in NYC." High visibility often equals heavy inspection in our modern society, so keep that in mind as you do business via the site. Just because it's happening via the web doesn't mean you're invisible. You still have to follow the rules, and it should be obvious that it's not that hard for authorities to track your online activities.

Doing Business As ...

One way to keep legal is to file a DBA (doing business as) in your local area. Information on how to do this can be found at Scott Allen's Entrepreneurs Guide. See http://entrepreneurs.about.com/od/businessstructure/a/doingbusinessas.htm. You'll learn that "dba" is referred to as "trading as" in the United Kingdom, and that "if you present your business under a name other than your proper legal name without proper notification, it may be considered fraud."

Skip's Tips

You can use the IRS for profit. While you're looking over tax information at www.irs.gov, you might also check out their auctions at www.ustreas.gov/auctions/irs/index.html. How does a house in Los Angeles with a starting bid of $10,300 sound? We found that while researching this book, and a lot more bargains.

If your business grows large enough, you may need to set up a corporation and get a Federal Employer Identification Number. You can read about how to do those things online at www.simplefilings.com. The site's information page on DBAs is extensive and should tell you everything you need to know about this simple and effective tool for legally establishing yourself in business. See it at www.simplefilings.com/dba/dba.php.

Keeping Your Business Legal

When you file a DBA you have to choose a name for the business, and with it you can legally open a bank account and operate under what is known as your "trade name." When you take it a further step and incorporate, that does more to protect your personal assets from being subject to seizure or attachment should you be sued. In short, it pays to look into these things. Another good place to study the differences and get a quick free education about them is at www.legalzoom.com/dba-guide/dba-defined.html. Learning the advantages and disadvantages of a DBA, what it means to have a corporation, and what a limited liability company (LLC) is all about are things you should do. For example, did you know that in a corporation or LLC, the owners are not personally liable for business debts?

Today, an LLC can be incorporated and an EIN number obtained in an hour or so at sites such as bizfilings.com and legalzoom.com. Before jumping in, you would be wise to research the corporate structures and rules on the websites, as well as in the excellent books published by nolo.com.

Sadly enough, a number of people start doing business via craigslist and the web, then catch up to the legalities later. At a certain level of business, they place unnecessary liability on themselves that could be averted if they simply formed a DBA, a corporation, or an LLC. They fail to take the simple procedure of filing 1099 forms on independent contractors in their employ, or do not deal with other taxes. Be good to yourself and do some reading at the links referenced above and on the **1099** (self-employment) craigslist discussion forum; you'll be forewarned and forearmed and happy you did it.

Shipping and Handling Tips

One thing you learn when you do business via eBay is that you can hurt yourself if you don't watch the cost of shipping and handling (S&H). Too often, people only learn the hard way to add in the cost of S&H, but customers are used to paying it. It comes with the territory in eBay and is factored in when you pay, as stipulated by the seller. You won't find information about S&H on craigslist because they want you to pay cash and deal locally.

Everything factors in: cost of shipping materials, insurance, the carrier you choose, and your time in putting together the shipment. Whether you're using DHL (www.dhl.com), Federal Express (www.fedex.com), United Parcel Service of America (www.ups.com), or the U.S. Postal Service (www.usps.com), they all base their shipping fees on distance, weight, and the method of shipping. Most people don't mind paying an extra fee for a USPS Priority Mail package to get something they want in two days. All the above services pick up and deliver, so check their sites for information and pricing.

Anything that makes your business stand out is great, as long as it's legal. That's why services like Stamps.com (www.stamps.com) offer unique "branding" possibilities like putting your own picture on stamps, but the USPS does that, too, via its "PictureItPostage" page. These days, lots of companies are scrambling for your business, so check them all out before just continuing in your same old habits.

How Net Neutrality Affects Your Bottom Line

Clicking on **defend net neutrality** on the craigslist home page gets you to http://savetheinternet.com/faq. One of the first things to be seen on that page is that "Network Neutrality ... is the guiding principle that preserves the free and open Internet." It further explains that "Net Neutrality prevents Internet providers from blocking, speeding up or slowing down web content based on its source, ownership or destination." If Net Neutrality is *not* maintained, that means that companies will be able to regulate how websites operate on your computer, and how easily they can be found. Let's say some of the lobbying done in Washington is successful, and laws are changed. What if struggling newspapers make deals with online providers to make the craigslist site load slowly? Then it might not sell as many ads, and could go out of business. As wild as that sounds, it could happen in theory, and if you're heavily involved in doing business via craigslist, you would suffer greatly.

> ### List Notes
>
> If you're interested in being an activist about anything that Craig Newmark is interested in, or if you just want to ask him a question, see www.cnewmark.com/2009/03/ask-the-president.html. It's part of his personal site **cnewmark**, where "craig from craigslist indulges himself."

Who Wants to Charge You More

The Save the Internet site says, "The nation's largest telephone and cable companies—including AT&T, Verizon, Comcast and Time Warner—want to be Internet gatekeepers, deciding which websites go fast or slow and which won't load at all." Quoting the *Washington Post*, *Business Week*, and *The Wall Street Journal*, the site lists all the people who would be most affected by such changes. Most notably for craigslist business-builders, these people include small businesses, "innovators with the next big idea," online shoppers, and telecommuters. See the details on that and more at www.savetheinternet.com/frequently-asked-questions. Just as craigslist depends on its users flagging site abusers, the Internet remaining neutral depends on users being active to keep it free. Don't take the craigslist warnings lightly.

What You Can Do About It

You might be able to find out if your Internet provider is lobbying in Washington via the Public Citizen site located at www.lobbyinginfo. org/tools. You can search out a lobbyist directly from that link, and the page also links and describes other sources of information including:

◆ Center for Public Integrity (www.publicintegrity.org/lobby)

◆ Influence (www.influence.biz)

◆ Political Money Line (www.politicalmoneyline.com)

Funny thing is, though, when using the Public Citizen lobbying link mentioned earlier, and searching using the "Choose A Company That Lobbies" button, the most recent year that we could find for lobbying from AT&T, Verizon, Comcast, or Time Warner was 2005. A much better lobbyist search is available from the Center for Responsive Politics at www.opensecrets.org/lobby/index.php. For example, by May of 2009, Comcast Corp. had according to the site spent $2,760,000 in 2009 alone. Results on companies are published quarterly. If you really want to know about lobbyists, use this site.

Using Government Resources

The U.S. federal government has an excellent site for all its information at www.usa.gov. Check out "Businesses and Nonprofits" at www. usa.gov/Business/Business_Gateway.shtml. You'll find links there that will not only provide information you need about doing business, but in acquiring surplus goods from the government that you can resell. Think you have anything to learn from the following topics?

◆ Buying from the Government

◆ Sell to the Government

◆ Launch a Business

◆ Managing and Growing a Business

◆ State Programs

◆ Data and Statistics

- ◆ Financial Assistance
- ◆ International Trade
- ◆ Exporting
- ◆ Laws and Regulations
- ◆ Business Taxes

There's state, federal, and international information. If you got through everything linked on that page, you'd have a rough equivalent of a minor degree program in business. With links to other government sites like Business.gov, "The Official Business Link to the U.S. Government," we believe you'll find that perhaps for once you'll be happy about what you're getting in return for your tax dollars, and be much better able to build a very profitable business using craigslist.

> ### List Notes
>
> Government and legal entities might be able to find out who you are from craigslist use (only via subpoena) but normal users cannot do that if you use an anonymized craigslist address, explained at www.craigslist.org/about/anonymize.

Dealing with the IRS

To find out everything you need to know to be tax-compliant with the Internal Revenue Service (IRS), click on the **Businesses** tab at www.irs.gov. That leads to the **Tax Information For Businesses** page. Under Businesses Topics on the left you'll find links to Starting a Business and Operating a Business that should tell you all you need to know about tax liabilities once you have a business going. You'll also find sites linked like State and Local Governments on the Net, "a directory of official state, county, and city government websites," at www.statelocalgov.net/index.cfm. If you look, everything you need regarding taxes and business rules can be accessed via the IRS site.

Employee vs. Independent Contractor

The IRS defines an employee as someone who performs "services that can be controlled by an employer (what will be done and how it will be done). This applies even if you are given freedom of action. What matters is that the employer has the legal right to control the details of how the services are performed." About independent contractors it states: "People such as doctors, dentists, veterinarians, lawyers, accountants, contractors, subcontractors, public stenographers, or auctioneers who are in an independent trade, business, or profession in which they offer their services to the general public are generally independent contractors." The IRS provides a thorough discussion of this titled "Independent Contractor (Self-Employed) or Employee?" at www.irs. gov/businesses/small/article/0,,id=99921,00.html. There's even Form SS-8 that you can file if you can't determine whether a worker is an employee or an independent contractor. Don't forget that you'll also have to deal with state and local governments. You can use the State and Local Governments on the Net site mentioned earlier to find information about that. The IRS has a **State Links** page at www.irs. gov/businesses/small/article/0,,id=99021,00.html leading to sites for all U.S. states, too.

Your Personal Responsibilities

Did you know there is a self-employment tax? According to the IRS, the SE tax "is a social security and Medicare tax primarily for individuals who work for themselves. It is similar to the social security and Medicare taxes withheld from the pay of most wage earners." If you have employees or independent contractors working for you, there will be forms that you'll need to file. You can learn which ones on the IRS site. According to the "Small Business Tax Calendar—Dates and Actions" page, on the first Monday of February you must "Furnish Forms 1098, 1099 and W-2G to recipients for certain payments made during [the previous calendar year], and Form W-2 to employees who worked for you during [the previous calendar year]." If you pay an independent contractor more than $600 U.S. dollars in a year, you must issue them a 1099 form. See www.wisegeek.com/what-is-a-1099-contractor.htm for more information. According to the IRS site:

Employers must file Form W-2 for wages paid to each employee from whom:

♦ Income, social security, or Medicare tax was withheld or

♦ Income tax would have been withheld if the employee had claimed no more than one withholding allowance or had not claimed exemption from withholding on Form W-4, Employee's Withholding Allowance Certificate.

Also, every employer engaged in a trade or business who pays remuneration for services performed by an employee, including noncash payments, must file a Form W-2 for each employee even if the employee is related to the employer.

The above information is merely a shorthand description of the basics of tax responsibilities. It might be cumbersome to spend a lot of time on the IRS and other government sites learning the rules, but for most small business owners that's much more cost-effective than hiring a tax professional. Even if you can afford a pro, it might still be wise to learn all the basics, so you'll have some idea if they make a mistake.

List Losers

Don't expect the 1099 "self-employment" discussion to be completely jammed with friendly, helpful people only interested in helping other people doing business. You'll find as many insults and off-topic threads there as you will on any Internet chatroom.

The 1099 Forum

On the right side of the **self-employment** page known as **1099** under **discussion forums,** you'll find a box that lets you search by handle (the name a person uses on the forum) or by keyword. Once you've spent enough time on the forum, you'll have an idea of who's a flamer and who's there providing good information, so searching by a handle then might be useful. Otherwise, particularly if you're new, use the keyword search box. It also works for a phrase like "independent contractor." When you get the results of the search, you'll see questions and answers posted by users, 30 at a time. It's a lot easier to scroll through those pages than to try to pick out relevant threads on the opening page of the forum. If the forum seems daunting, just remember, everyone there including the knowledgeable ones were probably once as uninformed as you may be, starting out, so you might get more sympathy than you expect.

Keeping craigslist and the Internet "Free"

In addition to the Save the Internet site linked under **defend net neutrality** on the craigslist home page, check out the Electronic Frontier Foundation (EFF) at www.eff.org. As the site states: "EFF is the leading civil liberties group defending your rights in the digital world." Although the EFF is in many ways an "anything goes and that's OK" type of organization, they do serve as a counterpoint to those who want to limit freedoms on the Net. For example, when the South Carolina Attorney General came after craigslist on the same charges of enabling prostitution that the site had settled with other states, EFF linked it on its "Deeplinks Blog" and pointed out that craigslist was protected by Section 230 of the 1996 Communications Decency Act, which immunized providers of "interactive computer service" (website operators, ISPs, domain name registrars) from state criminal liability for content posted by third parties. You don't need to browse through the EFF site to keep abreast of these things. You can sign up for RSS syndication feeds at www.eff.org/rss and you'll find a lot of other similar-minded links on the sign-up page.

Although it might seem like a waste of time to participate in such things when you're trying to make money, you have to keep in mind that you're using the Internet to build your wealth. That's a pretty big community, and being a member, it's only fair that you do your part.

The Least You Need to Know

- You can learn a lot about the benefits of a DBA ("doing business as") at Scott Allen's Entrepreneurs Guide at http://entrepreneurs.about.com.

- Net Neutrality is important because it "prevents Internet providers from blocking, speeding up or slowing down web content based on its source, ownership or destination."

- At www.usa.gov you can learn about buying and selling to the government, including where to get things at government auction that you can then sell via craigslist.

- Between the **Businesses** section of the Internal Revenue Service site at www.irs.gov and the linked state, county, and city government website at www.statelocalgov.net/index.cfm, you can learn all the tax information you need for your business.

- The Electronic Frontier Foundation at www.eff.org is an excellent place to keep track of all efforts to keep the Internet from being anything but free.

Chapter 20

Discussion Forums: How to Boost Your Business

In This Chapter

- The best forum—help!
- The Money Forum
- The legal forum
- Opportunities in education
- The Job Forum

By this point, we've established that ads are posted in the discussion forums, even though there are express stipulations against that from craigslist. We don't recommend that you do it, but there's something to be learned by studying such postings, so feel free. Sometimes you'll learn what people object to seeing, because the listings will be flagged and deleted. Follow some, you'll see.

At other times, you'll learn of opportunities that might actually be relevant to the topic of discussion. To see how active any given forum is, click on the **discussion forums** banner. You'll be taken to a page that lists them all, and to the right of each forum name you'll see the number of posts to that particular forum in the last 24 hours (24h). For example, when we checked while writing this chapter, the **women's issues** forum on the Los Angeles craigslist site had 10 times as many posts as any other forum. That should tell you something about how many women were using that particular site.

If you want to make some friends in your field of endeavor and trade tips, the forums can definitely be used for that, even though, like all Internet discussion locations, the words can get heated at times. How you handle that will probably have a lot to do with how you do in developing a craigslist friend network.

A Most Important Forum—Help!

Here's craigslist's description of this forum:

> The help desk is for users to help each other with problems related to using craigslist. Our help pages cover all the basics, such as:

> ◆ system status

> ◆ how to submit a post

> ◆ where is my self-publishing email?

> ◆ where is my post

> ◆ how to edit or delete a post

> ◆ common acronyms & terms

That's in the right column of the **help** forum page, which also has a line: "forums help is also available" with a clickable link. For that reason, **help** is probably the most important forum, even though it probably won't have the most activity.

As with all forums, if you're looking for specific information about a
problem you'll probably find it difficult to scroll through the post title
lines looking for your subject, so use
the search box.

You can also simply post your question, but to do that you'll need to
have a forum account established. If
you haven't already done that, just
click on **register** on the top right
and you'll see how to do it. Once

you're registered, you can click on **subscriptions** in the right side column, and get emails with responses to your post. You'll also have the
choice of looking in your local area, or **all.** That choice is found at the
top left of the page.

The help forum is, compared to some other forums, relatively tame, so
it might be the one you'd want to browse through first. Plus, it'll help
you learn the site!

Profiting from the Money Forum

When you click on a posted thread in the left side column of any
forum, it appears in the right side column and you have four choices:

> reply to this post
>
> email it
>
> rate
>
> flag

The **money** forum is one where you might find yourself emailing various posts to yourself or others. It can be very informative. You can
reply to the post without being logged in, but for the other options
you'll have to be logged in to your account.

As with most forums where people are a bit more serious, you won't
find a lot of flames here. There's also a lot of humor in this forum that

is reflected in the quote in the right side column when you arrive on the page: "inflation is taxation without legislation." In short, free thinkers and informed capitalists might well be alive on this page. You'll find people talking about market rallies, collection, and consumer credit, among other things.

The site links to the tax forum and also to the self-employment forum from the right side column, and offers this disclaimer:

> DISCLAIMER—craigslist is not responsible for, and you may not rely upon, the accuracy of any information or advice posted here— this forum is provided for educational and entertainment purposes only—you should consult with a licensed financial advisor prior to acting on any information found here.

Translated: There may be a lot of people here who know what they're talking about money-wise, but if you take their advice and lose your shirt, don't even think about suing.

Keeping Your Money; the Forum for It

Clicking on **frugal** gets you to the "frugal living" forum, which can be surprisingly enlightening. You'll find few flamers here. A lot of the posters are the type of person you might find using www.freecycle.org and the **free** category under **for sale.** It is, however, one of the forums where you'll probably want to click on the **24h** in the upper left of the left side column. That separates the threads and their replies so that it doesn't look like one thread after another, and they're easier to read.

One popular thread we found when researching this forum was about the best craigslist find/buy deal that others had found. For the poster, it was paying $90 for an iPod Touch first generation 8 gig. One responder reported taking time and finding cars on three separate occasions from people who had lost a job, or were moving out of the country, or going back to school. The buyer drove each car five years, then sold each for more than the original purchase price.

> **Online Heat**
>
> Many craigslist discussion forums are not displayed. On the Los Angeles site, **farm** is at http://losangeles.craigslist.org/forums/?forumID=3276. You'll find them mentioned in posts and on the rather well-known www.forumslister.com.

Little tidbits like that can provide ideas about deals on craigslist and give you some idea of what to search for and where to search, so the frugal living forum might be good to spend time browsing through.

Lawyer, What Lawyer? (The Legal Forum)

The **legal** forum, like the **money** forum, has a disclaimer in the right side column, with the addition of the term *res ipsa loquitur.* That's a Latin term that means "the thing itself speaks." When the term is used in court, it means an injury was caused by the negligent action of another party. In other words, craigslist is saying "Don't blame us if the free legal advice you get here doesn't work out, we didn't give it to you."

Nevertheless, you'll find advice there from actual lawyers, as well as people who are experienced in legal situations that are brought up. This doesn't mean you should file a lawsuit or go to court based on that advice, however.

That's why craigslist advises this upfront. Just because someone uses "lawyer" in their "handle" doesn't mean that they possess a valid law degree. Nevertheless, you'll find that you can pose a legal question in the forum and get some logical answers. If you want to follow up offsite with a person who gives good answers, fine, but make sure you have proof that person is a lawyer licensed to practice in your state before you trust him or her.

Many professionals spend time in discussion groups relating to their profession, sometimes to pick up clients. While it might not seem to equate that lawyers would be spending time on craigslist, which many people equate with "cheap," anyone who's known wealthy people understands that many of them got that way by spending as little as possible to get what they needed and wanted.

Opportunities in the Education Forum

Accessed via **educ,** the education forum features a quote from Ralph Waldo Emerson on the right side column that begins: "If the colleges were better, if they really had it, you would need to get the police at the gates to keep order in the inrushing multitude."

You'll find a few more flames here, but if you're contemplating going back to school to finish a degree or get another one, you'd do well asking around this forum. *Hint*: Don't necessarily stick with your local area, unless the educational institution you're contemplating is located there. If you've been offered a job teaching high school in Phoenix, Arizona, find that city's page and ask about the quality of high school education there. Chances are, people will open up to you rather quickly.

Many people who are looking into another career, particularly in the modern economy, want to know about the schools offering courses and degrees that will help their transition. Also, keep in mind that you have the **all** option on the top left, which lets you access the forum threads across craigslist.

One more thing to keep in mind is that if you teach something in particular and offer the courses online, you could let people know in this forum. Let's say you offered writing courses like you'll find at www. skippress.com. It wouldn't be wise to mention them in the education forum because you'd probably get flagged, but you could always survey people to get their experience in taking similar courses. As the thread goes along, you could reveal you're asking because you teach such a course and wanted to glean opinions from writing students. People in the education forum are usually looking to improve themselves in some way, and can be more receptive than others.

Skip's Tips

If you need a break, click on the **jokes** forum and do some reading. Be sure to click on **24h** to separate out the threads. Be forewarned, some of the humor can be pretty raw, but you'll probably be laughing before long and feel better about the day or night.

Getting Employed in the Jobs Forum

The right side column on the **jobs** forum page exclaims: "please, no job postings!" Maybe it's just a coincidence, but this can be a fairly "hot" forum in a "flame" sense. It's not a place to find a job, rather one about "hiring practices, job market trends, recruiters, career development, resumes, interviewing tips, you get the idea" according to craigslist.

Nevertheless, you'll find listings with links about various jobs that people are experiencing across the country. To get more specific to your area, click off the **all** default to your locale on the top left of the page. There is also a link at the top left called **search Job Market** that takes you (oddly enough) to the same page you get when clicking on the **discussion forums** banner on the main page. The **search Job Market** link sets the search buttons to **ALL** and **Job Market** respectively. Enter a job title such as "teacher," then click on the "search" button, and you'll get postings from across the country, some of which are from people looking for folks to fill a specific job. The discussion postings are presented 30 at a time.

One post we saw using that criteria was from a person who said: "I'm looking for a korean teacher in gainesville but i'm not really sure where to advertise." Obviously, if you were a teacher of Korean in Gainesville or willing to move there, you could reply to the post and maybe end up gainesvilley employed.

You will also find other people who are in the same job market as yourself, and you might be able to build up your own personal craigslist community by getting to know them.

Using the **jobs** discussion forum in this way might seem a bit of a long shot, but you'll be able to find out within a few minutes. And who knows, if you start a thread saying something like, "Looking for an engineering job, any leads?" you might just hear from someone who knows a company that's hiring.

Other Discussion Possibilities

There are 72 forums listed on the craigslist home page, and as you've read earlier, there are other craigslist forums that are listed there. While they certainly aren't all about moneymaking opportunities or possible jobs, they're all about people in the craigslist community posting about things that are on their mind. They might all be worth looking at, at least once. For example, **testing** gets you to a page that in the right side column tells you how to embed a link in your posting and also how to embed an image directly in your posting. Nice, huh?

Hey, it's a community thing, and that community stretches across almost the entire world. Look around, get to know it, and try to be a friend. We hope you enjoy it thoroughly, and that you make your dreams come true, financially and otherwise. Thanks for reading, and happy posting!

The Least You Need to Know

♦ If you run into a problem you can't get answered elsewhere, use the **help** forum and you'll probably get an answer more quickly than elsewhere.

♦ The people most serious about profits, and likely the most informed craigslist users, can be found on the **money** forum.

♦ The **legal** forum often has good advice, but more from people who have hard-won experience, not lawyers. There are, however, lawyers who frequent the forum.

♦ The **educ** (education) forum is a particularly good discussion place for people who are contemplating furthering their education.

♦ The **search Job Market** link at the top left of the **jobs** forum page can help you quickly find any jobs mentioned in the forum, and specific advice about job experiences from job seekers.

Glossary

There aren't a lot of special terms to be considered in using craigslist, but you might find it helpful to have a page to refer to for looking up what the various categories in the middle three columns on the home page expand into. We've left out the **personals** banner categories because they are not a focus within this book.

The categories are presented in the order they appear on the home page, not alphabetically. Please note: we have omitted defining any category that may be of a personal, political, religious, or sexual nature, or that doesn't offer much profit potential and therefore has little relevance to this book.

Under community

activities   Expands to "activity partners" meaning people to join you in workouts, etc.

artists   As stated, covering any and all types of personnel involved in the arts.

childcare   Everything from babysitters to day care and schools.

general The "general community" page that is a catchall, could be called "miscellaneous."

groups Can be anything from shopping groups to ads for network marketing.

events Expands to "event calendar" and is a repository for any activity to which you want to attract attendees.

musicians Everything from musicians looking for others to clubs looking for acts.

local news Expands to "local news and views" and is like a community bulletin board that you might find in the center of a village.

rideshare Rarely abused by off-topic ads.

volunteers Listings about everything from free help needed to paid medical experiments.

classes All types of instruction from online to in-person.

Under discussion forums

1099 Expands to "self-employment"—ads for and by people that prefer being their own boss.

apple Expands to "apple / mac" discussions about that type of personal computer.

arts The "arts forum" has far-ranging discussions about anything artistic and art activities.

autos Expands to "automotive" and covers any possibility in that category.

beauty Expands to "beauty / fashion" and offers lively discussion about topics generally attractive to women.

bikes Expands to "bicycling," meaning motorcycles and motorbikes are not covered.

celebs Expands to "celebrity gossip" and might be valuable for determining the value of celebrity collectible items.

comp   The "computer forum" for discussion of any type of computing.

crafts   The "crafts forum" is very helpful if you're active in items listed on the arts+crafts category.

diet   Expands to "dieting" and has ads along with discussions of the subject.

divorce   Potentially profitable for attorneys and those with divorce-related products and services.

dying   Expands to "death & dying" so might be relevant if you're selling related products.

eco   The "ecology" group discusses eco-products and activities worldwide.

educ   Under "education" you'll find ads for schools and classes as well as discussions.

etiquet   The "etiquette" discussions might be helpful in business, particularly in determining local customs.

feedbk   Expands to "cl – feedback" and offers a chance to "talk back" to the site about anything at all.

film   This "film & theatre" group is the perfect place to discuss anything having to do with post-performance products and everything else.

fitness   Products and programs are discussed here constantly.

fixit   Covers "fixit / home imp" (home improvement) and is particularly helpful for those in the building trades, or those hiring same.

food   The "food forum" can be helpful to anyone dealing in selling or preparing food items.

frugal   Expands to "frugal living" and is filled with tips about saving money.

gaming   This one is about computer games, not adult gambling as in casinos or online.

garden   In the "gardening" forum you can learn about what people are planting, what products they are using, etc.

gifts   The "gift ideas" forum that can be a blessing to those in the gift business.

haiku Expands to "haiku hotel" and might be useful if you're publishing or selling books of this type of poetry, as it's mostly filled with those poems.

health The "health & healing" forum covers all aspects of same, both traditional and alternative.

help The "cl - help desk" where users help each other and craigslist staff weigh in, too.

history The "history forum" might be interesting if you are selling historical items like clothing, games, or books.

housing Meaningful and helpful discussions for anyone needing answers about renting, leasing, or buying real estate.

jobs The "job market" forum helps you determine what's going on both locally and across all the craigslist sites.

jokes Good for a few laughs to break up your workday, but some of the jokes are raw.

l.t.r. The "marriage & ltr" (long-term relationship) discussion is perfect for gauging ideas and reactions to marriage and dating products.

legal The "legal forum" can actually give you reliable legal advice posted by lawyers on occasion, and otherwise the posts usually come from people with real experience in the issue under discussion.

linux For anyone who uses or is interested in software using the Linux operating system.

loc pol The "politics local" discussion group can be helpful in keeping up with local rulings, regulations, and laws.

money Though often filled with off-topic posts, the forum can be a good place for advice about and mentioning various business ideas.

motocy The "motorcycle" forum stays pretty much on-topic with discussions by enthusiasts, dealers, and others.

music The "musical beat" forum is excellent for reaching musicians and getting ideas about musical products.

npo The "nonprofits forum" is very active due to the Craigslist Foundation attention to this area of public activity.

outdoor   This "outdoors" forum is excellent for anyone involved in marketing outdoor products or destinations.

over 50   The "over 50 club" gives you an opportunity to commune with the Baby Boomer generation (and older), which is a very desirable demographic for marketers.

p.o.c.   The "People of Color" forum designed primarily for non-Caucasians.

parent   The "parenting" forum offers subforums via the right side column: parents' giving forum, parents' picture forum, trying to conceive forum, and single parent forum.

pets   The "pet & animal" forum is excellent for those who want advice on marketing items to this demographic.

politic   The "politics world" forum can offer assistance in keeping up with what's going on at a government level with regard to affecting your business and life.

psych   If you have employees or a difficulty in understanding someone you're dealing with in business, a question posed on the "psychology" forum might get you a quick answer.

recover   The "recovery" forum offers insight into those dealing with substance abuse and similar problems, so if you, an employee, or business partner are dealing with such problems, you could find friends in this group.

science   The "science & math" forum has subject listings that often cross over into how science is involved in business.

shop   The "shopping forum" is largely filled with product mentions and business opportunities, along with discussions about doing business.

t.v.   The "television" forum might offer some benefit if you're dealing in TV-related products and want to know what shows and celebrities are on people's minds.

tax   The "tax forum" is filled with advice about all aspects of this concern of businesses and individuals.

testing The "XYZ testing" group is for checking out how your pictures and links will display within ads when posted.

travel The "travel forum" offers helpful discussion that can range from better deals to interesting destinations.

vegan The "vegan forum" has lively discussions for anyone interested or involved in this dietary lifestyle.

wed The "wedding forum" is where anyone selling products or services relating to brides and bridegrooms, or those planning weddings, come to discuss this huge industry.

wine From deals to vintages, wine business people and customers keep the threads flying.

women As explained by craigslist on the page, the "women's issues" forum "is a place to discuss issues of particular interest to women, a place for lively, honest conversations about a wide variety of subjects and experiences."

writers The "literary & writing" forum is open for discussion of literature but also frequented by professional writers and editors.

Under housing

apts / housing Expands to "apts/housing for rent" so not the right category for selling.

rooms / shared The "rooms & shares" discussion group might be wise to search if you're locating to another city for a short time for work.

sublets / temporary Similarly, this group for housing solutions for business people could be helpful, particularly if you want a home office bigger than a room.

housing wanted This "all housing wanted" forum is a place where property owners look for potential tenants.

housing swap Trade locations with someone coming to your city when you're going there.

vacation rentals If you're looking for profit on your unused vacation real estate, this is the place to put an ad.

parking / storage   Probably the easiest place to find this type of required space.

office / commercial   Leasing and buying, often without dealing with a broker.

real estate for sale   The "real estate – all" category is where you'll find single-family homes but also other properties for sale.

Under for sale

barter   For any excellent "horse trader" this category can be a source of great profit.

bikes   The "bicycles" category is the place for all listings of interest to bicycling enthusiasts.

boats   Listings of all types of boats, from rowing to yachts, and everything associated with same.

books   Covering "books & magazines" of all types, mostly collectibles.

business   The "business/commercial" category offers businesses for sale, but also items needed by business, such as desks and chairs.

computer   All products having to do with personal computers, across all platforms.

free   The "free stuff" category is exactly what it implies, nothing for sale. (But that doesn't mean you couldn't resell things found here.)

furniture   The "furniture - all" category generally means household furniture, but office furniture can also be found here.

general   The "general for sale" category is where you'll find things for sale that you won't find elsewhere on the site.

jewelry   Adornment merchandise for sale by individuals and dealers.

material   This "materials for sale" category generally means materials that are used in building, and then things in homes and personal residences.

rvs   All "recreational vehicles" can be found here, from three-wheelers to Airstream trailers.

sporting The "sporting goods" category for both new and used items.

tickets Tickets to events of all types, generally local and sold by individuals.

tools Mostly used tools are listed here, of all types.

arts+crafts The "arts/crafts for sale" category is where artists sell their wares, and art is also sold by its owners.

auto parts The category where car parts are generally found more cheaply than any place except salvage yards.

baby+kids The "baby & kid stuff" category is where parents find bargains, usually on used items, but new items are sold here as well.

cars+trucks The "cars & trucks – all" category covers everything on four wheels or more.

cds/dvd/vhs The place where mostly prerecorded programming and equipment is for sale.

clothes+acc The "clothing & accessories" category for both men's & women's attire.

collectibles Some truly valuable bargains can be found here, with usually very little wrongly categorized merchandise.

electronics Any type of electronic equipment (but usually not computers) falls under this category.

farm+garden The "farm/garden for sale" category also includes farm animals such as pigs, cattle, horses, and goats.

games+toys In the "games/toys for sale" category you'll mostly find video games and equipment, but traditional games are also sold there.

garage sale Covering "garage & moving sales," this category is both the cyberequivalent of and advertising for these sales in your area.

household A category for "household items" that can range from small kitchen items to big appliances and anything else used in a home.

motorcycles Offering "motorcycles/scooters," this category also includes motorbikes and other types of two-wheeled motorized transportation.

music instr   You'll find "musical instruments" of all types here.

photo+video   The "photo/video for sale" category deals with cameras of all types and their accessories, including monitors.

wanted   In "items wanted" you can find buyers for things you have for sale, so it might pay to search there before bothering to place a listing.

Under services

beauty   Anyone who provides "beauty services" posts their ads here.

computer   The "computer services" personnel posting here are mostly technicians.

creative   In the "creative services" listings you'll find anything from classes to photographers and much more.

event   The "event services" listings offer locations, party planners, entertainment, and more.

financial   You'll find ads in "financial services" from accountants and anyone else that deals with other people's money and what they do with it.

legal   The "legal services" listings you'll find in this category can be something as simple as people who will handle auto registrations for you.

lessons   The "lessons & tutoring" ads here can be anything from pre-recorded lessons to classes given locally by instructors.

automotive   In "automotive services" you'll mostly find ads by people who work on cars, but you'll also see an ad here and there about parts.

household   The "household services" category includes cooks, maids, nannies, etc.

labor/move   This category expands to "labor & moving" and thus involves many types of laborers.

skill'd trade   In the "skilled trade services" area ads are place by handy-men, plumbers, even interior designers.

real estate   Under "real estate services" you can find anything from financing to brokers.

sm biz ads These "small biz ads" are placed by many types of people, including psychics.

therapeutic The "therapeutic services" advertised here might be caregivers or masseuses, or even medical professionals.

travel/vac You might find resorts under "travel/vacation services" or even a driver; it's a bit wide-open as a category.

write/ed/tr8 Covering "writing/editing/translation," this category is a source of work for freelancers worldwide and a place where publishers create listings on occasion.

Under jobs

accounting+finance The "accounting/finance jobs" here are posted by employers locally but often from across the country as well.

admin / office This category has become a major source of finding people for clerical help on every craigslist site.

arch / engineering Covering "architect/engineer/CAD jobs" (CAD being computer-aided design), jobs here are for the white-collar people of the construction industry.

art / media / design In "art/media/design jobs" you'll find occupations suitable for art school graduates and other creative persons.

biotech / science The "science/biotech jobs" listings also include ads for people needed for medical studies.

business / mgmt In "business/mgmt jobs" you'll find everything from interns to top management needs.

customer service The craigslist "customer service jobs" might include something as mundane as receptionist; the category is broad ranging.

education The "education/teaching jobs" listings generally are not placed by school districts. Rather, they're usually from other types of schools.

food / bev / hosp In "food/beverage/hospitality jobs" you'll find offers as far ranging as fast-food restaurants to hotel jobs.

general labor   The "general labor jobs" advertise for blue-collar workers, but also business franchises like carpet cleaning.

government   In the listings for "government jobs" you'll find that even the U.S. military has learned of the benefits of using craigslist.

human resources   The "human resources jobs" found in this category offer staffing positions from major companies as well as smaller businesses.

internet engineers   For most of the "internet engineering jobs" here, you'll have to be known to your friends and co-workers as quite a "techie."

legal / paralegal   Attorneys and law firms now advertise as readily in "legal/paralegal jobs" as they once did only in legal publications.

manufacturing   Though "manufacturing jobs" may be on the decline in the United States, skilled people like machinists will find plenty of listings in this category.

marketing / pr / ad   Listings for "marketing/advertising/PR jobs" could be anything from a layout artist to an experienced public relations professional.

medical / health   These are healthcare jobs and thus might ask for front office personnel all the way up to a licensed physician.

nonprofit sector   The "nonprofit jobs" might be for a director of a major organization, or simply an assistant. This is a broad category.

real estate   The "real estate jobs" listed here might be for an agent or broker, or they could be for a resident manager of an apartment building.

retail / wholesale   Defined as "retail/wholesale jobs," listings here are basically for salespeople, and usually for those working in retail stores.

sales / biz dev   There is little in the way of business development here, and thus you see "sales jobs" when you arrive on the page. It could be any type of sales, but rarely in retail stores.

salon / spa / fitness   The "salon/spa/fitness jobs" could be for a receptionist for a plastic surgeon, or someone to do nails in a salon.

security The category of "security jobs" rarely moves beyond guards and people who do dispatching of same.

skilled trade / craft Under "skilled trades/artisan jobs" you might find a need for a carpenter, or even an auto mechanic. A bit of a catchall category.

software / qa / dba Computer programmers and software engineers search under "software/QA/DBA/etc jobs" if using craigslist for work.

systems / network The "systems/networking jobs" in these listings are for personnel like the tech administrators found in firms with networked computers.

technical support Listings for "technical support jobs" might be anything from help desk personnel to a technical services engineer.

transport In "transportation jobs" you'll find a need for parking cashiers, drivers, and anything else having to do with things and people moved around in vehicles.

tv / film / video A broad-ranging category of "tv/film/video/radio jobs" that basically covers everything for broadcast media personnel.

web / info design Personal computer geniuses and web wizards find work in "web/HTML/info design jobs."

writing / editing The "writing/editing jobs" advertised here could be anything, including blogging.

[ETC] "et cetera jobs" could be anything? Are you up for participating in brain research?

[part time] Listings for "all jobs" are here and often enough they lead to permanent positions.

Under gigs

computer The "computer gigs" listings in this category usually are short-term for things like web design or "app" developers.

creative The "creative gigs" here could be anything, depending on the locale, from a fine artist to a poetry teacher.

crew   If you see "crew gigs" it usually means something to do with the arts, like film and TV, or music. It varies by locale; in some places it might mean a construction crew.

domestic   The "domestic gigs" could be a need for a babysitter, or for a handyman. Mostly, homeowners create these listings.

event   If you're a bartender or anyone else good at working around crowds, "event gigs" might be the category for you.

labor   Everything from construction workers to fine craftspeople are advertised for in the "labor gigs" category.

writing   Not only writers, but editors, bloggers, and translators find temporary jobs in "writing gigs."

talent   In the "talent gigs" category you might find short-term work if you're a model, mime, clown, juggler, or spokesperson.

Web Resources in Addition to craigslist

While craigslist is a fabulous resource, it's even better when used in conjunction with other sites. Throughout this book, we have attempted to provide links to other sites that will enhance your use of craigslist and help you in building a business. We present them again here, by chapter, for easy reference. If you think of others that we could tell others about, please let us know at skip@skippress.com.

Chapter 1–The Reach of craigslist: A World of Possibilities

www.whatismyip.com—A site used to discover the Internet Protocol (IP) address of your computer.

www.ftc.gov—The Federal Trade Commission online complaint form.

www.zazzle.com/craigslist—Site offering craigslist T-shirts.

http://craigslistfoundation.org—The site of the Craigslist Foundation geared toward "building a platform for civic engagement."

http://savetheinternet.com/faq—Site linked from the defend net neutrality link on the craigslist home page.

www.crazedlist.org—A way you can "search craigslist like a madman" both in the United States and worldwide.

www.trademart.in and www.ratantextiles.com—Examples of websites in India that could help you build an import business from that country.

Chapter 2—Navigating from the Basic Page

http://getsafeonline.org and http://wiredsafety.org—Sites linked from the personal safety tips link on craigslist.

http://24hoursoncraigslist.com—The movie about using the site linked at craigslist movie & dvd on the main page.

www.craigslistfoundation.org/bootcamp.html—The Craigslist Foundation instructional boot camps.

http://en.wikipedia.org/wiki/Captcha—Explanation of "captcha" words you enter on web pages like some on craigslist to verify that you're a human and that a software robot isn't placing the ad.

www.eskimo.com/~newowl/Flagged_FAQ.htm— "Unofficial Flag FAQ: Answers to Frequently Asked Questions about flags and your craigslist ad."

Chapter 3—Profiting Across the Listings

www.postlets.com and www.vflyer.com—Sites that help you create craigslist pages with special fonts, elaborate pictorials, and layouts.

Chapter 4—Placing and Responding to Ads

www.craigslistaddesign.com—One of the professional services available for writing or designing craigslist ads.

http://en.wikipedia.org/wiki/5_Ws—The "five Ws"— who, what, where, when, why, along with the how of the matter in question—long used by newspaper journalists.

www.listpic.com/about.html—Ryan Sit's site that lets you take a visual tour through craigslist listings.

http://www.howtodothings.com/computers-internet/how-to-enhance-and-resize-photos-for-craigslist—Good article about how to fix up your web pictures, specific to craigslist.

www.network-science.de/ascii—A site that helps you make up fancy images with keyboard characters, called ASCII images, using text in different fonts.

www.degraeve.com/img2txt.php—Site that converts already online images such as those you find via Google images into ASCII images.

Chapter 5—Software and Other Shortcuts

http://craigslisteditor.com—Software that formats your ad in HTML language for craigslist.

www.download.com and www.versiontracker.com—Free software download sites.

www.craigspal.com—Software that does a multisite search of craigslist across categories, with the content set by you, with instant notification of new results.

www.craigslistnotifier.net—A Windows tool that allows you to receive notifications on listings that interest you via email, text (SMS, cell phone), and onscreen.

www.motiont.com—Site offering Craigslist Reader, a free application that gathers information off craigslist and notifies you about changes that you specify.

www.f5.com/products/big-ip—The company that made the proprietary system that runs craigslist.

http://sam308.com/html/craigslist_s_classified_ad_pos.html—Craigslist Classified Ad Posting Utility, the Microsoft Excel–based utility that lets you apply HTML formatting to your ads with "style, color, and character."

www.craigslistextractor.com—Craigslist Ad Extractor, a robust product that lets you get data across all categories, cities, and countries on craigslist and extract all data and emails from the ads, with results saved in Excel format.

http://www-marketingpros.com/software/clg.html—Makers of Craigslist Genius, which promises to cut your ad posting time "to mere seconds!"

www.cldesktop.com—CL Desktop (Craigslist Desktop) lets you browse craigslist without saving the search settings, with results presented in a visual way.

www.marketplacemac.com—Marketplace, Mac software advertised as "Craigslist, without the ugly" that lets you search any craigslist region around the world, across any category or subcategory, and "get all the results in one convenient window."

www.whatisrss.com—A full explanation of Reader or News Aggregator software that grabs RSS (Rich Site Summary) feeds and sends them to your browser.

http://rssblog.whatisrss.com—Details on RSS feeds.

http://wordpress.com—Wordpress, the free blog website that seems to have become the site of choice for those who create high-traffic blogs.

www.consumersearch.com/job-sites—A rating of job websites. (craigslist came out #1 in best online classifieds.)

www.internettutorials.net/boolean.asp—An explanation of Boolean searches.

www.google.com/support/websearch/?ctx=web—A thorough primer on effective web searching.

www.forsalebyownercenter.com and http://homesineasttexas.com—Real estate sites that can help you compare prices found on craigslist sites.

www.dogpile.com—A metasearch site that combines four search engines—Google, Yahoo!, Bing, and Ask—in one search box and can be added to your browser's search bar with a simple click.

www.yousuckatcraigslist.com— "Exactly what it says on the tin." A humorous site that any craigslist user will enjoy.

Chapter 6–Keeping Your Account in Good Standing

www.getafreelancer.com—Site for jobs for independent writers.

http://en.wikipedia.org/wiki/File:Craigslist01.jpg—The Victorian house in San Francisco's Sunset District that houses craigslist.

www.cnewmark.com—The blog of Craig Newmark, founder of craigslist.

http://en.wikipedia.org/wiki/Craigslist—Wikipedia page on craigslist.

www.eskimo.com/~newowl/Flagged_FAQ.htm—The Unofficial Flag FAQ about craigslist that explains how and why your ads might be getting flagged by the site or other users.

http://en.wikipedia.org/wiki/Internet_troll—Wikipedia page that explains the most troublesome creature on the web.

Chapter 7–Why Some Listings Work and Others Don't

www.bulldogreporter.com—Superb site for public relations professionals that offers things like a "PR University."

www.wikihow.com/Post-Ads-to-Craigslist—A simple posting primer.

http://en.wikipedia.org/wiki/Geo_(marketing)—Wikipedia entry about the science of geomarketing.

www.rurdev.usda.gov—U.S. government site that provides information on things like the injection of government money into expanding broadband Internet into rural areas.

Chapter 8–How to Handle a Scam

www.haltabuse.org—Working to Halt Online Abuse, the most active and informative site for cybervictims on the web, founded by writer Jayne Hitchcock, providing lawyer referrals, forensic, and other resources, even links to private investigators.

www.tucofs.com/tucofs.htm—The Ultimate Collection of Forensic Software for every computer platform, even Personal Digital Assistants (PDAs).

www.ic3.gov/default.aspx—The Internet Crime Complaint Center (IC3), a partnership between the Federal Bureau of Investigation (FBI), the National White Collar Crime Center (NW3C), and the Bureau of Justice Assistance (BJA).

www.phonebusters.com—The Canadian PhoneBusters hotline, the central Canadian agency set up to collect information on telemarketing complaints in Canada to prosecute criminals in Canada violating telemarketing fraud laws.

www.recol.ca—The Reporting Economic Crime On-Line (RECOL) site set up by the Royal Canadian Mounted Police.

www.westernunion.com—Western Union, possibly the best method of receiving payments from some countries outside the United States.

www.paypal.com—PayPal, owned by eBay, offers secure transactions, the ability to send an invoice via email, and a customer can pay with most credit and debit cards.

www.pgpi.org/doc/faq/pgpi/en/#What—The international version Pretty Good Privacy, broadly known as PGP.

www.pgpi.org—Pretty Good Privacy software.

Chapter 9–Separating the Payers from the Painful

www.irs.gov—The Internal Revenue site, which will explain among other things that barter is taxable in the United States.

www.recalls.gov—U.S. government site listing products that have been recalled.

www.barterbart.com—Auction-style barter and trade site.

www.barterquest.com—Goods and services in many categories, locally and internationally.

www.mytradeamerica.com—The world's largest barter marketplace, a barter and trade exchange similar to a chamber of commerce.

www.swap-it-now.com—"The Internet's flea market" where you can "swap DVDs, books, automobiles, toys, compact discs, autographs, and everything in between."

www.swaptreasures.com—An online swap community where members can swap, barter, buy, and sell goods and services.

www.swaptree.com—A site for swapping books, CDs, DVDs, and video games.

www.switchplanet.com—A site for trading books, CDs, DVDs, and video games.

http://titletrader.com—A book, movie, and music swap club.

www.TradeAFavor.com—A site enabling trading anything with anyone on Facebook.

http://u-exchange.com—The largest free swap site that specializes in every type of trade.

www.barternews.com—Good hub of barter information.

www.nate.org—National Association of Trade Exchanges (NATE) offering the BANC (Barter Association National Currency), a scrip that allows "independent barter exchanges to do business with each other, without the need for back-to-back reciprocal trading."

www.bartercard.com—A credit card for your barter trades.

http://freegan.info and www.freecycle.org—Sites for giving things away or getting things free.

www.investopedia.com/terms/l/lossleader.asp—A full explanation of the practice of offering a product or service that loses money but draws in customers, known as "loss leaders."

www.amazon.com—Amazon often offers lower prices than other merchants on items like computers.

www.ecrater.com—A free web store builder and online marketplace where sellers can create a free online store and browse and compare between thousands of products.

www.epier.com—A bit of a cross between craigslist and eBay that puts an emphasis on featured sellers.

www.hopeiwin.com—Free listings and stores, with a $25 bonus for signing up.

www.ioffer.com—A San Francisco–based site that "allows you to buy, sell, and trade just like you would in real life by negotiating."

www.listitforabuck.com—List any item in any category for 30 days "for only a buck."

http://classifieds.livedeal.com—The Live Deal Online Marketplace lets you search by zip code, city, or state in the United States and in many product and service categories. It also offers Yellow Pages and City Pages searches.

www.onlineauction.com—Auctions with free unlimited listings.

www.oodle.com—Allows you to see "local listings from over 80,000 websites" and sends you email updates when new matches pop up.

www.tagsaler.com—Organized, modernized, and free classifieds.

www.ubid.com—"Your connection to excess inventory from the world's most trusted brands."

http://ads.thekittyletter.com—The Kitty Letter, a newsletter in southern California that goes out to 50+ Realtor offices each week.

www.moneyfactory.gov/section.cfm/7/35—An explanation of money counterfeiting measures such as the watermark, color-shifting inks, fine-line printing patterns, enlarged off-center portraits, and a low-vision feature.

http://yourfavorite.com/checkwriter/verify.htm—Site that allows you to verify a U.S. bank routing number for free.

www.fraudaid.com—A 501(3) nonprofit site devoted to fraud victim advocacy, offering law enforcement support.

www.alertpay.com, http://payments.intuit.com, and www.swreg.org—Competitors of PayPal.

www.business.com and www.rocketlawyer.com—Sites offering free template employee contracts.

www.complaintsboard.com and www.consumeraffairs.com/online/ craigslist.html—Sites where complaints about craigslist can be lodged.

www.statelocalgov.net/50states-courts.cfm—Directory of courts in the United States.

www.legalzoom.com—Paid legal site that offers a lot of free information via an Education Center offering Small Claims Education, a FAQ, and Glossary.

www.internetlawcenter.net—The Internet Law Center, which focuses on "helping businesses navigate the challenges of the digital economy" while providing "comprehensive solutions for businesses both online and offline."

Chapter 10—Using Similar Sites

www.backpage.com—The biggest competitor of craigslist, organized by metro area.

www.kijiji.com—Site created by eBay to compete with craigslist.

www.oodle.com—Site created by former Excite and eBay executives to compete with craigslist.

www.classifiedads.com—Yet another free craigslist competitor.

www.gumtree.com—A United Kingdom craigslist-like site that ranks higher than any other for traffic, according to the web traffic site Alexa. com.

www.angieslist.com—Site founded by Angie Hicks in 1995 for listing service companies and health-care professionals in over 400 categories that has become so successful it now pays for media ads to draw people to the site.

www.trustys.com—Similar to Angie's List but has a much more small-town feel, and it's free.

http://siteslikecraigslist.com/the-ranked-list-of-sites-like-craigslist—List of sites similar to craigslist, ranked by traffic signatures.

Chapter 11–Understanding the Jobs and Gigs Categories

http://employeeissues.com/probationary_period.htm—Explanation of the 30-day to six-month probationary period for new personnel before they're considered permanent.

www.hitwise.com/info/us-competitor-report-offer.php—Free deal from Hitwise to help you beat your competitor.

Chapter 12–Major Companies and craigslist

www.consumersearch.com/job-sites—ConsumerSearch site about the top job sites on which employers pay to list.

http://hotjobs.yahoo.com—Deemed "best large job site" by ConsumerSearch.

www.TheJobSpider.com—Free employment information exchange job board created by Chris McGarry, inspired by craigslist.

www.dice.com—"The Career Hub for Tech Insiders" chosen as best job site for technology fields by ConsumerSearch.

www.monster.com—Most popular job site according to ConsumerSearch.

www.careerbuilder.com—An "aggregator job site" favored by ConsumerSearch.

www.state.gov—The U.S. State Department site that offers a page for "Job Search by region and country" with links for job searches across the world.

www.goinglobal.com/countries/usa/usa_work.asp—Site recommended by the U.S. State Department.

www.bls.gov/OCO—Site offering the Bureau of Labor Statistics Occupational Outlook Handbook.

Chapter 13—Maximizing Your Resume

www.samspade.org—Site offering free "Whois" lookup of Uniform Source Locators (URLs) and other web tools.

www.godaddy.com—Popular site for registering domain names that also offer Whois searches for sites registered there.

http://hotjobs.yahoo.com/resume—An excellent step-by-step series of articles about putting together a professional resume, connected to Yahoo!'s excellent job search engine.

www.dailywritingtips.com/resume-writing-tips—Site containing 44 resume writing tips.

www.damngood.com—From author and resume expert Yanna Parker, has free templates and advice.

www.pongoresume.com—Offers paid services as well as thorough free advice.

www.provenresumes.com—Comprehensive site that offers examples of resumes that were rewritten to get salary increases and jobs.

www.resume-help.org—Examples and tips and pro services.

www.rockportinstitute.com/resumes.html—Extensive site that offers a literal education in resumes including information on powerwords.

Chapter 15—Staffing Your Company from craigslist

www.strengthfinder.com—Personnel evaluation tools based on the book *Now, Discover Your Strengths* by Marcus Buckingham and Donald O. Clifton, Ph.D.

www.sba.gov—Website of the Small Business Administration.

www.eeoc.gov—Website of the U.S. Equal Employment Opportunity Commission.

www.leadingforloyalty.com/free_employee_assessments.html—Free downloadable employee assessment tools.

www.gallup.com/tag/Jobs.aspx—Information about the current job scene.

http://wellhire.com/Public/how-it-works.aspx—Site that allows you to include a job test in your craigslist ad; Well Hire will assess and track job applicants for you.

Chapter 16—From Recycling to Real Estate

http://dictionary.law.com—Excellent source of legal definitions and understanding.

www.tradeafavor.com—Application for Facebook that facilitates barter site trading.

www.marketingteacher.com/Lessons/lesson_pricing.htm—Free educational resources on the topic of marketing.

http://en.wikipedia.org/wiki/Pricing_strategies—Wikipedia description of different types of pricing.

http://entrepreneurs.about.com—Scott Allen's excellent free resource for creative business people at About.com.

http://sfbay.listpic.com—Virtual classifieds browser that resembles craigslist but is not affiliated.

Chapter 17—Opportunities Outside the United States

www.ehow.com/how_2191334_import-electronics-from-japan.html—Article explaining the steps necessary to import Japanese items.

www.pricejapan.com—Site for ordering items directly from Japan.

www.cia.gov/library/publications/the-world-factbook—The CIA World Factbook available online and updated with new material every two weeks.

www.work.com/doing-business-in-china-461—Excellent primer on business in China.

www.export.gov/china—Link offering the "Are You China Ready?" test at the U.S. Government Export Portal.

www.made-in-china.com—Site for locating trade shows and suppliers in China, among other things.

http://search.ebay.com/india—Link for viewing all the items being offered for sale from India on eBay by people in that country and elsewhere.

www.buyusa.gov/europe—Page from the U.S. Commercial Service at U.S. Embassies and Consulates designed to work with companies "to increase exports to Europe of U.S. products and services."

www.ehow.com/how_2183450_calculate-exchange-rates.html—Tool with the most up-to-date information on exchange rates around the world.

www.xe.com/ucc—Universal Currency Converter.

Chapter 18—craigslist vs. eBay: Using Both Effectively

http://stores.shop.eBay.com/_stores/hub—Page on how to set up your own store on eBay.

http://reseller.eBay.com/ns/FAQs.html—eBay's Reseller Marketplace, explained.

www.goldfellow.com—Valuable metals buying site that lets you print a FedEx shipping label from its site so that you can track (and insure) the shipment.

http://shopping.yahoo.com—Yahoo! site good for searching keywords to discover what's in demand among buyers.

http://pages.ebay.com/community/boards/index.html—Workshop/ Discussion forums on eBay.

Chapter 19—Financial Safety and Legal Necessities

http://entrepreneurs.about.com/od/businessstructure/a/ doingbusinessas.htm—Free information on filing a DBA (doing business as) in your local area.

www.ustreas.gov/auctions/irs/index.html—Treasury Department site offering items seized by the Internal Revenue Service.

www.simplefilings.com, bizfilings.com, legalzoom.com—Extensive site on DBAs, corporations, and other business possibilities.

Nolo.com—Excellent books on business, entrepreneurship, intellectual property, and incorporating.

www.dhl.com, www.fedex.com, www.ups.com, www.usps.com, and www.stamps.com—Sites for shipping and mailing.

www.lobbyinginfo.org/tools—Public Citizen site that can help you find out if your Internet provider is lobbying in Washington.

www.publici.org/lobby—Another site for determining who is lobbying in Washington, D.C.

www.influence.biz—Yet another lobbying search site.

www.politicalmoneyline.com—Find out who's spending money to try to gain political influence.

www.opensecrets.org/lobby/index.php—The best lobbyist search site from the Center for Responsive Politics.

www.usa.gov—Central site for all U.S. government information.

www.statelocalgov.net/index.cfm—State and Local Governments on the Net, "a directory of official state, count, and city government web-sites."

www.wisegeek.com/what-is-a-1099-contractor.htm—Information on what to do for the IRS when you pay an independent contractor more than $600 U.S. dollars in a year.

www.eff.org—Site of the Electronic Frontier Foundation, the "leading civil liberties group defending your rights in the digital world."

Chapter 20—Discussion Forums: How to Boost Your Business

www.forumslister.com—Site that reveals the craigslist discussion forums that are not displayed on the home page.

www.skippress.com—Personal site of the author of this book. Send him an email!

Index

I